Prolife Feminism
Yesterday & Today

**Edited by Mary Krane Derr,
Linda Naranjo-Huebl and Rachel MacNair**

Sulzburger & Graham Publishing, Ltd.
New York

Publisher: Neil C. Blond, Esq.

Copy Editor: David Gregory

© 1995 Sulzburger & Graham Publishing, Ltd.
P.O. Box 20058
Park West Station
New York, NY 10025

Contents

Preface and Acknowledgments

This book is a compilation of feminist writings on the issue of abortion from the early nineteenth century to the present. Divided into two parts comprising writings by "yesterday's" feminists in part one (from approximately 1800 to 1965) and by contemporary feminists in part two (1965 to the present), the book attempts to document the continuum of feminist prolife thinking.

Terminology is a touchy subject to adherents of both sides of the abortion debate. The editors know that no matter what terms we use, there will be accusations of bias and manipulation. We certainly do not deny that we have an opinion on the abortion issue—this book's stated purpose is to present the feminist prolife argument—but out of respect for those who do not share our views, we have tried to use the terms that advocates for the respective positions prefer for themselves: "prolife" and "prochoice." Occasionally we use the term "abortion rights advocates" when we feel it more accurately reflects the political nature of the position. We have not, however, edited the terminology of the individual writers featured herein.

Mary Krane Derr wishes to thank the following people for their help, interest, and encouragement in her research on early feminists: her family; Jeff Donels; Rose Evans; Geoff Goodman; Nat Hentoff; Laurie Ramsey Jaffe; Kelly Jefferson; Evelyn K.S. Judge; Rachel MacNair; Frederica Mathewes-Green; Linda Naranjo-Huebl; Marvin Olasky; Charlotte Paris; Richard Stanley; staff at Americans United for Life; the University of Chicago Library, the Newberry Library, Chicago Historical Society, and the Women's Christian Temperance Union, Evanston, Illinois; the Coleman Library of Tougaloo College, Tougaloo, Mississippi; and anyone else she may have failed to mention.

Rachel MacNair and Linda Naranjo-Huebl would like to thank Cindy Osborne, Pat Goltz, Catherine Callaghan, Jessica Pegis, Martha Crean, Pam Cira, Paulette Joyer, Mary Meehan, Sharon Richardson, Mary Bea Stout, Gail Grenier-Sweet, Juli Loesch-Wiley, Kay Castonguay, Carol Crossed, Barbara Willke and others for their help in providing historical and biographical information on the contemporary feminists included in Part Two. Linda would particularly like to thank Scott, Micaela and Maura for their support and understanding of that part of her life that has her glued so often to the computer keyboard (a postmodern reality) and helping make her a life away from it.

All of the editors would like to thank the numerous contributors to *Sisterlife* who have laid such a solid foundation for contemporary feminist prolife theory, many of whom publicly held their position before they learned of the weight of history behind them.

Part One

RECLAIMING OUR PAST:
The Historical Beginnings of Prolife Feminism

If we live in a society where women's knowledge and theories are notable by their absence, in which women's ideas are neither respected or preserved, it is not because women have not produced valuable cultural forms but because what they have produced has been perceived as dangerous by those who have the power to suppress and remove evidence ... So while men proceed on their developmental way building on their inherited tradition, women are confined to cycles of lost and found, only to be lost and found again—and again ... We can see that what we are doing today is not something new but something old: this is a source of strength and power.

—Dale Spender, *Feminist Theorists: Three Centuries of Key Women Thinkers*

Introduction

Although it currently receives little attention, there is a motif in feminism which began long ago and has endured to the present day. This is the theme of abortion as an injustice against fetal life which originates with injustice against female life. As early as 1792, Mary Wollstonecraft articulated it in her ground-breaking *Vindication of the Rights of Woman*. She spoke of how male domination made women "weaker in mind and body than they ought to be." As a result, they "have not sufficient strength to discharge the first duty of a mother" and "either destroy the embryo in the womb, or cast it off when born." Wollstonecraft deemed this practice "a savage custom." As this anthology will show, Wollstonecraft anticipated the view of many of her nineteenth and twentieth century sisters.[1]

For all their seemingly intractable disagreements, many people on both sides of the contemporary abortion debate would be surprised that such a position could be voiced in the name of women's rights, for they share the firm conviction that feminism is necessarily grounded in an unconditional moral and legal right to abortion. This assumption betrays their common lack of knowledge about an overlooked but critical facet of women's history: the undeniable fact that our feminist foremothers staunchly opposed abortion.

Many early feminists committed acts of nonviolent civil disobedience to protest laws they condemned as unjust.[2] They recognized full well that morality and legality were not necessarily tantamount to each other. They refused to pay taxes to a government that would not represent their sex and its interests. They entered polling places and insisted on casting their own votes. They picketed, marched, and went on hunger strikes. Believing that domestic and public life were of one piece—i.e., that "the personal is political"—they intervened in abusive practices which their opponents attempted to exempt from criticism on the grounds of personal privacy. They sheltered blacks fleeing from slavery and women fleeing from tyrannical husbands.

Interestingly, the early feminists never included antiabortion laws in the many they challenged. Most of their public writings on abortion came with the wave of prolife legislation that swept the United States in the latter half of the nineteenth century. They praised this legislation and called for more effective enforcement of it. For example, the *Revolution*, the newspaper put out by Elizabeth Cady Stanton and Susan B. Anthony, refused without exception to advertise patent medicines.[3] In doing this, the paper quite knowingly deprived itself of a major source of revenue to periodicals of its era.[4] Why did it adopt such a policy? The explanation is that these drugs were often thinly disguised abortifacients—as shown by an editorial statement praising a bill to restrict them. "Restellism has long found in these broths of Beelzebub, its securest hiding place."[5] "Restellism" was a contemptuous term for abortion derived from the name of Madam Restell, perhaps the most notorious abortion profiteer of the nineteenth century.

The early feminists unanimously agreed that a legal ban *alone* would not entirely eliminate the practice of abortion. Some, such as Tennessee Claflin, despaired that "abortion cannot be put down by law," for it "is one of the fixed institutions of the country; one of the marked characteristics of the age; one of the indicative symptoms of the ripening and rotting of our present state of society!"[6] Yet Claflin was not *denouncing* antiabortion laws. She was simply expressing a certain view of legislation as too "superficial" to effect desirable social change in and of itself. Clearly, in citing abortion as a prime sign of what was wrong with society, she was not offering a defense of it.

Although often eager to uncover and reclaim the long history of their movement, most present-day feminists suffer from total amnesia on the history of its attitudes toward abortion. Thus numerous participants in abortion rights marches have donned the white of the suffragists without any sense of irony. So strongly do they believe that a right to abortion is the bedrock of feminism, they cannot imagine that perhaps once it was not—let alone that it might not be today. Not surprisingly, many of them have reacted with vehement disbelief when confronted with historical material that does not dovetail with their belief system.

In 1990, several progressive magazines ran a Feminists for Life advertisement featuring quotations on abortion, complete with citations, from such notables as Elizabeth Cady Stanton. The magazines received a number of irate and incredulous responses. "I wish I could tell you the total rage and disappointment I feel," wrote one individual to the editor. "Something so anti-woman in this woman-centered journal is an affront. What happened to the vision?"[7] "My heart stopped cold," wrote another. "I was appalled that you would allow such faulty misrepresentation of an issue, without considering the ramifications (and truth!) of what you might be printing …"[8] Yet another asked: "Would you take an ad from Jews for a Nazi America? How about from Black Panthers for a Klan-controlled America? … I implore you not to debase and demean the words of some of history's most notable women by allowing them to be quoted on your pages out of literary and historical context for the purpose of rescinding modern women's right to control our own reproduction."[9]

At Antioch College, an institution that prides itself on its liberal open-mindedness, a student attempted a more extensive presentation and analysis of the feminist foremother quotations in a paper. The instructor accused her of fabricating them. The student then submitted photocopies of the original articles from which the quotes were taken. The instructor grew even more furious. She demanded not only that the student footnote every single sentence in the essay, but supply entire issues of the periodicals in which the quotes initially appeared.[10]

Other prochoice feminists, too sophisticated and knowledgeable about history to opt for such indignant denial, have nevertheless tended to treat their foremothers' position on abortion as briefly and dismissively as possible. They have attributed it exclusively to reasons which now seem absurdly old-fashioned or "politically incorrect." For instance, Rosalind Pollack Petchesky, without thoroughly examining primary sources, faults the early feminists for buying into a species of "false consciousness," namely the oppressive Victorian mystique about motherhood.[11] James Mohr concludes that they unquestioningly accepted Victorian sexual ethics, especially an abhorrence of nonprocreative intercourse.[12] Others cite the dangers abortion posed to women's health— dangers which presumably have been eradicated by legalization and by advances in medical technology.[13]

These explanations of the early feminist position are incomplete, if not misplaced or even inaccurate. It is true that the early feminists celebrated motherhood as a uniquely female power and strength which deserved genuine reverence. Isabella Beecher Hooker even went so far as to suggest that female reproductive capacity was a source of female superiority. She wrote to her friend John Stuart Mill: "[O]f late I have been impressed more and more with the close likeness to the divine nature which woman seems to bear, in that she is more sensibly, if not more truly, a creator than man is. Add to this her more intimate fellowship with the child of her womb during the antenatal period, and the power of sympathy that comes through this, and you have given her a moral advantage that man can never have, and for which he has no equivalent or compensation."[14]

Yet not even Hooker was fooled for one minute into oblivious-ness towards the real-life conditions under which mothers labored. Hooker and her peers affirmed the *experience* of motherhood while rejecting the *institution* of it.[15] They identified the motherhood mystique as a cover-up for the denigration of women, and actively encouraged members of their sex to see through it. Elizabeth Cady Stanton, for instance, responded in the following way to a delegation of Orthodox Jewish women who insisted that their religious authorities did genuinely "reverence" them as mothers: "I asked them why, if this were all so, one heard in the synagogue service every week the 'I thank thee, O Lord, that I was not born a woman.' ... Suppose the service read, 'I thank thee, O Lord, that I was not born a jackass.' Could that be twisted in any way into a com-pliment to the jackass? They smiled ..."[16]

Not surprisingly, given their incisive criticisms of the mother-hood mystique, the early feminists recognized full well that women had creative capacities other than that of the womb. Thus they fought for women's entrance into higher education and the professions, and a good many of them were courageous pioneers themselves in these areas. But they refused to accept the patriarchal dictum that their own physiology in and of itself was a barrier to public achievement. Rather, they put the blame on a society which refused to accommodate and authentically respect their reproductive potential, like all their other capacities. In a litany of wrongs against the female sex, Susan B. Anthony, Elizabeth Cady Stanton, and Matilda Joslyn Gage declared: "How completely de-moralized by her subjection [woman] must be, who does not feel her personal dignity assailed ... when she finds that which should be her glory—her possible motherhood—treated everywhere by men as a dis-ability and a crime!"[17]

From the beginnings of their movement, the early feminists' at-titudes toward motherhood led naturally to their outspoken criticisms of sexual puritanism. In *Vindication of the Rights of Woman,* Mary Wollstonecraft identified the sexual double standard as a major weapon in patriarchy's war against women.[18] So did the feminists who came together in 1848 at Seneca Falls, New York, to organize an American women's movement. The Declaration of Sentiments issued from their Convention contained this grievance: "[Man] has created a false public sentiment by giving to the world a different code of morals for men and women, by which moral delinquencies which exclude women from society, are not only tolerated, but deemed of little account in man."[19]

In their challenge to the double standard, feminists affirmed the value of sex for pleasure and communication, not just procreation—for men and women alike. Dr. Frederick Hollick wrote: "Those who suppose that sexual enjoyment is altogether immoral and unworthy of rational beings … are in error."[20] He frankly described the clitoris and stated that women were "capable of considerable excitement."[21] Elizabeth Cady Stanton chided Walt Whitman for speaking "as if the female must be forced to the creative act, apparently ignorant of the great natural fact that a healthy woman has as much passion as a man."[22] Victoria Woodhull stated that nothing was so expressive of sexual inequality as men's insensitivity to the gratification of that passion: "There is nothing so destructive as that intercourse carried on habitually without regard to perfect and reciprocal consummation … I need not explain to any woman the effects of unconsummated intercourse … But every man needs to have it thundered in his ears … that the other party demands a return for all he receives, demands that he shall not be enriched at her expense, demands that he shall not, either from ignorance or selfish desire, carry her impulse forward only to cast it backward with its mission unfulfilled to prostrate the impelling power and breed nervous debility or irritability and sexual demoralization."[23]

The early feminists also defied conventions regarding female sexuality in their enthusiastic support for sex education and family planning, including, in a number of cases, so-called artificial methods of contraception. A number of them skirmished with the Comstock Law of 1873, which prohibited open discussion of sexually related matters in the United States. As historian William Leach notes, even as they "bemoaned the horrors of abortion," they "nevertheless insisted upon limitations upon fertility" and upon guarding women "against the deceit, exploitation, and conflict that inevitably ensued from sexual ignorance."[24] Indeed, as we shall see shortly, they frequently argued that "voluntary motherhood," which was made possible by effective sex education and family planning methods, was vitally necessary because it would help put abortionists out of business.

Why was abortion advocacy expressly excluded from the early feminist challenge to sexual puritanism? It was not simply because of the health risks abortion posed to women, although feminists deplored these. As prochoice historian Carl Degler honestly acknowledges, endangerment to women's health was not their only or even main concern.[25] If it had been, they would have retracted their objections after the development of sterile technique made the procedure safer. They would not have spoken of abortions that killed women as the loss of not one but two lives. They would not have habitually referred to the procedure as "ante-natal murder," "child-murder," "ante-natal infanticide," or simply "infanticide." In their view, killing a child before birth was so much like killing a child after birth, the two acts could be subsumed under the same term.

Why did the early feminists place such value on fetal life? It was not because they slavishly adhered to archaic religious dogmas about ensoulment. James Mohr has established that religious orthodoxy played very little part in the nineteenth century campaign to outlaw abortion.[26] Even if it had played a larger role that still would not explain the feminist position. Of the feminists in this anthology whose religious orientation is known, most *were* deeply spiritual people. However, these women, for all the depth of their religious conviction, were often willing to work alongside people who did not share it.

In addition, these women, drawing on their religious faith, critically questioned and challenged those religious precepts that justified or encouraged social injustice. Many had links to Spiritualism, which, as religion professor Ann Braude observes, sanctioned their commitment to women's rights: "At a time when no churches ordained women and many forbade them to speak aloud in church, Spiritualist women had equal authority, equal opportunities, and equal numbers in religious leadership. While most religious groups viewed the existing order of gender, race, and class relations as ordained by God, ardent Spiritualists appeared not only in the woman's rights movement but through most radical reform movements of the nineteenth century."[27] Victoria Woodhull, Tennessee Claflin, and Laura Cuppy Smith were well-known Spiritualist "mediums," i.e., ministers. Paulina Wright Davis, Alice Bunker Stockham, Henry Clarke Wright, and Isabella Beecher Hooker all identified themselves as Spiritualists. Matilda Joslyn Gage, Susan B. Anthony, and Frances Willard did not label themselves as such, but sympathized with Spiritualists and sought to construct their own alternatives to patriarchal religion.

What possible explanation might be left for the early feminists' desire to protect fetal life? Theirs was an era when men still argued in all seriousness that women were less than human because of their biological "inferiority" and their purported lack of souls.[28] Not surprisingly, then, feminists were strongly inclined to reject the argument that other groups of human beings—fetuses included—were nonpersons. Feminists were fully conscious that the rationale for oppressing one group—namely that its members were not full-fledged human beings—could be readily used to oppress another. This consciousness was joined to a new scientific understanding of fetal development as continuous from the moment of conception, not simply from the point of "quickening" (i.e., the moment when a pregnant woman first detects fetal movement). Degler has offered this commentary on the valuation of fetal life at all stages:

> Seen against the broad canvas of humanitarian thought and practice in Western society from the seventeenth to the twentieth century, the expansion of the definition of life to include the whole career of the fetus rather than only the months after quickening is quite consistent. It was in line with a number of movements to reduce cruelty and to expand the concept of the sanctity of life. The reduction, in the course of the nineteenth century, in the use, or the elimination of the death penalty, the peace movement, the abolition of torture and whipping in connection with crimes all represented steps in that centuries-long movement. The prohibiting of abortion was but the most recent effort in that larger concern.[29]

In addition to their advocacy of women and unborn children, feminists were active in all the movements that Degler mentions, along with abolitionism, already-born children's rights, and in some cases, animal rights.[30] These efforts against violence of all kinds were clearly linked in the feminist mind. For example, the alternative medical periodical *Water Cure Journal* published a poem about the ironic case of Mary Ann Hunt, a pregnant woman whose execution was stayed until after her child's birth. Why on earth, the poet wondered, was the reverence for life behind the sparing of the unborn child not extended to the mother?[31]

Nowhere did the early feminists more strongly and explicitly hold to a "consistent ethic of life" than in their stance against abortion. Feminists' concern for unborn children did not preclude, but instead was interwoven with, a larger concern for the women who bore them. Feminist antiabortion sentiment was grounded in an acute sensitivity to the problems of women who bear and raise children. It is not to be confused with the misogynist diatribes of conservatives like Dr. Horatio Storer. Storer claimed that aborting women "care nothing for ethical considerations," and dismissed their motivations as "excuses and pretexts," arguing that they were merely indulging in "a tide of fashion" started by the women's movement.[32]

Indeed, such invective outraged feminists—not only because it misrepresented their own position, but because they sympathized with unintentionally pregnant women. They organized a campaign against imposing the death penalty on Hester Vaughan, a poor woman accused of infanticide on shaky evidence, and offered aid to other women in crisis pregnancies. As much as they objected to abortion, they knew very well that women would not submit themselves to such a physically risky and psychologically painful procedure without compelling reason. Victoria Woodhull was speaking for the entire women's movement when she retorted: "Men must no longer insult all womanhood by saying that freedom means the degradation of woman. Every woman knows that if she were free, she would never bear an unwished-for child, nor think of murdering one before its birth."[33]

Precisely because feminists recognized how abortion was part and parcel of women's oppression, they repeatedly insisted that laws against it had to be supplemented by vigorous efforts against its root causes. These underlying causes included culturally enforced ignorance about sexual and reproductive physiology, including pregnancy prevention and fetal development; men's sexual and parental irresponsibility and coercion; women's economic dependency and lack of opportunity; the stigma placed on women, but not men, who conceived out of wedlock; an overall dearth of communal supports for those who bore and reared children; the cultural belief that pregnancy was a disease; and women's vulnerability to a profiteering industry which touted abortion as a panacea for all these injustices.

Most of these social conditions affected women of every social class and ethnic group, but they fell most heavily upon African-Americans. From early in life, female slaves were systematically subjected to sexual and reproductive traumas: rape and enforced impregnation by their masters; deprivation of the proper rest and nutrition required for healthy gestation; wet nursing of white children to the exclusion of their own; and coerced, permanent separations from their children and consensual male partners. Slavemasters rationalized their behavior with an especially pernicious and victim-blaming variant on the double standard. They believed that white women were paragons of purity who deserved chivalrous male protection; black women were said to "ask for it" because they were purported to be wanton, rapacious and destructively lustful by nature.[34]

As did their white allies, feminist ex-slaves such as Sojourner Truth and Frederick Douglass spoke out against these degradations. Sojourner Truth described her personal sorrow at having to wet-nurse white babies while all thirteen of her own children were taken from her, and she believed God alone heard her sorrowful lament.[35] Yet the currently known historical record seldom directly addresses the link between black women's lack of sexual and reproductive freedom and the practice of abortion/infanticide. According to some present day commentators, "child murder" by slave women was a desperate, self—and other—destructive effort to revolt against miserable conditions.[36] This dynamic is imaginatively reconstructed in Toni Morrison's 1987 novel *Beloved*, which is based upon an actual historical incident. The protagonist, Sethe, escapes from slavery but is haunted by the ghost of the cherished daughter she had killed long ago to spare her from the adversities of a life of captivity.[37]

Only a handful of nineteenth-century African-American women, however, before or after the Emancipation Proclamation, had the chance to speak out in their own voices about *anything*, let alone "indelicate" subjects related to sexuality. Illiteracy was mandated, and public speaking was even more out of the question than for white women. Most writings by black female authors were largely forgotten until quite recently—that is, if they were preserved at all. In these ways, as in so many others, African-American women were metaphorically aborted from society. The possible historical links between "child murder" and oppression of other groups—Native Americans, Americans of Latin heritage, disabled persons, for instance—have been articulated even less. Hopefully, the links will become clearer with time, as more historians seriously engage themselves with issues of cultural diversity and more long-forgotten historical resources come to light.

This much said, the early feminists' insistence on the misogynist underpinnings of slavery was obviously related to their demand of "voluntary motherhood" for all women. Not surprisingly, abolitionist Sarah Grimké was one of the first to pen the case for voluntary motherhood.[38] It is also clear that feminists, whatever their differences on other matters, all agreed wholeheartedly about this demand. As historian Linda Gordon has noted, the early feminists—from the conservative church-women involved in temperance reform to the anarchistic, often antireligious "free lovers"—were all united in their belief that "voluntary motherhood," more than any other measure, would put this industry out of business.[39] Their advocacy of voluntary motherhood, but not abortion, may strike the modern reader as contradictory. In the present debate the phrase "enforced motherhood" denotes the denial of women's purported right to abortion. It meant something entirely different to our feminist foremothers, who viewed abortion not as a right but as an *abrogation* of rights. Given this disapproval of abortion, what could they have possibly meant by "enforced motherhood"? They meant motherhood resulting from sexual intercourse forced on women at times when they did not deem it in their best interests to risk childbearing or childrearing. When the early feminists spoke of woman's right to her own body or right over herself, they meant her right to be free from sexual coercion and irresponsibility on the part of men. This was a most significant demand, for rape was not only widespread outside of marriage, but *legal and expected* within it. Even in cases where sex appeared to be consensual, socioeconomic conditions demanded that women, both single and married, subjugate themselves sexually to men in order to survive. And women were punished for the resulting pregnancies, while no blame was affixed to their male offenders. This differential treatment rankled feminists, especially since conservative men excoriated aborting women as frivolous and self-indulgent, without saying a word about the men who impregnated them.

Voluntary motherhood was important to safeguard not only women but children, as shown by the contention that it would prevent abortion. In addition, it was widely believed in the Victorian period that the conditions surrounding a child's conception and gestation made a long-lasting impression on his or her well-being. Thus, children conceived through coercive, inegalitarian sexual relations would grow up to be sickly, insane, or retarded. This fear was based on more than a folk belief. It derived from the reality of congenital syphilis, often transmitted to women and hence unborn children by men who regarded their wives as "baby machines" and prostitutes as instruments for their pleasure. This was a eugenic argument, but one initially made in order to safeguard individual rights rather than to advance a reactionary social engineering agenda.[40] The feminist case against abortion and for voluntary motherhood did at times become intertwined with prejudices against disabled persons, blacks, and immigrants. Elizabeth Cady Stanton's piece "Infanticide and Prostitution," for example, is clearly tainted by such attitudes. However, such prejudices were not inherent or even central to the historical feminist argument for a woman's right to her own body and an unborn child's right to life. Indeed, as Part Two of this volume demonstrates, contemporary activists believe that such prejudices *con-*

tradict prolife feminism, hence their frequent challenges to right-wing abortion opponents.

The early feminists agreed wholeheartedly on the benefits that voluntary motherhood would bring to women and children, especially the elimination of abortion. As noted earlier, they agreed that women needed access to sex education and family planning knowledge in order to exercise free choice in regard to motherhood. But they differed over *which* family planning methods were acceptable means to the end of voluntary motherhood: abstinence or contraception. Many spoke of abstinence as the best solution to the problem of unintended pregnancy. This was not necessarily because they were utterly repelled by sex, or felt that its *only* purpose was procreation. Rather, it was because abstinence according to a woman's own choice afforded her the most control over her situation. Nineteenth-century birth control methods were either male-controlled (withdrawal or condom), or, even if female-controlled, not as effective as a woman might need them to be (douches or "womb veils"—devices like a diaphragm or cervical cap, but without accompanying spermicide). Those who argued for abstinence as opposed to contraception also were concerned that the latter would actually work against women's interests. They felt that given the power disparities between men and women, contraception might encourage more male exploitation. Dr. John Cowan devoted a whole chapter of his sex education manual *Science of a New Life* to praise of the women's movement. The book was hailed by a number of prominent feminists. Yet Cowan cautioned that contraceptives would give men's "licentiousness full play without restriction," giving rise to all the "pains, the troubles … the woman has to experience through man's lust."[41] In other words, there was a sense in which contraception was equivalent to abortion.

Others were convinced that women willing to accept the risks of contraceptive failure should have access to other preventive measures. This was because intercourse had functions other than making babies; and contraception, in great contrast to abortion, did not take life. Indeed, an effective separation between procreation and the other purposes of sex would actually prevent the destruction of life that takes place in abortion. "I am confident," wrote Dr. Hollick, "that much of the horrible practice of procuring Abortion, now so prevalent among married people, is caused by the want of simple and reliable means of prevention."[42]

English activists Charles Bradlaugh and Annie Besant, who were tried for distributing Charles Knowlton's birth-control treatise *Fruits of Philosophy*, similarly made a sharp distinction between abortion and other methods of fertility control. "The advocacy of all checks ... is lawful except such as advocate the destruction of the fetus after conception or of the child after birth ... I admit in the fullest sense that any advocacy of the destruction of human life is not simply illegal under statute, is not simply illegal under common law, but is illegal under that moral law which obtains wherever there is an intelligent appreciation of what morality should be."[43] American physician and radical Edward Bond Foote concurred: "Any interference with the natural growth development of [the embryo] at any stage of its uterine life causes an abortion, and is therefore destructive of a living entity; but if the two elements necessary to conception fail to come together there is no impregnation, no beginning of a new life, and physiologically speaking, there is no sin in merely preventing the union of the two microscopic elements by artificial means which for want of a single appropriate word I will call contraceptics ..."[44]

But advocates of "contraceptics" did agree with Cowan that "if there is one direction more than another in which Woman's Rights should assert itself, it is in this one of choice of time for sexual congress."[45] As a means of preventing abortion, voluntary motherhood, even in this sense, is of more than historical interest. Indeed, some contemporary feminists have conflated abortion and rape, despite their belief in a right to abortion.

In a memoir of her work as an abortion clinic nurse, Sallie Tisdale reports a dream "that two men grabbed me and began to drag me away. 'Let's do an abortion,' they said with a sickening leer, and I began to scream, plunged into a vision of sucking, scraping pain, of being spread and torn by impartial instruments that do only what they are bidden."[46] In *Of Women Born*, poet and lesbian-rights activist Adrienne Rich has written: "In a society where women entered sexual intercourse willingly, where adequate contraception was a genuine social priority, there would be no 'abortion issue' ... Abortion is violence: a deep, desperate violence inflicted by a woman upon, first of all, herself. It is the offspring, and will continue to be the accuser, of a more pervasive and prevalent violence, the violence of rapism."[47]

Catharine MacKinnon, the esteemed law professor known for her efforts to combat pornography and sexual harassment, evokes Rich's analysis in her own commentary on *Roe v. Wade*, the 1973 case legalizing abortion on demand in the United States. "Sexual intercourse, still the most common cause of pregnancy, cannot simply be presumed co-equally determined. ... Sex doesn't look a whole lot like freedom when it appears normatively less costly for women to risk an undesired, often painful, traumatic, dangerous, sometimes illegal, and potentially life-threatening procedure than to protect themselves in advance. Yet abortion policy has never been explicitly approached in the context of how women get pregnant, that is, as a consequence of intercourse under conditions of gender inequality; that is, as an issue of forced sex."[48]

But MacKinnon is mistaken that abortion policy has never been approached in this manner. As we have seen and will continue to see, it has been approached in this manner throughout the history of feminism. It is time for feminists to reclaim their past and discover how much insight it can yield into the present abortion controversy. Decades of feminism have tremendously improved people's lives. Yet abortion is still very much with us, and still is caused by many of those same injustices against women identified by early feminists. Women today continue to struggle with male irresponsibility and other forms of discrimination against them and against their children, born and unborn. Thus the prolife tradition in feminism cannot be summarily dismissed as old-fashioned and outdated. It not only invites thoughtful people to question an automatic equation of feminism with the cause of abortion rights; it invites them to consider whether this equation has actually worked against women's interests. For there is still wisdom in Lucy Stone's portrayal of abortion as a sign and symbol of the grave injury which patriarchy inflicts upon all human beings:

> I have seen the acorn men and woman, but never the perfect oak; all are but abortions. The young mother, when first the babe nestles in her bosom ... finds herself unprepared for this new relation in life, and she sends forth the child scarred and dwarfed by her own weakness ... as no stream can rise higher than its fountain.[49]

Dr. Charlotte Denman Lozier
(1844–1870)

Charlotte Denman Lozier was an accomplished and independent-minded woman: a wife, a mother, a respected physician, and a firmly committed activist.[50] Her biography was all the more remarkable for the fact that she lived in an age when it was widely proclaimed that the physiological functions unique to women—menstruation, pregnancy, lactation—necessarily confined the "weaker sex" to the domestic sphere.[51] But Lozier was never one to be cowed into obedience by such misogynist fulminations.

From a very early age, she clearly showed that she was her own woman. Orphaned at twelve on the western frontier, she supported her younger siblings by teaching. She then earned a degree at the New York (City) Medical College for Women, an institution which outraged conservatives not only because of the gender of its students, but because it was the first to incorporate the study of hygiene into the curriculum. Specifically attacking the College, Dr. Augustus K. Gardner raged that medical training sinfully exposed women to "the horrors and disgusts of life," which they found "disgusting … accustomed [as they are] to softness and the downy side of life."[52]

As a student at this scandalous institution, Charlotte Denman successfully protested against Bellevue Hospital's refusal to extend clinical privileges to medical women. After graduation, she joined the faculty of her alma mater and served as First Vice-President of the Working Women's Association. While continuing her career, she married and had three children with the physician son of College founder Dr. Clemence Lozier, another woman with a remarkable life history.[53] Like other pioneering women physicians such as her mother-in-law, Elizabeth Blackwell, and Harriot K. Hunt, Charlotte firmly believed in empowering female patients to understand and care for their own bodies and those of their children, despite the widespread prejudice that "it's not fitting for women to know about themselves; it makes them nervous!"[54]

This prejudice is so formidable and deeply entrenched in the culture that it has persisted well into the late twentieth century, even in the minds of people who profess to be champions of women. The United States Supreme Court has ruled more than once that a woman contemplating abortion need not be informed about pregnancy, fetal development, the possible health hazards of the procedure, or alternatives to it. The Court's rationale has been that legally requiring such information "may serve only to *confuse* and punish [a woman] and to heighten her anxiety."[55] Feminist scholar Rosalind Pollack Petchesky has not been alone in condemning such informed consent requirements as "an intimidation tactic meant to scare women out of having an abortion, and to make them feel guilty if they do."[56]

Dr. Lozier and her professional and ideological contemporaries would have been puzzled by people who expressed such opinions in the name of woman's rights. Early feminists considered information about pregnancy, fetal development, and the destructiveness of abortion *empowering* to women. And they supported legislative disincentives to abortion. This is demonstrated by the following account of Lozier's effort to uphold an antiabortion statute while offering assistance to the pregnant woman in the case. Her action was praised not only in the popular press, but by the influential and progressive *Springfield Republican,* which was edited by feminist sympathizers, and most of all by *The Revolution,* the radical weekly put out by Elizabeth Cady Stanton and Susan B. Anthony.[57] Although it has largely been forgotten, a short biography of Charlotte Lozier remains to this day in the Library of Congress. It bears some notes made by Susan B. Anthony in 1903.[58]

Restellism Exposed:
The Resistance of Dr. Charlotte Denman Lozier

Dr. Charlotte Lozier of 323 West 34th Street, of this city [New York] was applied to last week by a man pretending to be from South Carolina, by name, Moran, as he also pretended, to procure an abortion on a very pretty young girl apparently about eighteen years old. The Dr. assured him that he had come to the wrong place for any such shameful, revolting, unnatural and unlawful purpose. She proffered to the young woman any assistance in her power to render, at the proper time, and cautioned and counseled her against the fearful act which she and her attendant (whom she called her cousin) proposed. The man becoming quite abusive, instead of appreciating and accepting the counsel in the spirit in which it was proffered, Dr. Lozier caused his arrest under the laws of New York for his inhuman proposition, and he was held to bail in a thousand dollars for appearance in court.

The *[New York] World* of last Sunday contained a most able and excellent letter from Dr. Lozier, in which she explains and most triumphantly vindicates her course in the very disagreeable position in which she was placed. It is certainly very gratifying and must be particularly so to Dr. Lozier, to know that her conduct in the affair is so generally approved by the press and the better portion of the public sentiment, so far as yet expressed. The following are only extracts from extended articles in the New York *World* and Springfield *Republican* relating to it:

> The laws of New York make the procuring of a miscarriage a misdemeanor, punishable by imprisonment for not less than three months, nor more than a year; they define the committing of an abortion resulting in the death of either child or mother to be manslaughter in the second degree. It was this latter crime that Dr. Lozier was asked to commit, and she insists that as the commission of crime is not one of the functions of the medical profession, a person who asks a physician to commit the crime of ante-natal infanticide can be no more considered his patient than one who asks him to poison his wife. Thus Dr. Lozier makes out her case, and seems to prove conclusively that neither law nor professional honor forbids physicians handing over to the police persons who apply to them to commit murder; but that law, professional honor, moral obligation, and social duty all unite in compelling them to thus aid in the punishment of these attempts to procure the slaughter of the innocents. This being so, how does it happen that it has been left for this woman to be the first to perform this duty? The pulpit and the press for months have been ringing with declamations against the frequency of the offence of ante-natal infanticide among the most respectable classes of American society. Has there been no cause for these accusations; or do physicians generally hold opinions of their duty in this matter wholly different from those entertained and acted on by Mrs. Lozier?

And the Springfield *Republican* says:

> A woman physician at New York, Mrs. Dr. Charlotte D. Lozier, took the very unusual step, on Saturday, of having a man and a woman, who had applied to her to assist in procuring an abortion upon the latter, arrested and committed to jail for trial, under the New York statute, which has long been practically a dead letter,

but which makes the bare solicitation or advising to commit this crime a state prison offence.

The woman, whose name is Caroline Fuller, first went alone to the office of Doctress Lozier, and on stating her purpose was kindly warned of the sin and danger of such a course, and allowed to depart. But the next day she returned with her paramour, Andrew Moran of Anderson Court House, S.C., and he boldly demanded that the operation should be performed, offering to pay roundly and to shield Mrs. Lozier from any possible legal consequences, should there be a fatal termination. Upon this Mrs. Lozier promptly sent for a policeman, who arrested both Moran and Miss Fuller, though the latter was discharged when brought before the justice for examination. Moran is held for trial, having failed to bribe Mrs. Lozier not to appear against him by offering her $1,000. Moran and Miss Fuller came all the way from South Carolina to have the abortion performed, and Moran's wife made a third in the party, though one would hardly suppose she would enjoy a trip to the metropolis under such circumstances. May we not hope that the action of Mrs. Lozier in this case is an earnest [sic] of what may be the more general practice of physicians if called upon to commit this crime, when women have got a firmer foothold in the profession? Some bad women as well as bad men may possibly become doctors, who will do anything for money; but we are sure most women physicians will lend their influence and their aid to shield their sex from the foulest wrong committed against it. It will be a good thing for the community when more women like Mrs. Lozier belong to the profession.

—*The Revolution*, December 2, 1869.

Paulina Wright Davis (1813–1876)

S hortly after her "exposure of Restellism," Charlotte Denman Lozier died in childbirth. She was not yet twenty-six. The journal *Herald of Health* did not deem the manner of Lozier's death proof of the societal conventions that she had always defied. Rather, an editorial lamented, "Mrs. Dr. Lozier had but a few days previous to her death engaged to become a contributor [to *The Herald*] on important subjects. She had important matters to communicate to our readers, good words that will now never be said." If her untimely death proved anything, it showed that physicians, both male and female, needed to protect themselves from overwork. The advancement of medical knowledge would help them to care better for themselves, so that they could continue caring for others.[59]

Parker Pillsbury, an eminent abolitionist and an editor of the *Revolution*, noted in her obituary that "an earthly career of the very brightest promise has been arrested. … Her funeral was very largely attended, the church being nearly full, and a more sorrowing audience is seldom seen … How large was the loss both in a private and domestic and in a public view."[60] A week later, the paper featured a eulogy from another editor: Paulina Kellogg Wright Davis, long a highly esteemed suffragist and abolitionist.

As a girl on the then-frontier of Western New York, Davis was stung by the injustice of her puritanical church's refusal to allow even gifted women to speak in mixed assemblies. Although the prevailing culture justified slavery on supposedly Scriptural grounds, Davis outspokenly opposed it, so much so that in 1835 a mob of slavery advocates threatened her house. As early as the 1840's, Davis and freethinker Ernestine Rose agitated for married women's property rights. These were denied under the common-law doctrine, often reinforced by clergymen, that a wife's legal personhood was subsumed into that of her husband. In 1853, Davis started the Providence, Rhode Island-based *Una*, one of the first women's-rights periodicals in the United States. During its three years of publication, the *Una* served as an important public forum for feminist leaders to state their newly developing critiques of marriage and the confinement of women exclusively to the home.[61]

As noted in the 1871 compilation *History of the National Woman's Rights Movement,* Davis's work not only "commenced before the woman's rights conventions were held," but addressed the crying need of women to learn about their bodies:

> As early as 1844 [Davis] commenced the study of anatomy and physiology, and gave lectures on these subjects. She sent to Paris and imported the first *femme modele* that was ever brought into the country. She has told many amusing anecdotes of the effect of unveiling this manikin in the presence of a class of ladies. Some would leave the house, others faint in their seats, others draw their veils, and a few only had the moral hardihood and scientific curiosity to appreciate it and examine the fearful and wonderful manner in which they were made. In course of time, however, these natural "weaknesses and disabilities" were over-come, and many of Mrs. Davis's classes are today professors and pupils in our medical colleges, hospitals, and dissecting-rooms, the result of her early efforts in urging the medical education of women. Many who are now comfortably supporting themselves in that profession gratefully acknowledge her influence in di-recting the whole course of their lives.[62]

Davis was, then, a most fitting person to pay tribute to Dr. Lozier. In her eulogy, Davis compares Lozier to Elizabeth Garrett, the first En-glishwoman to enter the medical profession, who never forgot the brave women who had made her success possible. And of all Lozier's admi-rable actions, it is interesting—and telling—which one Davis found the most commendable.

"A True Woman"
by Paulina Wright Davis

Miss Garrett has founded two scholarships for women who wish to study medicine in London. When will some of the rich women of our country go and do likewise, instead of endowing Professors' chairs in theological seminaries for "poor but pious young men"?

How many fairs have been held? how many poor eyes tortured almost to blindness, doing fancy work to support students in theological seminaries, and aid young men to get a liberal education, we will not attempt to ascertain—suffice it to say, that when women became strong enough to demand admission to colleges, theological seminaries, and medical schools, and found that there was no place for them, they saw that they must do their own work, that no college would ever voluntarily open its doors to them, and again fairs, with all their petty toil of pin-cushions, furbelows, raffles of doubtful morality, post-offices and clap-traps of all kinds, in order to make money, were resorted to; but now, that they are chartered and endowed and it is a fixed fact that women are in the professions, and are successful in practice, nothing more is re-quired except to enlarge and to give till they have all the means and appliances that young men have.

It is certainly complimentary to their genius, capacity and power for grasping questions so intricate and lumbered with technicalities, that they have been able to succeed at all, with the meagre opportunities which they have had. They claimed the right as theirs by divine adapta-tion, and they have proven that the claim was true. Custom and preju-dice said, No, it is not your sphere. Spiritual intuition said, Go on, study when, where, and how you can; and when you have acquired give to others.

We have been led to these reflections by the unexpected death of Mrs. Charlotte Lozier, who was one of those richly gifted women who seized instinctively medical science, so far as there is any settled prin-ciples, and imparted as freely as she received.

Her steady, persistent, unwavering integrity, and her high sense of duty were strongly marked. Her recent action, prompt and decisive, against a high-handed crime cannot be too much commended. She chose to bear reproach and bitterness, rather than a stain upon her conscience. The impression will long remain with us of her pure, womanly grace and sweetness. Her real strength did not reveal itself in the brief inter-view we had with her; it was not till she came out firmly to stay the prevalent sin of infanticide that we knew the woman in all her greatness.

Her sense of justice would not allow her to let the wrong-doer escape the penalty of the law, while at the same time she pitied and tenderly cared for the victim. We have been amazed to hear her denounced for this brave, noble act on the ground of professional privacy. It is said she had no right to expose the outrage of having one thousand dollars offered her to commit murder.

The murder of the innocents goes on. Shame and crime after crime darken the history of our whole land. Hence it was fitting that a true woman should protest with all the energy of her soul against this woeful crime.

—*The Revolution,* January 20, 1870.

Dr. Elizabeth Blackwell (1821–1910)

The Miss Garrett praised in Davis' eulogy was inspired to enter medicine after attending a lecture series given in England by none other than Dr. Elizabeth Blackwell.[63] Blackwell is widely remembered as the first female physician in the United States; more accurately, she was the first American woman to earn what has become the most prestigious of medical degrees—the M.D. In the nineteenth century, there were a wide variety of medical credentials, including the homeopathic degree held by Clemence and Charlotte Lozier; and, of course, throughout history there have been midwives practicing the healing arts without official sanction of any kind. Recognizing women's earlier contributions to the field of medicine, however, does not diminish Blackwell's accomplishments.

Blackwell came from a prosperous and reform-minded family which included many notable women. Her sister Emily Blackwell followed her into the practice of medicine.[64] Elizabeth's brother, Henry, the abolitionist, was married to Lucy Stone, the suffragist who paved the way for married women who wish to keep their birth names. Another brother, Samuel, was married to Antoinette Brown Blackwell, one of the first women ministers in the United States and an influential writer.[65]

At a young age, Elizabeth Blackwell decided she would not passively enjoy a life of privilege. She wanted to give something back to the world, so she decided to become a doctor, fully cognizant of the gender discrimination that she would face. Her decision was clinched by an item in the *New York Herald* regarding Madame Restell. She wrote in her diary: "The gross perversion and destruction of motherhood by the abortionist filled me with indignation, and awakened active antagonism. That the honorable term 'female physician' should be exclusively applied to those women who carried on this shocking trade seemed to me a horror. It was an utter degradation of what might and should become a noble position for women."[66]

Blackwell was strengthened in her resolve by her readings of the eighteenth century Scandinavian mystic Emmanuel Swedenborg. Swedenborg's works inspired Spiritualism and other challenges to Christian orthodoxy. Blackwell was especially attracted to his belief in the power of compassionate works, akin to the Mayahana Buddhist emphasis on generating good karma to liberate all sentient beings, seen and unseen, from their sufferings. "Being at that time a reader of Swedenborg, and strongly impressed by his vivid representation of the unseen world, I finally determined to do what I could 'to redeem the hells' and especially the one form of hell—abortion—thus forced upon my notice."[67]

Blackwell's long moral struggle began with the fight to get into medical school. After a dozen rejections, Blackwell was finally admitted to Geneva Medical College in Syracuse in 1845 as a prank on the part of the faculty and the student body. The entire four years, she was relentlessly harassed by her male classmates despite, or possibly because of, her superior performance. Following graduation, she received two more years of training in Europe, where she was cordially received, for the most part. In contrast, when she went to New York City and attempted to establish herself professionally, she found herself shunned and alienated by her peers. Undaunted, in 1854 she adopted a seven-year-old orphan girl, a remarkable choice for a woman who had also opted long ago to remain single. Three years later, she, along with her sister Emily and a German physician, Marie Zakrzewska, opened the New York Infirmary for Women and Children, the first American hospital with an entirely female staff. In 1865, the Infirmary received a charter to begin a women's medical college. Although in competition with Clemence Lozier's medical school for women, the Infirmary's approach to patient care and medical education also emphasized prevention and self-help. During this time Elizabeth Blackwell openly challenged the Restell business.[68]

Throughout her career, Blackwell lived out the passionate concern for women and children that informed her antiabortion stance. She became known as a sexual reformer. She wrote about the ill effects of prostitution on women who practiced it.[69] She insisted that women's capacity for sexual passion and enjoyment be recognized.[70] And she called upon pregnant women to revere and actively care for the miraculous new lives growing within their bodies, as she does in this passage from one of her earliest publications, a sex education manual for girls.

"Look at the First Faint Gleam of Life ..."
by Dr. Elizabeth Blackwell

Look at the first faint gleam of life, the life of the embryo, the commencement of human existence. We see a tiny cell, so small that it may be easily overlooked; the anatomist may examine it with scalpel or microscope, and what does he discover? Nothing but a delicate, transparent membrane, containing one drop of clear water; the chemist may analyze it with the most scrupulous care, and find nothing but the trace of some simple salts. And yet there is in that simple germ-cell something wonderful—life!—it is a living cell; it contains a power *of progressive growth, according to laws, towards a definite type,* that we can only regard with reverent admiration. Leave it in its natural home, tended by the rich life of the healthy maternal organism, and it will grow steadily into the human type; *in no other by any possibility.* Little by little the faint specks will appear in the enlarging cell, which mark the head, the trunk, the budding extremities; tiny channels will groove themselves in every direction, red particles of inconceivable minuteness will appear in them—they move, they tend towards one central spot, where a little channel has enlarged, has assumed a special form, has already begun to palpitate; finally the living blood in the small arteries joins that in the heart, and the circulation is established. From every delicate incomplete part, minute nerve-threads shoot forth, they tend invariably towards their centres, they join the brain, the spinal marrow, the ganglia. The nervous system is formed. The cell rapidly enlarges, its attachments to the maternal organism becomes more powerful, for increasing amounts of fresh nourishment must be conveyed to the growing being, the work advances to perfection, each organ is distinctly formed, placed in the cavities of head, chest, and abdomen, that are now completely closed; the human type is surely attained, and after a brief period of consolidation the young existence, created from that simple cell, will awake to a further development of independent life. Throughout this period of early life we remain spectators merely of the wonderful growth; it would be impious folly to attempt to interfere directly with this act of creation; but even here, in this early stage of existence, we have *important aid* to render ... Such favoring influences are found in the daily life of the mother, during the early period of the embryonic existence, in the cheerful sunshine of the spirit that should so naturally enfold the new centre of many hopes, in the observance of those important rules of hygiene, regular habits, early hours, periodic exercise, cold bathing, plain wholesome food, and loose comfortable clothing; these rules are simple, easily understood, not difficult to be observed, yet they are of *immense importance*—they are the *favoring circumstances* of growth, they are *our part* in the work of creation. Then, surely, they never can be neglected by the wise mother who has once clearly recognized their use.

—Elizabeth Blackwell, M.D., *The Laws of Life, With Special Reference to the Education of Girls*, New York: Putnam and Sons, 1852, 70–73.

Dr. Anna Densmore French

D r. Anna Densmore French was another pioneering woman physician who championed sex education for the sake of maternal and child welfare. She was a founding member and leader of Sorosis, an organization of professional women in New York City whose efforts won respect even outside the feminist community. She persuaded the New York City Board of Education to grant her, by unanimous consent, the use of school property for a radical project: given the limited number of female physicians and their restricted availability for health education work, she wished to train schoolteachers for this task. Women schoolteachers were far more numerous and had daily access to the young people who needed so much to learn about their bodies. Her training sessions attracted an unusually large number of enthusiastic women.[71] The piece below is a letter written to the *Revolution* by a satisfied participant.

Lectures of Dr. Anna Densmore

New York, March 18, 1868
Editors of the *Revolution:*

When reading your valuable paper this morning my attention was specially drawn to two articles, one entitled "The One Thing Needful," the other "Child Murder."

In the first article, we find these expressions: "There is much, very much, to be said to women that cannot be printed, that must come from thoroughly taught women to their sisters. And until it is said, and the truths acted upon, the world must continue to suffer. Only women can save us."

While inwardly commenting upon the force of the above quotation it seemed to me that perhaps you might not be aware that there is a movement now in successful operation in our own city that is destined to do more for women in the way of widespread physiological knowledge among them than has ever been accomplished.

Dr. Anna Densmore, of our city, delivered a course of lectures to ladies, at Bunyan Hall, in the month of January last, which were more largely attended than any course of scientific lectures on medical topics ever given in this city.

Many of the teachers in our public schools were present, and both principals and subordinates were much delighted with the valuable instruction afforded them. At the close of the courts, Dr. Densmore proposed to form a class for teachers exclusively, to qualify them to instruct young women and girls in those departments of Physiology and Hygiene, that are specially important to their future as wives and mothers, and in the language of your Boston correspondent, "that must come from thoroughly taught women to their sisters." 'Tis a verity in this connection that "only woman can save."

She should present this topic for our consideration, she said, because it is the one least understood, and the one of all others necessary to be *well* comprehended in order that the duties and responsibilities of maternity and child culture should be realized in sufficient force to compel a *radical change* in the wifehood and motherhood of American women.

Further assuring us that it is only in the light of such knowledge that young women can expect to cope with temptation successfully under all the various forms in which it is disguised, and that it is only necessary for women to know themselves *thoroughly,* in all that pertains to the varying attributes of girlhood, wifehood, and maternity; for true morality to attain a sound enduring foundation, against which the artifices of past times can make but a light impression. And that to ignorance of the laws that govern her life in all these particulars, are due to the sad advances that Frivolity, Invalidism, and Crime, have made in all communities of women.

I can assure you that we were deeply touched, as well as interested, by the earnest appeal made to us as teachers to improve the large and valuable opportunities that our position and extensive intercourse with the young and others of our sex can command, to carry on the work of Physiological training on a large and successful scale.

Every woman physician, she said, should herself be a teacher, and make it a cardinal rule to spread the knowledge she has gained, in reference to the prevention of disease and the possibility of imparting better constitutions to our children than is now done. But, from the nature and multiplicity of our professional duties, they could not as a class be as largely useful in this direction as they ought and desire to be, *unless* they could make available the talent and energy of some other class of women that could carry on the work continuously, after suitable preparation, from the point where the woman physician was compelled by circumstances to relax her efforts.

She then demonstrated to us in a forcible and happy way that we were the great connecting link between woman physicians and the vast numbers that were perishing from want of instruction, and the only class of women that could make such knowledge readily and extensively available.

The class was formed in a few days, and we number from one hundred and fifty to two hundred, I do not know the exact number.

The Board of Education granted us the use of the main hall of the Twelfth Street Public School by a unanimous vote, and we are progressing rapidly, to say nothing of the engrossing interest with which the entire subject is invested by Dr. Densmore.

All teachers are cordially imparted to partake of these advantages without money and without price, and I will add that the hall will not seat more than *two hundred*. In reading the article on "Child Murder," I could not repress the wish that the whole world could have heard Dr. Densmore's remarks at Bunyan Hall upon that theme. Those who had the privilege will never forget the startling effect of the truths that she revealed relative to the primitive and ever present vitality of the developing embryo, as evidenced by the fainting of several self-convicted participators in the crime of premeditated child destruction before birth.

And now, I should not be true to my womanly instincts if I failed to write a few of those things that your Boston correspondent would probably class as among those that should be taught by women, but *not* written.

And I do it, because I am *sure* that women would rarely dare to destroy the product of conception if they did not *fully believe* that the little being was devoid of life during all the earlier period of gestation.

This was my own impression, and I know that the majority of women have never had any other opinion. In fact, we have been taught it from our mothers.

But Dr. Densmore demonstrated to us fully and clearly that the fulfillment of life processes were going on from the very beginning of embryonic development, and showed us how, step by step, was added bone, muscle, and nerve, and that even before any intimate connection was made between the little structure and the parent, that by the process of endosmosis an albuminous product that was furnished by the mother was absorbed and nourished the embryo to the extent of adding to its substance, and forming distinct enveloping membranes that continued to develop and remain as permanent structures till the child was born.

And that even before the mother could assure herself that she was to wear the crown of maternity by realizing the movements of the child, that the educated ear of the physician could often distinguish the beating of its heart. These are the facts that women need to know.

We have not such an amount of inherent depravity, nor such a degree of reckless daring to our composition, nor such a deficiency in the motherly instinct and other elements that go to make up the true woman, as to lead us into the commission of this most *deadly* crime *realizing it to be so.*

Give us *knowledge* before accusing us of crime, and do not forget to gauge the calibre of our sins by the light furnished to guide us.

Do not tell us that it is indelicate for us to know ourselves, and then ask us to discharge our responsibilities to ourselves and our children in a manner creditable to us and them and acceptable to the Almighty!

Let every God given function be stripped of the mysterious mantle with which the darkened mind of man has enshrouded it, and we shall no longer, wittingly or unwittingly, stain our hands with the blood of the innocent.

—A Teacher
—*The Revolution*, March 19, 1868.

Dr. Alice Bunker Stockham
(1833–1912)

D r. Alice Bunker Stockham continued the feminist women's health agenda begun by women like Davis, Blackwell and French. She, too, insisted on sex education as a measure that would prevent abortion and promote the best interests of women. She authored two popular medical books. Although little known today, Stockham lived a long, active, and achievement-filled life. She married, raised a family, and eventually became "a proud grandmother, but is not inclined to diminish her efforts on that account, as she is yet in the prime of life." As a profile in the *Chicago Tribune* declared, she enjoyed a most productive medical career, was "an enthusiastic worker in reform movements" and "above all, [was] a loyal friend to her sex." Born of Quaker parents, she started her professional life as a teacher, but then decided that she preferred medicine. While maintaining her Chicago practice, she became involved in suffrage and "Social Purity," the feminist campaign against the sexual double standard. She was involved in an organization that assisted prostitutes and other unintentionally pregnant women. She operated a free kindergarten, where she pursued an interest in experimental methods of education.[72] She travelled to Russia to personally meet with novelist Leo Tolstoy, and wrote a book extolling his spiritually based philosophy of nonviolence—which included vegetarianism, opposition to war and capital punishment, and an abhorrence of infanticide coupled with compassion for the desperate women who resorted to it.[73]

This book was one of many Stockham put out under the auspices of the publishing house she operated in partnership with her daughter Cora. A number of her widely selling works popularized medical knowledge in a manner that thoroughly challenged prevailing dogmas about female sexuality. Above all, she felt that people had a right to knowledge about their own sexuality, from childhood on. She believed that sex education should be an integral part of the elementary school curriculum. As she stated in 1878 to the Illinois Social Science Association, "we should make it obligatory upon ourselves to see to it that every child should get special instruction in procreation and reproduction."[74] Her marriage manual *Karezza* (1898) offered birth control advice and asserted that sexuality was *not* a matter of "man's necessities and woman's obedience to them." *Karezza* also proclaimed the healthfulness of sexual pleasure for its own sake, and indicated that women were just as capable of it as men were.[75]

Tokology, which went through many editions and was translated into five languages, functioned as the *Our Bodies, Ourselves* of its day. Numerous women received their only sex education from this widely distributed book. *Tokology*, which Stockham dedicated to her daughter, instructed knowledge-hungry readers about female physiology and pre-natal self-care. In contrast to most of her medical contemporaries, Stockham did not at all consider female bodily functions inherently pathological. Pregnancy, for instance, was not naturally the painful and debilitating disease that so many women experienced it to be; rather, it was made into one by an improper diet, a lack of exercise, the wearing of corsets, and by a general failure of society to treat it as a normal, healthy state of being. She considered the disease model of pregnancy as a contributing factor to abortion: "This period is transformed from one of hope, of cheerfulness, of exalted pleasure, into days of suffering, wretchedness, and direful forebodings. It is one long nightmare, and childbearing is looked upon as a curse and not a blessing. Motherhood is robbed of its divinest joys ... Ordinarily pregnancy is classed by both physicians and women among the diseases. Physical sufferings and mental agonies are the common accompaniments of the condition. Murderous intent fills the mother's heart, and the fearful crime of feticide is daily committed."[76] Stockham, then, traced this "fearful crime" back to a violent disregard for women's bodies—a disregard that women were socialized to practice against themselves, and against their unborn children at the same time. In her day, attempts to heal the alienation of women from their bodies were literally considered criminal. For her courageous work, Stockham was fined under the Comstock Law.[77]

Feticide
by Dr. Alice Bunker Stockham

Feticide is a produced abortion, whether by drugs, intentional shocks, electricity, or by instrumental interference, either by one's own hand or by the hand of a surgeon.

Many women have been taught to think that the child is not viable until after quickening, and that there is no harm in arresting pregnancy previous to the feeling of motion; others believe that there is no *life* until birth, and the cry of the child is heard.

A high legal authority says: "The absurdity of the principle upon which these distinctions are founded is easy of demonstration. The fetus, previous to the time of quickening, must either be dead or living. Now, that it is not the former, is most evident from neither putrefaction nor decomposition taking place, which would be the consequence of an extinction of vital principle. The embryo, therefore, before the crisis, must be in a state different from that of death, and that can be no other than life."

When the female germ and male sperm unite, then is the inception of a new life; all that goes to make up a human being—body, mind, and spirit, must be contained in embryo within this minute organism. *Life must be present from the very moment of conception.* If there was not life there could not be conception. At what other period of a human being's existence, either pre-natal or post-natal, could the union of soul and body take place? Is it not plain that the violent or forcible deprivation of existence of this embryo, the removal of it from the citadel of life, is its premature death, and hence the act can be denominated by no more mild term than murder, and whoever performs the act, or is accessory to it, is guilty of the crime of all crimes?

The life of the babe in her arms is to the mother more precious than all else; her heart is thrilled with a pang of agony at the thought of the least danger to its life. By what false reasoning does she convince herself that another life, still more dependent upon her for its existence, with equal rights and possibilities, has no claim upon her for protection? More than this, she deliberately strikes with the red hand of murder and terminates its existence with no thought of wrong, nor consciousness of violated law.

The woman who produces abortion, or allows it to be produced, risks her own life and health in the act, and commits the highest crime in the calendar, for she takes the life of her own child. She defrauds the child of the right to its existence.

By a wise provision we are placed in this world for growth, development and preparation for another life. As we leave this life, we must enter the other. In so far as a human being is deprived of this existence, to that extent he is deprived of schooling and preparation for the other life. Pause for one moment and think of the thousands of stunted, dwarfed beings that are prematurely ushered into an existence that can not be normal and designed. Were infants to have been born into spirit life, provision would have been made to that effect. That they are born into this life is proof that this world is best adapted for their growth and education.

There may be no harm in *preventing* the conception of a life, but once conceived it should not be deprived of its existence in that world which in all its appointments is specially adapted to its development.

What are some of the incentives to produce abortion? An unmarried woman, seduced under false representation by a man who feels no responsibility for his own offspring, suffers alone all the shame and contumely of the act, and is tempted to cause miscarriage to shield her good name.

Married women who fear that maternity will interfere with their pleasures, are guilty of forcibly curtailing embryonic life. Others again, who are poor or burdened with care or grief, or have licentious or drunken husbands, shrink from adding to an already overburdened existence.

The first class, the girls who have lost their virtue under promise of marriage—are most deserving of sympathy and commiseration, though none receive less. "Let him who is without sin cast the first stone." At the least imputation against a fair girl's character, even those professing to be the followers of the loving Christ, often have so little leniency, so little of the Father's love in their hearts, that they hug their Christian robes to their bodies, lest they be contaminated by the polluting touch of the victim. They "pass by on the other side" and leave the poor broken-hearted child bleeding by the wayside.

The girl's lessons of life and purity have been learned mainly from one she loved and trusted, only to be betrayed. What wonder that in her ignorance of the value of life she should be tempted to add a second wrong to the first! She knows the shadow that has darkened her path; she realizes:

> "Alas! if for the rarity
> Of Christian charity
> Under the sun."

And if she can conceal the evidence of her guilt, she may hope by honest endeavor to retrieve her good name, and thus is tempted to produce an abortion.

Two wrongs cannot make a right ... When girls are given proper instruction upon the relations of the sexes and understand how to govern and guard themselves; when young men are taught that virtue has as high a meaning for one sex as for another, that the protective chivalry of which they boast does not imply that they shall force the woman with whom they associate to the defensive; and that the *paternal* interest in, and responsibilities for a child are equal to the *maternal,* then the temptation to produce abortion for the purpose of shielding one's character will not exist.

Of the second class, who produce miscarriage for pleasure and for selfish interest, there is little to say in extenuation. They may be victims of ignorance or of a false education. The maternal instinct is inherent in every woman's heart. It seems strange that any morbid idea of pleasure could antagonize the natural aspirations to such an extent that one could destroy the viability of her own offspring.

I will remember years ago the wife of a well-to-do lawyer making application to me to produce abortion. She had but one child, and he three years of age, and was surrounded by every comfort a prosperous business could afford. I sought the cause of the unnatural promptings of this intelligent woman's heart. It seems that a trip to Europe was contemplated and planned for in the early summer, and that this unanticipated and chance maternity would thwart their expectations. With all the arguments I then possessed, I showed her the wrong she sought to do, but nothing seemed to weigh against the proposed trip. She returned the second and third time even, armed with a lawyer's sophistry to endeavor to persuade me to be accessory to the diabolical deed. No doubt one cause of her persistency was fear of trusting her secret to me unless she could persuade me to be an accomplice.

She probably found someone to assist her out of the "trouble," for she took the proposed trip, but I was not astonished to learn three or four years later that she was lying at death's door with consumption. How many times she produced abortion I know not, but I was told that for months she suffered from uterine hemorrhages and in the weakened state of her system a violent cold settled upon her lungs which soon terminated her life. This was the physical result of the crime she had committed.

Of the last class, who have an apparent need to limit the size of the family, what can be said in extenuation of their committing this crime? Shall not the mother who already has many children, who is herself sick, nervous, and prostrated, or else has a husband who is diseased or a drunkard, leaving her the support of the family, save herself additional care by arresting the life of the embryo? The heart goes out in sympathy for all such, but even the most aggravating circumstances cannot atone for the crime. The whole nature of every true woman revolts against forced maternity.

Thoughtful minds must acknowledge the great wrong done when children are begotten under adverse conditions. Women must learn the laws of life so as to protect themselves, and not be the means of bringing sin-cursed, diseased children into the world.

The remedy is in the prevention of pregnancy, not in producing abortion. When men and women have learned the wise control of the procreative functions, then may we hope that children will be begotten in love and unselfishness. It is the undesired and undesigned maternity that is revolting to the nature of woman. As long as men feel that they have a right to indulgence of the passions under law, no matter what the circumstances, what the condition of the wife, or the probabilities of maternity, so long will the spirit of rebellion take possession of women and the temptation enter their souls to relieve themselves of this unsought burden. May the day soon arrive when men will learn that even passion should serve reason, and that gratification at least should not be sought at the expense of conjugal happiness and *unwelcome children.*

—*Tokology: A Book for Every Woman,* Second Edition, Chicago: Sanitary Publishing Company, 1887, 245-51.

Elizabeth Cady Stanton (1815–1902)

Today, people who affirm the value of fetal lives are often accused of contempt for women's lives, of obliviousness to the circumstances that prompt them to seek abortion. But Alice Stockham was certainly not afflicted by such misogyny. Neither was Elizabeth Cady Stanton, whose fearless and unflinching six-decade defense of women still inspires feminists today. In her own time, she was perceived as so radical that other, more conservative suffragists were afraid she would lose them any public respectability they had gained. From observing her father's legal practice, she resolved at a very early age to change the unjust laws that denied women control over their economic and family lives. She married an abolitionist, and, like Lucretia Mott and others, became disaffected by the hypocritical failure of the anti-slavery movement to include women as equals. Out of this discontent came the 1848 Seneca Falls Convention which marked the beginning of organized feminism in the United States. Even while raising her seven children, Stanton fought for "the Cause"—as a writer for the feminist press, an editor of *The Revolution,* a travelling lecturer, a leader of the National Woman Suffrage Association, co-editor with Susan B. Anthony and Matilda Joslyn Gage of the first three volumes of the monumental *History of Woman Suffrage*, and author of the controversial *Woman's Bible.*[78]

Stanton repeatedly asserted that personal liberation for women required the increased valuation of motherhood in the culture, but she decidedly rejected the notion that maternity was women's *only* creative power and that every woman had to be a mother. "Let us remember," she cautioned, "that womanhood is the great fact, wifehood and motherhood its incidents."[79] Indeed, she stated outright that societal pressures to make every woman bear children *degraded* motherhood: "It is not the duty of all men and women to be parents and because this has been regarded as their duty, infanticide is common and will continue to be until there is a changed attitude in regard to childbearing."[80]

As her declamations against abortion, infanticide, and other injustices clearly indicate, she felt that women as a sex would benefit by "taking back" motherhood from patriarchy in every way possible. She exulted in her subversive ability to remain healthful and vigorous throughout pregnancy and labor, particularly when she had her first daughter: "I have never felt such sacredness in carrying a child as I have in the case of this one. She is the largest and most vigorous baby I have ever had, weighing 12 lbs … And yet my labor was short and easy … What refined, delicate, genteel, civilized woman would get well in so indecently short a time? Dear me, how much cruel bondage of mind and suffering of body poor women will escape when she takes the liberty of being her own physician of both body and soul!"[81]

In a speech delivered around the country to women-only groups, she insisted: "We must educate our daughters that maternity is grand, and that God never cursed it, and the curse, if there be any, may be rolled off."[82] In the hope of "rolling off the curse," she addressed many subjects considered unfit for public discussion or consideration: the unfair denial of child custody to divorced women, the limitations of patriarchal religion, the desirability of family planning, the suffering inflicted upon mothers by the disease model of pregnancy, and the dire economic and social conditions which compelled so many women to resort not only to prostitution but to such equally "degrading" (her word) practices as abortion and infanticide. Like other early feminists, Stanton equated these two acts. She viewed them as violence not only against helpless children but against their mothers. In fact, she was at the forefront of the feminist defense of Hester Vaughan, a poor woman impregnated and abandoned by her employer, then accused of infanticide. The following pieces, including her plea on behalf of Vaughan, make clear not only her conflation of abortion and infanticide, but her belief that they were both atrocities resulting from the subjugation of women, both single and married, rich and poor. Thus, she held that legal action against women who resort to these practices must be tempered by a merciful desire not to blame the victim.[83]

Infanticide
by Elizabeth Cady Stanton

The remarkable mortality among natural or illegitimate children is a topic agitating the Press very largely just now in America, England, and France. The system of boarding them out for slow murder (that is about what it comes to) is alarmingly on the increase among the well-to-do in this country and England, as is evidenced by the cases that now and then rise to the surface, and are seen; while the advertisements of those

willing to take the "infants to board" tell a sure tale of the demand they propose to supply. In the late debate of the Corps Legislatif on the Emperor's new Army bill, M. Jules Favre made a tremendous point against the enforced celibacy of so large a proportion of young Frenchmen, declaring that it must result in an increase of illegitimate births ... It is impossible to shut our eyes to these facts ... Where lies the remedy?

—*NY Times*

In the independence of woman. "Give a man a right over my subsistence," says Alexander Hamilton, "and he has right over my whole moral being." When the world of work is open to woman, and it becomes as respectable as it is necessary to happiness for women of the higher classes, as well as others, to have some regular and profitable employment, then will woman take her true position as dictator in the social world.

The common excuse that young men give in our higher circles for not being married is, that they cannot afford to support a wife. Our idea is, that every woman of sound mind and body, with brains and two hands, is more noble, virtuous, and happy in supporting herself. So long as woman is dependent on man, her relation to him will be a false one, either in marriage or out of it; she will despise herself and hate him whose desires she gratifies for the necessaries of life; the children of such unions must needs be unloved and deserted. When women have their own property and business, they will choose and not be chosen; they will marry the men they love, or not at all; and where there is love between the parents, children will ever find care and protection. The strongest feeling of a true woman's nature is her love for her child; and the startling facts in the above extract, multiplying as they are on every side, warn us that all things are inverted. Objectors cry out to us who demand our rights, and the ballot to secure them, "Do not unsex yourselves." It is against this wholesale unsexing we wage our war.

We are living to-day under a dynasty of force; the masculine element is everywhere overpowering the feminine, and crushing women and children alike beneath its feet. Let woman assert herself in all her native purity, dignity, and strength, and end this wholesale suffering and murder of helpless children. With centuries of degradation, we have so little of true womanhood, that the world has but the faintest glimmering of what a woman is or should be.

—*The Revolution*, Jan. 29, 1868.

Child Murder

by Elizabeth Cady Stanton

The public attention has been much drawn to this frightful subject of late. The disclosures made are appalling to the highest degree. The social system is too corrupt, it would certainly seem, long to survive. Infanticide is on the increase to an extent inconceivable. Nor is it confined to the cities by any means. Androscoggin County in Maine is largely a rural district, but a recent Medical Convention there unfolded a fearful condition of society in relation to this subject. Dr. Oaks made the remark that, according to the best estimate he could make, there were *four hundred murders annually produced by abortion* in that county alone. The statement is made in all possible seriousness, before a meeting of "regular" practitioners in the county, and from the statistics which were as freely exposed to one member of the medical fraternity as another.

There must be a remedy for such a crying evil as this. But where shall it be found, at least where begin, if not in the complete enfranchisement and elevation of woman? Forced maternity, not out of legal marriage but within it, must lie at the bottom of a vast proportion of such revolting outrages against the laws of nature and our common humanity.

—*The Revolution*, March 12, 1868.

Infanticide and Prostitution

by Elizabeth Cady Stanton

Social Evil Statistics

The annual inspection report of the Captains of the Metropolitan Police of New York City and Brooklyn, gives the number of houses of prostitution as 523; of houses of assignation, 92; and of prostitutes, 2,097. This estimate, however, must be considered as only approximate, on account of the migratory character of the women to whom it relates, and because many of them reside in tenement houses and other dwellings, where their real character is unknown, and, it may be, unsuspected.

—*Sun.*

Child Murder

The horrible developments published the other day respecting a notorious "boarding-house" in this city where mothers, married or unmarried, can be delivered of their offspring in the strictest confidence, and relieved of all the bothers of maternity, awaken serious reflection as to what ought to be done for the repression of the terrible social evil of which such establishments are at once the outgrowth and the promoters. The evil, we are sorry to believe, is on the increase. The murder of children, either before or after birth, has become so frightfully prevalent that physicians, who have given careful and intelligent study to the subject, have declared that were it not for immigration the white population of the United States would actually fall off. In a populous quarter of a certain large Western city it is asserted, on medical authority, that not a single Anglo-American child has been born alive for the last three years. This is incredible; but, making all due allowances for exaggeration, it is plain enough that the murder of infants is a common thing among American women.

—*Tribune.*

Scarce a day passes but some of our daily journals take note of the fearful ravages on the race, made through the crimes of Infanticide and Prostitution.[84]

For a quarter of a century sober, thinking women have warned the nation of these thick coming dangers, and pointed to the only remedy, *the education and enfranchisement of women;* but men have laughed them to scorn. Let those who have made the "strong-minded" women of this generation the target for the jibes and jeers of a heedless world repent now in sackcloth and ashes, for already they suffer the retribution of their own folly at their own firesides, in their sad domestic relations. Wives sick, peevish, perverse; children deformed, blind, deaf, dumb, and insane; daughters silly and wayward; sons waylaid at every corner of the streets and dragged down to the gates of death, by those whom God meant to be their saviors and support. Look at these things no longer as necessary afflictions, sent to wean us from earth as visitations from Providence; but as the direct results of the violation of immutable laws, which it was our duty to study and obey. In the midst of all these miseries, let us regard ourselves as guilty sinners and not helpless saints. God does not wink, even at the sin of ignorance.

We ask our editors who pen those startling statistics to give us *their* views of the remedy. We believe the cause of all these abuses lies in the degradation of woman.

Strike the chains from your women; for as long as they are slaves to men's lust, man will be the slave of his own passions.

Wonder not that American women do everything in their power to avoid maternity; for, from false habits of life, dress, food, and generations of disease and abominations, it is to them a period of sickness, lassitude, disgust, agony and death.

What man would walk up to the gallows if he could avoid it? And the most hopeless aspect of this condition of things is that our Doctors of Divinity and medicine teach and believe that maternity and suffering are inseparable.

So long as the Bible, through the ignorance of its expounders, makes maternity a curse, and women, through ignorance of the science of life and health find it so, we need not wonder at the multiplication of these fearful statistics. Let us no longer weep, and whine, and pray over all these abominations; but with an enlightened consciousness and religious earnestness, bring ourselves into line with God's just, merciful, and wise laws. Let every thinking man make himself to-day a missionary in his own house. Regulate the diet, dress, exercise, health of your wives and daughters. Send them to Mrs. Plumb's gymnasium, Dio Lewis's school, or Dr. Taylor's Swedish movement cure, to develop their muscular system, and to Kuczkwoski to have the rhubarb, the sulphur, the mercury and "the sins of their fathers" (Exodus XX.5.) soaked out of their brains.

—*The Revolution*, February 5, 1868.

Trial by a Jury of Our Peers
by Elizabeth Cady Stanton

... [W]e demand in criminal cases that most sacred of all rights, trial by a jury of our own peers. The establishment of trial by jury is of so early a date that its beginning is lost in antiquity; but the right of trial by a jury of one's own peers is a great progressive step of advanced civilization. No rank of men have ever been satisfied with being tried by jurors higher or lower in the civil or political scale than themselves; for jealousy on the one hand, and contempt on the other, has ever effectually blinded the eyes of justice. Hence, all along the pages of history, we find the king, the noble, the peasant, the cardinal, the priest, the layman, each in turn protesting against the authority of the tribunal before which they were summoned to appear. Charles the First refused to recognize the competency of the tribunal which condemned him: for how, said he, can subjects judge a king? The stern descendants of our Pilgrim Fathers refused to answer for their crimes before an English Parliament. For how, said they, can a king judge rebels? And shall woman here consent to be tried by her liege lord, who has dubbed himself law-maker, judge, juror, and sheriff too?—whose power, though sanctioned by Church and State, has no foundation in justice and equity, and is a bold assumption of our inalienable rights. In England a Parliament-lord could challenge a jury where a knight was not empaneled; an alien could demand a jury composed of half his own countrymen; or, in some special cases, juries were even constituted entirely of women. Having seen that man fails to do justice to woman in her best estate, to the virtuous, the noble, the true of our sex, should we trust to his tender mercies the weak, the ignorant, the morally insane? It is not to be denied that the interests of man and woman in the present undeveloped state of the race, and under the existing social arrangements, are and must be antagonistic. The nobleman cannot make just laws for the peasant; the slaveholder for the slave; neither can man make and execute just laws for woman, because in each case, the one in power fails to apply the immutable principles of right to any grade but his own.

Shall an erring woman be dragged before a bar of grim-visaged judges, lawyers, and jurors, there to be grossly questioned in public on subjects which women scarce breathe in secret to one another? Shall the most sacred relations of life be called up and rudely scanned by men who, by their own admission, are so coarse that women could not meet them even at the polls without contamination? and yet she shall find no woman's face or voice to pity and defend? Shall the frenzied mother, who, to save herself and child from exposure and disgrace, ended the life that had but just begun, be dragged before a tribunal to answer for her crime? How can man enter into the feelings of that mother? How can he judge of the agonies of soul that impelled her to such an outrage of maternal instincts? How can he weigh the mountain of sorrow that crushed that mother's heart when she wildly tossed her helpless babe into the cold waters of the midnight sea? Where is he who by false vows thus blasted this trusting woman? Had that helpless child no claims on his protection? Ah, he is freely abroad in the dignity of manhood, in the pulpit, on the bench, in the professor's chair. The imprisonment of his victim and the death of his child, detract not a tithe from his standing and complacency. His peers made the law, and shall law-makers lay nets for those of their own rank? Shall laws which come from the logical brain of man take cognizance of violence done to the moral and affectional nature which predominates, as is said, in woman?

Statesmen of New York, whose daughters, guarded by your affection, and lapped amidst luxuries which your indulgence spreads, care more for their nodding plumes and velvet trains than for the statute laws by which their persons and properties are held—who, blinded by custom and prejudice to the degraded position which they and their sisters occupy in the civil seal, haughtily claim that they already have all the rights they want, how, think ye, would you feel to see a daughter summoned for such a crime—and remember these daughters are but human—before such a tribunal? Would it not, in that hour, be some consolation to see that she was surrounded by the wise and virtuous of her own sex; by those who had known the depth of a mother's love and the misery of a lover's falsehood; to know that to these she could make her confession, and from them receive her sentence? If so, then listen to our just demands and make such a change in your laws as will secure to every woman tried in your courts, an impartial jury. At this moment among the hundreds of women who are shut up in prisons in this State, not one has enjoyed that most sacred of rights—that right which you would die to defend for yourselves—trial by a jury of one's peers.

—From an address to the New York State Legislature, February 1854, reprinted in *The History of Woman Suffrage,* Volume 1, eds. Elizabeth Cady Stanton, Susan B. Anthony, and Matilda Joslyn Gage, New York: Fowler and Wells, 1881, 597-98.

Hester Vaughan
by Elizabeth Cady Stanton

Not long ago, one day a pretty English girl, poor and friendless, was wandering in the streets of Philadelphia, seeking employment. Seeing a respectable-looking man, she asked him if he could tell her where she could find a good place to work. Yes, he promptly replied, he would take her to his country home. So she went with him and remained in his family several months.

But alas! her protector proved her betrayer, and she was turned into the street at the very time she needed shelter, love, and care. With the wages she had saved, for she was an industrious, frugal girl, she took a small room in a tenement house, and there, in the depth of the winter, without a fire, a bed, or one article of furniture, with no eye, save that of Omnipotence, to witness, and no human heart to pity her sufferings, she laid one morning with a newborn child, exhausted on the floor. In vain she had called for help, no one heard or heeded her cries, feverish with pain and thirst, she dragged herself to the door to beg some passerby for water, and when, at last, help came, she was found in a fainting condition, and the child dead by her side. She was taken to the station house, and soon after imprisoned for infanticide. Tried and condemned, with most inadequate proof, she now lies in a Philadelphia prison waiting the hour of her execution, and in the great State of Pennsylvania not one woman has protested against the barbarism of this whole procedure, nor petitioned Gov. Geary for the girl's life. In the name of womanhood, we implore the mothers of that state to rescue that defenceless girl from her impending fate. Oh! make her case your own, suppose your young and beautiful daughter had been thus betrayed, would it not seem to you that the demands of justice should take the life of her seducer rather than her own? Men have made the laws cunningly, for their own protection, for they can never weigh the sufferings and sorrows of their victims. So long as by law and public sentiment maternity is made a disgrace and degradation, the young and inexperienced of the poorer classes are driven to open violence, while money affords the rich the means of fraud, protection, and concealment.

How can a man understand the terrible mortification and sorrow of a girl's life when betrayed into a false step, when in the crisis of her danger, she denies herself, through fear, all human sympathy, has no hope of future love and happiness, when every natural pulsation of the human heart, the deepest and holiest affections of a mother's nature must, of necessity, be crushed in concealment and violence, as the young victim stands trembling and appalled before future exposure, disgrace, and degradation?

What a holocaust of women and children we offer annually to the barbarous customs of our present type of civilization, to the unjust laws that make crimes for women that are not crimes for men! Years ago, a large circle in high life was suddenly startled by a Hester Vaughan of their own class, in reduced circumstances, who threw her new-born child into the ocean. God and the angels pitied that pale mother, as she stood alone upon a beach, in the grey light of that November morn. They saw and weighed the human agony in that sad hour, as the young mother fondly kissed the soft cheek of the new-born infant, pressed it for a moment to her breast, then wildly tossed it into the blue waters of a stormy sea. Had God and the angels been the only witnesses, she might have escaped the world's gaze, its falsehood and revenge; for in the Court of Heaven that act was not registered to her account, but to a priest who had fled to foreign lands. Unpitying human eyes had witnessed that sad burial, and the unhappy mother was imprisoned for infanticide.

The day of trial dawned. The halls of justice were crowded; old men and young, wise and foolish, learned and unlearned, virtuous and vicious, all pressed in to get one look at the trembling captive, pale, hopeless, deserted, and in all that trembling multitude not one woman was there to pity her misfortunes, or to shield her by her sympathy and presence. She, too, was doomed; but before the day of execution, the angel of death in mercy opened her prison and set her bruised spirit free.

—*The Revolution,* November 19, 1868.

[Hester Vaughan experienced a kinder fate, thanks to the call to action issued by Stanton. Stanton, Susan B. Anthony, Eleanor Kirk, Dr. Clemence Lozier, Dr. Harriet Hopkins, and Ernestine Rose petitioned the Governor of Pennsylvania to lift the death sentence from Vaughan and release her from prison. Their campaign, which included visits to Vaughan's jail cell, succeeded. Vaughan was pardoned and assisted back to her home in England.[85] —Ed.]

Matilda Joslyn Gage (1826–1898)

Matilda Joslyn Gage was another bold and richly talented woman who led the suffrage movement for decades, even while raising a family and suffering from recurrent ill health. Although she seldom found other like-minded reformers in her upstate New York village, as early as the 1850's she joined the temperance movement. Her home had been part of the "Underground Railroad" which enabled runaway slaves to escape to Canada. She first came to the attention of feminists at the 1852 Syracuse National Convention. Without knowing any of the leaders, she bravely rose up and gave an impressive speech on women's historical accomplishments which Lucretia Mott asked to reprint and distribute as part of the official movement literature.[86] She remained a courageous laborer for women's rights until her death in 1898. She helped organize the National Woman Suffrage Association in 1869, served as one of its officers, and edited its paper, *The National Citizen and Ballot Box*. She linked a variety of issues to suffrage, from prostitution to the United States government's mistreatment of Native Americans. In 1872, when Susan B. Anthony was tried for attempting to vote, Gage defended her with the stirring oration "The United States on Trial—Not Susan B. Anthony."[87] In the 1880's, out of admiration for her eloquence and powerful intellect, Anthony and Elizabeth Cady Stanton asked her to help them document the history of their movement. Gage eventually became frustrated with what she saw as their over-concentration on the vote and founded the radical Women's National Liberal Union.

Throughout her whole career, Gage used gifts she had inherited from her remarkable parents—remarkable because they had regarded her education and self-development as important as a son's. "From her earliest years, it was a law of the household that her childish questions should not be put off with an idle reply, but must be reasonably answered; and when she was older, [her father] himself instructed her in mathematics, Greek, and physiology. But that for which she feels most indebted to him, as she often says—the grandest training given her—was to think for herself. She was taught to accept no opinion because of its authority, but to question the truth of all things. Thus was laid the foundation of Mrs. Gage's reform tendencies and of her non-acceptance of masculine authority in matters of religion and politics. Nor was she, in a certain way, less indebted to her mother, a woman of refined and elevated tastes, universally respected and beloved. From this side Mrs. Gage inherited her antiquarian tastes and habits of delving into old histories, from which she has unearthed so many facts bearing upon woman's degradation."[88]

Gage had hoped to attend medical school but was barred because of her sex. She then channeled her talents into political activism. Gage was famous for incisively criticizing male domination wherever she found it—not just in the voting booth—and for bolstering her arguments with forgotten historical information that she had painstakingly gleaned from archives and libraries. These hallmarks of her work are evident in her masterpiece *Woman, Church, and State,* a work that has been praised by contemporary theologians such as Mary Daly. Dedicated to Gage's mother, this tome asserts that "woman's degradation is not the normal condition of humanitiy, neither did it arise from a settled principle of evolution, but is a retrogression, due to the grossly material state of the world for centuries past, in which it has lost the interior meaning or spiritual significance of its own most holy words."[89] Marshalling newly uncovered facts on a range of cultures, Eastern and Western, Gage postulates that the human race had in ancient times enjoyed an age of "Matriarchate, or Mother-Rule," in which "all life was regarded as holy ... Even the sacrifice of animals was unknown. The earliest phase of life being dependent upon [woman], she was recognized as the primal factor in every relation."[90] The "divinity of the feminine" was honored along with the "femininity of the divine."

Gage argues that Scripture itself, if properly interpreted, "plainly recognizes the feminine as well as the masculine element in the Godhead, and declares the equality of the sexes in goodness, wisdom, and power."[91] She identifies many forms of woman-abuse as corruptions of authentic spirituality by the "Patriarchate." These include the blaming of original sin upon the female sex; the denial that women have human souls; the exclusion of women from the clergy; sexual abuse of women by clerics; and ecclesiastical collusion in the sexual double standard, wifebeating, and ageism. Yet women, in Gage's view, have ingeniously and bravely found ways to develop and use their spiritual gifts, even when subjected in large numbers to such dire punishments as witchburnings. "A brighter day is to come for the world," Gage wrote, "a day when the intuitions of woman's soul shall be accepted as part of humanity's spiritual wealth."[92]

Gage's critiques of organized religion so disturbed some of her contemporaries that information about her was suppressed after her death. In an admiring essay from the anthology *Feminist Theorists,* Lynne Spender comments, "To read Matilda Joslyn Gage is in many respects to be shocked; shocked that this powerful and perceptive analysis of society should have been formulated a century ago, and not built upon, shocked that in the late 1960's we had to begin again without benefit of those valuable insights which she herself forged over a lifetime, but shocked too that a woman of the nineteenth century should have so clearly and uncompromisingly spoke out against men … It is time this remarkable woman was reclaimed as she herself reclaimed so many women before her. She must not be lost again."[93] These remarks are not inapplicable to Gage's perspective on abortion.

Is Woman Her Own?
by Matilda Joslyn Gage

The short article on "Child Murder" in your paper of March 12, touched a subject which lies deeper down into woman's wrongs than any other. This is the denial of the right to herself. In no historic age of the world has woman yet had that. From the time when Moses, for the hardness of his heart, permitted the Jew husband to give his unpleasing wife a letter of divorcement—to Christ, when the seven *male* sinners brought to him for condemnation the woman taken in adultery—down through the Christian centuries to this nineteenth, nowhere has the marital union of the sexes been one in which the women has had control over her own body.

Enforced motherhood is a crime against the body of the mother and the soul of the child.

Medical jurisprudence has begun to accumulate facts on this point, showing how the condition and *feelings* of the mother mould not only the physical and mental qualities of the child, but its moral nature.

Women keep silence upon many points, not breathing their thoughts to their dearest friends, because of their inner reticence, a quality they possess greatly in excess of men.

And, too, custom has taught them to bear in silence.

But the crime of abortion is not one in which the guilt lies solely or chiefly with the woman. As a child brings more care, so also, it brings more joy to the mother's heart.

Husbands do not consult with their wives upon this subject of deepest and most vital interest, do not look at the increase of family in a physiological, moral, or spiritual light, but almost solely from a money standpoint. It costs. Tens of thousands of husbands and fathers throughout this land are opposed to large families. And yet so deeply implanted is the sin of self-gratification, that consequences are not considered while selfish desire controls the heart.

Much is said of the wild, mad desire of the age for money. Money is but another name for power, it is but another name for bread, it is but another name for freedom, and those who possess it not are the slaves of those who do.

How many states in the Union grant the wife an equal right with the husband to the control and disposal of the property of the marital firm? But two.

How long is it since a married woman in this state had the right to control of her own separate property? Barely twice ten years.

How long since she could control her own earnings, even those of a day's washing? Not yet ten.

History is full of the wrongs done the wife by legal robbery on the part of the husband. I need not quote instances; they are well known to the most casual newspaper reader. It is accepted as a self-evident truth—that those "who are not masters of any property, may easily be formed into any mould."

I hesitate not to assert that most of this crime of "child murder," "abortion," "infanticide," lies at the door of the male sex.

Many a woman has laughed a silent, derisive laugh at the decisions of eminent medical and legal authorities, in cases of crimes committed against her as a woman. Never, until she sits as a juror at such trials, will or can just decisions be rendered.

This reason and that reason have been pointed to by the upholders of equal rights, to account for the oppression of women during past ages, but not one that I have ever heard offered has looked to the spiritual origin of that oppression.

If my health and eyes enable to me to do so, I shall be glad to write occasionally as you request. Perhaps a series of short articles upon the above point will be timely. Individual freedom is emphatically the lesson of the nineteenth century.

—*The Revolution,* April 9, 1868.

Mattie H. Brinkerhoff

Far more than Gage herself, Martha (Mattie) H. Brinkerhoff, a Missouri native, is one of those forgotten women of the past who can be retrieved only through laborious Gage-style research. Yet in her day she was a popular and effective lecturer in the Midwest. In 1867, Brinkerhoff canvassed the state of Kansas with Susan B. Anthony, Elizabeth Cady Stanton, and Reverend Olympia Brown (the first ordained woman minister in the U.S.). They helped to restore the temporarily diminished morale of prosuffrage forces there.[94] The next year, Brinkerhoff toured Illinois and then, as reported in *The History of Woman Suffrage,* "made a very successful lecture-tour through the northern counties of Iowa. She roused great interest and organized many societies, canvassing meanwhile for subscribers to *The Revolution.*"[95] As one might expect, *The Revolution* gave her efforts a most favorable review: "She is modest and lady-like in her deportment, earnest and candid in her reasoning, interesting and entertaining as a speaker."[96]

The newspapers in the small towns where she spoke also responded enthusiastically to her, even though in many cases she was the first suffrage worker they had ever encountered. The *Fort Dodge North West* remarked that it did not matter much that Brinkerhoff was young and relatively new at public speaking, for "her style is easy and graceful and womanly—her arguments clear, logical, and pointed—and there is a calm earnest eloquence in her address that carries conviction to the hearer." Even the *Dubuque Herald,* a paper normally swayed by the popular stereotype of suffragists as shrewish old maids, found Brinkerhoff persuasive. Its pages noted that she was "a wife and mother" whose speech was "earnest and truthful... What she says will be remembered when an extravagant scold leaves only an unpleasant impression but never brings conviction."[97]

Yet Brinkerhoff eventually failed to receive the acclaim she deserved—this ardent and successful activist whose main difficulty in her work was finding the time to accept half the speaking invitations she received. Because she left her husband and married another man, she was deliberately written out of suffragist history: a warning example of how even feminists, people who are generally inclined to uncover suppressed information, have censored their own history when they have found it unpalatable.[98] The following piece gives an inkling of why such censorship is unfortunate.

Woman and Motherhood
by Mattie H. Brinkerhoff

In number 25, vol. 3d of THE REVOLUTION, I noticed from the editor of a German paper in this state [Illinois] these words: "American women have long been ardently engaged in the endeavor to free themselves, in a mechanical way, from the discharge of those functions which are essential to the continuance of society, and which cannot be shared with them, or performed for them, by men." The gallant editor unquestionably refers to the office of maternity. This and similar articles have from time to time been so ably answered in your paper, that it seems almost unnecessary to add anything further upon the subject; but the boldness with which many men blame women for the crime of infanticide without assuming themselves, in the case, a shadow of responsibility, I should think would rouse every *mother*, at least, to utter words in self-defence. That American women are more guilty of this practice than women of any other nation, I do not doubt; but is there not a reason for this?

Knowledge and slavery are incompatible. Teach a slave how to read, and he wants to be his own master—and as the masses of American women not only know how to read and write, but so much of the "tree of knowledge" have many of them eaten, that they have learned it should be for them to decide when and how often they shall take upon themselves the sacred duties of motherhood, but as law and custom give to the husband the absolute control of the wife's person, she is forced to not only violate physical law, but to outrage the holiest instincts of her being to maintain even a semblance of that freedom which by nature belongs to every human soul.

When a man steals to satisfy hunger, we may safely conclude that there is something wrong in society—so when a woman destroys the life of her unborn child, it is an evidence that either by education or circumstances she has been greatly wronged. But the question now seems to be, how shall we prevent this destruction of life and health?

Mrs. Stanton has many times ably answered it—"by the true education and independence of woman."

Our German writer seems to think that the whole aim of a woman's life should be motherhood. Suppose this were true, is the mission of so little importance that no preparation be required to fill it? If, to be a first class artist, or lawyer, it requires years of thought and culture, what preparation should be made to carve the outlines and justly balance the attributes of an immortal soul. Are little children, the germs of men and women, of so little importance that it matters not whether their mother be physically healthy or unhealthy, cultivated or uncultivated in mind; expanded or dwarfed in soul? Some or no culture must be desirable in the mother. If some culture, then how much? Shall she have strong arms but weak legs, strong stomach but weak lungs, keen imagination but devoid of reason, large perception but no reflection? We are forced to ask, by what law shall we decide when woman is sufficiently developed in body and mind to be a good mother? Before what tribunal shall she be judged? Does not reason answer, the council chamber of her own being?

If she is by nature talented, is not this a silent declaration that her talents should be cultivated to their fullest extent? If we require any culture in the mother, the legitimate conclusion is, the more the better. If woman enters the seminary and finishes a preparatory course, the natural sequence is she has a right to a collegiate course. When here she has become acquainted with science, what course of reasoning shall we pursue to prove she should not cull the flowers to test her knowledge of botany, or gather stones to apply her knowledge of geology. Admit she may do all this, then how can we consistently deny her the privilege of studying our laws, to learn how far, as a nation, we are in advance of the ancient Greeks and Romans of whom through history we have become acquainted.

If she discovers that our legislation is superior to theirs, but thinks it might still be improved, shall we deny her the privilege of expressing her opinions here? If not, then we have in spirit granted the right of suffrage, and with it the right to hold office, and what follows.

The ability to frame laws, making the husband and wife equal owners in the property accumulated by their united industry and economy, making the mother the guardian of her own children, the owner of her own body, in short, the controller of her own destiny. Admit woman may learn the alphabet, and you admit she may cultivate every faculty of her mind, every attribute of her soul and every function of her body to its fullest capacity.

I will not refer to our jails and prisons, our institutions for the blind, the deaf and dumb, the idiotic and insane, to illustrate the necessity of such a type of womanhood, but simply to the editor who wrote the clause we have quoted, and to all men and women who answer amen to his sentiments.

If we would make woman free, let us teach her the alphabet of human *life*, make her understand and value true womanhood. Then she will scorn to be man's petted slave. She will scorn his smiles and courtesies, when they are proffered only as an excuse for justice.

Oh motherhood! which our opponents say is woman's holiest mission. We cannot have true mothers without having true womanhood first. Let us see that our daughters are developed into true women, and the office of maternity will take care of itself. Remove woman's shackles and she will soon create a public opinion that will declare it a disgrace for a man to outrage the woman he has sworn to protect. Then, and not till then, will man's shackles fall, for noble manhood must be the legitimate fruit of free and exalted womanhood. Brothers, 'tis for you, as well as ourselves we plead. Will you neglect so great a salvation?

—*The Revolution*, Sept. 2, 1869.

Susan B. Anthony (1820–1906)

Susan B. Anthony is as famous as Mattie H. Brinkerhoff is obscure. Today, no other woman is so identified with nineteenth-century American feminism, largely because of the ill-fated Susan B. Anthony dollar coin of a few years back. Her many decades of persistent devotion to social justice deserve a better remembrance than that. While supporting herself as a teacher (one of the few professions then open to women), she became involved in temperance and abolition work during the 1840's. These experiences prepared her for her career in the women's rights movement. This began after she grew frustrated with the male-dominated power structures of the temperance movement, and after she met Elizabeth Cady Stanton, with whom she was to have a close and enduring friendship. Among their most important joint projects over a period of five decades were numerous speaking tours and women's rights conferences, the publication of *The Revolution* from 1868 to 1870, and the first three volumes of the monumental *History of Woman Suffrage*.

Anthony's primary efforts focused on gaining the vote for women, and in 1872, she was tried for attempting to cast a ballot. However, her spiritually based philosophy of radical egalitarianism, which grew out of her Quaker heritage, moved her to extend her efforts well beyond woman suffrage. Starting with her anti-slavery agitation, she sought to link women across class and cultural differences. She spoke out against the legalization of prostitution, believing that this would legitimate the economic discrimination that compelled women into this trade.

Remembering the female workers in her father's upstate New York mills, she founded the Working Women's Association and attempted to build other bridges to labor. It was at this time that she illegally sheltered the abused wife and child of a wealthy and prominent man. Prefiguring the modern feminist contention that "sisterhood is global," she organized the International Council of Women in the late 1880's—the first such group ever.[99]

Unlike most other women's rights leaders of her time, Anthony opted not to direct any of her considerable maternal energies into marriage and parenthood. In the autobiography of her friend Frances E. Willard, she explained the significance she attached to this decision. A male friend said to Anthony that "with your great head and heart, you, of all women I have met, ought to have been a wife and mother." She replied: "I thank you, sir, for what I take to be the highest compliment, but sweeter even than to have had the joy of caring for children of my own has it been to me to help bring about a better state of things for mothers generally, so that their unborn little ones could not be willed away from them."[100]

Her sense of sisterhood with all women, including those who had made different life choices, afforded her tremendous insight into maternity, voluntary and involuntary, and other aspects of female sexuality. Indeed, as her biographer Kathleen Barry notes, "because she was unmarried, [she] had a particular vantage point from which to consider sexuality and its role in the exploitation of women. ... Anthony must have known what happened to women who experienced their sexuality in the context of unequal relationships, for she understood well the potential of sex as a form of human fulfillment—something she considered an epitome of human experience. But when relationships were unequal, in sex women were reduced to objects 'recognized as fit only to minister to man's animal instincts.'"[101] These themes figure in the piece below— along with her lifelong proclivity for getting to the "root" of an evil, and along with her radical egalitarianism—so radical it could encompass both unborn babies and their mothers.

Marriage and Maternity
by Susan B. Anthony[102]

In a late REVOLUTION is an extract from the New York *Medical Gazette* rebuking a practice common among married women, and demanding a law for its suppression.

Much as I deplore the horrible crime of child-murder, earnestly as I desire its suppression, I cannot believe with the writer of the above-mentioned article, that such a law would have the desired effect. It seems to be only mowing off the top of the noxious weed, while the root remains.

We want *prevention*, not merely punishment. We must reach the root of the evil, and destroy it.

To my certain knowledge this crime is not confined to those whose love of ease, amusement and fashionable life leads them to desire immunity from the cares of children; but is practiced by those whose inmost souls revolt from the dreadful deed, and in whose hearts the maternal feeling is pure and undying. What, then, has driven these women to the desperation necessary to force them to commit such a deed? This question being answered, I believe we shall have such an insight into the matter as to be able to talk more clearly of a remedy.

Women are educated to think that with marriage their individuality ceases or is transferred to their husbands. The wife has thenceforth no right over her own body. This is also the husband's belief, and upon which he acts. No matter what her condition, physical or mental, no matter how ill-prepared she may feel herself for maternity, the demands of his passion may never be refused.

He thinks, or cares nothing, for the possible result of his gratification. If it be that an immortal being, with all its needs, physical, mental, and moral, shall come into the world to sin, to suffer, to die, because of his few moments of pleasure, what cares he?

He says he is ready to provide for his children, therefore he feels himself a kind father, worthy of honor and love. That is, he is ready to provide for them food and clothing, but he is not willing to provide for them, by his self-denial, sound bodies, good tempers, and a happy antenatal existence. He gives his wife wealth, leisure, and luxury, and is, therefore, a devoted husband, and she is an *undutiful*, unloving wife, if her feelings fail to respond to his.

Devoted husband? Devoted to what? To self-gratification at the expense of the respect of his wife. I know men who call themselves Christians, who would insist that they are *gentlemen*, who never insult any woman—but their wives. They think it impossible that they can outrage them; they never think that even in wedlock there may be the very vilest prostitution; and if Christian women are *prostitutes* to Christian husbands, what can be expected but the natural sequence—infanticide?

Women who are in the last stages of consumption, who know that their offspring must be puny, suffering, neglected orphans, are still compelled to submit to maternity, and dying in childbirth, are their husbands ever condemned? Oh, no! It was only his right as a husband he claimed, and if maternity or death ensued, surely he could not be blamed for that. He did not desire it. The usual tenor of men's conduct in this respect seems on a par with that of Henry VIII, who when asked if the life of his wife or of his child should be saved, as it seemed needful that one should be sacrificed, answered, "O the child, by all means. Wives are easily obtained."

Women whose husbands are habitual drunkards and whose children are therefore idiotic, deformed creatures, and who feel assured that such must be the case with all their offspring, must yet submit. And if such a woman as the dying consumptive, rather than bring into the world such miserable children, rather perhaps than give life to a daughter to suffer all that she has endured, destroys the little being, so she thinks, before it lives, she would be punished by the law, and he, *the real murderer*, would go unrebuked, uncondemned.

All the articles on this subject that I have read have been from men. They denounce women as alone guilty, and never include man in any plans proposed for the remedy of the evil.

It is clear to my mind that this evil wholly arises from the false position which woman occupies in civilized society. We know that in the brute creation, the female chooses her own time, and ... among Indians ... yet what Christian woman, wife of a Christian husband, is free to consult her own feelings even in these most delicate situations?

Guilty? Yes, no matter what the motive, love of ease, or a desire to save from suffering the unborn innocent, the woman is awfully guilty who commits the deed. It will burden her conscience in life, it will burden her soul in death; but oh! thrice guilty is he who, for selfish gratification, heedless of her prayers, indifferent to her fate, drove her to the desperation which impelled her to the crime. It is very fine to say:

My Author and Disposer, what thou willst
Unquestioned I obey—Thus God ordains,
God is my law, thou mine.

But God has never given woman's individuality into the hands of man. If He has, why hold her responsible for this crime? If man takes her individuality he must also take her responsibility. Let him suffer.

No, I say, yield to woman her God-given right of individuality. Make her feel that to God alone is she responsible for her deeds; teach her that submission to any man without love and desire is prostitution; and thunder in her ear, "Who so defileth the body, defileth the temple of the Holy Ghost!" Let maternity come to her from a desire to cherish love and train for high purposes an immortal soul, then you will have begun to eradicate this most monstrous crime.

Teach man to respect womanhood whether in the person of his own wife or the wife of another; teach him that as often as he outrages his wife he outrages Nature and disobeys the Divine Law, then you will have accomplished still more.

Oh, there is a dreadful volume of heart-histories that lies hidden in almost every family in the land! It tells of trust betrayed, of purity violated under sanction of law, of every holy feeling outraged and purest love turned to fear and loathing. If the moral feeling in the heart of woman was not stronger than death itself, the crimes we now chronicle against them would be virtues compared with the depths of wickedness and sin into which they would be driven. But God is stronger than man and he holds us true to our higher natures, martyrs though we be. If, on the other hand, women were not so weak and disgracefully submissive, they would rise to the dignity of womanhood and throwing off the degrading touch, would say, "I am free. And to God alone will I unquestioningly yield myself."

I believe all that is needed is for the eyes of men to be opened up to the true state of affairs. They have received without a thought the faith of their fathers. The misery and degradation have not been personally felt by them. But let every wife dare to be honest, let her open her heart freely to her husband, and I know there are few whose better natures would not be touched, few who would not be awakened to a nobler life, to a more exalted view of marriage.

Then would marriage assume its high and holy place. Then would our children be truly olive plants, types of peace, lovingly desired, tenderly cared for, body and soul. Then the wife, looking with love and respect upon the husband, who has never caused her to fear his manhood, could say: "I am thine, and these are they whom God at our desire has given us."

—*The Revolution,* July 8, 1869.

Henry Clarke Wright (1797–1870) and an Anonymous Correspondent

When feminists formulated their position on abortion, they agreed with Susan B. Anthony that it was absolutely vital to take seriously the "heart-histories" of women. The strong desire of feminists to ground their stance in women's experience is confirmed by the works of Henry Clarke Wright, which preserve women's own voices.

Wright's long career as a reformer and itinerant lecturer was devoted to challenging one form of violence after another. He was known for his radical writings and speeches on behalf of the abolitionist movement's "nonresistant" wing and pacifism in general. He believed that peace began by educating young children in nonviolent methods of conflict resolution. Quite consistently, Wright paid special attention to the violation of women's and children's rights.[103]

The interrelatedness of Wright's reform concerns is evident from the resolutions he sponsored at the 1858 Rutland Free Convention, an important gathering of Spiritualists. "Resolved, that Slavery is a wrong which no power in the Universe can make right … Resolved, that it is always wrong and inexpedient for man to take the life of man; therefore, Capital Punishment, war, and all preparations for war, are wrong, and inconsistent with the safety and best interests of individuals and of society … Resolved, that the most sacred and important right of woman, is her right to decide for herself how often and under what circumstances she shall assume the responsibilities and be subjected to the cares and suffering of Maternity; and man can commit no greater crime against woman, as a wife and a mother, against his child, against society and against Humanity, than to impose on her a maternity whose responsibilities and sufferings she is not willing to accept and endure. Whereas, the assumed superiority of Man over Woman has held her in submission and entailed slavery and dependence on the sex and misery on the race; therefore, resolved, that immediate steps should be taken to remove that error and its consequences, and place woman politically, educationally, industrially, and socially on perfect equality with Man."[104]

In Wright's view, voluntary motherhood would prevent a particularly tragic and dire consequence of female subjugation: the act of violence he called "ante-natal murder." He compellingly articulates his perspective on this practice in his *The Unwelcome Child, or, the Crime of an Undesigned and Undesired Maternity. The Unwelcome Child's* case for voluntary motherhood derives from much more than purely abstract principles of justice. It owes much to the letters which Wright received from abortion recipients and included in its pages. One of these letters is reprinted below. Although its author lived over a century ago, her emotions nevertheless evoke those of many contemporary women who have suffered the pain of abortion—even women who have resorted to it legally.

"My Womanhood Rose Up In Withering Condemnation"

Dear Friend:

The following experience of a woman, given in her own words, will make its appeal to all that is pure, manly, and noble in manhood. It is the cry of anguish from woman's riven heart to man, to save her from the agony and blighting curse of a maternity whose sufferings she is not prepared joyfully to meet, and from which her entire nature shrinks with dread and loathing; to save her from the revolting alternative of killing her child before it is born or of giving life to one whose very existence is loathed by her. Several times the crime of an undesired maternity had been perpetrated upon her by her husband, and the child had been killed by herself or by a doctor, before its birth. She was asked how she felt under these outrages, and what was the result on her physical, social and spiritual nature. The following is her answer:

"How did I feel? I felt that I was committing a damning sin. My soul shrank from the deed with intense horror and loathing. The remonstrances of a guilty conscience I could not silence. I had submitted to the relation in which maternity originates, thinking it my duty, as a wife, to do so whenever my husband demanded. I told him that my very soul shrank from maternity; that I was not yet prepared for its responsibilities and agonies, and begged of him not to impose that burden upon me till I could joyfully welcome it, which I felt that I should, in due time. But he heeded not my prayer. He insisted on the relation. Conception and maternity ensued.

"My soul died within me. An ever-present loathing of the new life that was being developed within mine was in my heart. My own soul, and the God whose voice was heard within, repudiated its existence. I could not help the feeling. The spirit of murder, towards the unconscious child in embryo, was ever present to me; yet my soul shrank with horror from the deed. Shall I kill my child before its birth, or give existence to one whose birthright inheritance is, *a mother's curse?* was the question I found myself debating continually; for my curse was on its very life.

"I consulted a woman, a friend in whom I trusted. I found that she had perpetrated that outrage on herself and on others. She told me it was not murder to kill a child any time before its birth. Of this she labored to convince me, and called in the aid of her 'family physician' to give force to her arguments. He argued that it was right and just for wives thus to protect themselves against the results of their husband's sensualism—told me that God and human laws would approve of killing children before they were born, rather than curse them with an undesired existence. My only trouble was, with God's view of the case. I could not get rid of the feeling that it was an outrage on my body and soul, and on my unconscious babe. He argued that my child, at five months, (which was the time,) had no life, and where there was no life, no life could be taken. Though I determined to do the deed, or get the 'family physician' to do it, my womanly instincts, my reason, my conscience, my self-respect, my entire nature, revolted against my decision. My Womanhood rose up in withering condemnation. And after the deed was done, I felt that I could never respect myself again; that I could never again appear in society; that if I did, all that was pure and true in manhood and womanhood would shrink from me as a polluted, disgusting object.

"I tried to cast the blame on my husband, who had imposed the necessity upon me. I tried to feel that the outrage and the guilt were all his own; that had he heeded my prayer, and dealt justly by me, I should have never been driven to the dread alternative of ante-natal murder, or of giving birth to a child I did not want. But I saw and felt, that however great the wrong he had done to me, the fact still remained—my nature was outraged, if not by my consent, yet by my sufferance. I knew I could have saved myself from maternity, had I been resolute to do so; and that, having submitted to the relation in which it originated, I had no right to add to the outrage by killing my child. I felt myself to be a crushed, prostituted, abandoned woman. Can any apology be offered for a woman who commits the crime of ante-natal murder, after she has voluntarily yielded to the relation that leads to maternity?

"Maternity, with its prospective agonies and its abhorred responsibilities, (for I did not yet call for a child,) was again thrust upon me in a few months; but I shrunk from destroying my child again. I gave birth to two living children. Then my soul rebelled against having more; but my husband was deaf to my prayers and my tears, though he himself was opposed to having any more children, and insisted it was my fault if I did, though he persisted in his right to sensual indulgence. How could I avoid having any more children, when he was continually demanding of me the relation which naturally leads to offspring? 'Kill them,' was his reply, 'before they are born, or do something to prevent conception!'

"His injustice and heartless selfishness cut me to the quick—stung my very soul. 'This is the man,' I said to myself, 'who has promised to love, cherish, and *protect* me; who expects me to love him tenderly and evermore; whom I have promised to love till death separates us; and yet, this is the man who, without regard to my wishes and condition, insists on his right to gratify his passion, though at the expense of my body and soul!' My soul rose in rebellion against him. It became evident to me, that the gratification of his passion was his only object in seeking me as a wife; that this was the only claim he had upon me, or wished to have, and that he had no higher idea of marriage than as a means of licensed, reputable indulgence.

"I became desperate. I could not leave my children. I knew if I left him, I could give no reason for the step, except my aversion to having maternity thrust upon me in defiance of the demands of my own nature and I knew that all would condemn me, if I left him to escape from such an outrage, as this was not considered a wrong to me, but his right. Every feeling of my soul revolted against his taking possession of my person, without my consent, to blight and curse my body and soul to gratify his animal nature.

"I came to the conclusion to stand by my own rights, and defend my person against his sensualism. I told him, candidly, how I felt, and that I must protect myself, in this respect, for he would not. I told him I was living daily in deadly fear of his passion, and of maternity; that the relation in which it resulted had become repulsive to me, and that he had brought me to view myself as a loathed, abject, and prostituted woman. His wrath was roused; and finally, from fear of breaking up my family and having my helpless living children taken from me, I submitted to a hell which had no mitigation, until separation gave it to me.

"In my intercourse with men, I have found few who did not view marriage and a wife as my husband did, as a mere means of sensual gratification. Companionship, intellectual, social and spiritual growth, and elevation, they think little of, in connection with a wife. They see no soul, no God, in the wife; only the mere animal, to administer to the brute in them."

—*The Unwelcome Child, or, the Crime of an Undesigned and Undesired Maternity*, Boston: Bela Marsh, 1858, 101-104, from the Department of Special Collections, University of Chicago Library.

Elizabeth Edson Evans (1832–1911)

From youth, Elizabeth Edson Evans was a prolific writer of verse, novels, and essays. She was married to scholar Edward Payson Evans, known for his work in modern languages and literatures and his activism on behalf of animal welfare.[105] Edward dedicated his 1898 treatise *Evolutional Ethics and Animal Psychology* to Elizabeth in acknowledgement of her intellectual as well as personal companionship. This book made a case for animal rights and declared: "We have happily rid ourselves somewhat of the ethnocentric prepossessions ... to regard all other peoples as barbarians; but our perceptions are still obscured by anthropocentric prejudice which prevents us from fully appreciating the intelligence of the lower animals and recognising any psychical analogy between these humble kinsmen and our exalted selves."[106]

Elizabeth's first book concerned the rights and welfare of unborn children and their mothers. As Carl Degler notes, she was "certainly a friend of women," yet strongly, even vehemently, opposed to the violence of abortion.[107] Like Wright's *The Unwelcome Child*, her *The Abuse of Maternity* recounts women's real-life experiences of abortion and the devastation it can cause them.

The Abuse of Maternity, Through Its Rejection
by Elizabeth Edson Evans

And now let us listen to the regretful complaint of one whose early feelings [about overextending herself in the care of others] were not so kindly consulted ... "In my childhood," she says, "I was remarkable for an over flowing and unselfish affection for every living thing that was smaller and more helpless than myself; dogs, cats, chickens, birds, and all other household pets were the delight of my heart; and as for babies, I loved them to idolatry. And so it came to pass that not only were my services called for in season and out of season by all members of the family in behalf of the little ones of our own nursery, but my visits to neighbors and friends were made use of in the same way; while the children of any guests who might be staying with us were given over almost wholly to my loving and patient care.

"This distinction was rather a pleasure than a trouble to me so long as I remained myself a careless, playful child, but as years went on and my mind began to expand with a desire of knowledge, and I longed for silence and solitude in order to carry on the ponderings and questions of an active intellect and an earnest soul, I became impatient of the restraints which had so long bound me; I felt that I ought to be allowed more individual opportunity, instead of being so completely involved with the younger lives that were developing around me. But circumstances were too powerful for my resistance, and the only result of my struggle was, that I gradually lost, through my perceptible discontent, the reputation for amiability which I had hitherto enjoyed, and which had tempted others to impose an unjust share of their responsibilities upon me. At last I became free through my marriage, but when, soon afterwards, the prospect of a nursery of my own dawned upon me, I turned away in utter weariness, and would have none of its once so fascinating fatigues. I imagined that I hated children, and believed that the instincts of my early years had not sounded the real key-notes of my character. Now, when I recall the tender love I used to feel for my dolls, and the still-more exquisite enjoyment I formerly took in the contemplation and care of infants, I am wild with regret at my folly in rejecting the (alas! only once-proffered) gift of offspring. My only comfort is in the fact that my crime has not lost me my rare power of attracting the affection of dumb animals and speechless babes—the dogs of strangers still turn gladly to meet my caressing hand, and I can always woo the cherished child from the arms of its doting mother."

… Said a woman who has never ceased to regret an early sin against her motherhood, "While I was debating the subject in my own mind—being tempted to the crime chiefly through the fact that my sister had suffered extremely during childbirth, and the corresponding fear that I, who was even more slight and delicate than she, would surely lose my life in the struggle—my mother-in-law—who had not yet overcome the natural jealousy caused by seeing another holding the first place in the affections of a favorite son—took occasion, one day, while talking with a neighbor, to expatiate with all the eloquence of truth upon the frightful agonies she had suffered during parturition; saying, by way of climax, that, old as she was, it made the cold sweat start at every pore only to recall that long-past experience. What possessed her to speak in this manner, suspecting, as I think she did, my situation at the time, I cannot imagine; at all events, in my then excitable state, her words were daggers to my heart, and I left the room fully resolved to take speedy measures to spare myself the full measure of the tortures I could not expect entirely to avoid."

… Said one of these victims of early [physiological] ignorance, "During the first years of my repentance, when I was almost insane with unavailing sorrow, I became acquainted with one of the purest and loveliest specimens of my own sex that I have ever known. From the first she manifested a preference for my society, and soon showed a disposition to select me as a confidential friend. But this distinction I felt myself unworthy to accept, and I finally resolved to confess the secret to her and be guided concerning my future estimate of myself, by her judgment as to my sin. She listened to the story with surprise and pity, but without any signs of aversion, and, in trying to lighten my evident despair, she begged me to consider the fact as a mistake; sad and eventful certainly, but by no means indicative of my real character, nor decisive as to its power to blast my future career. This true woman, true wife, true mother, true friend, saved me from myself at a terrible crisis, and her unabated confidence and affection have since been as a strong shield against the keen darts of remorse which, ever and anon, have threatened to overcome my courage."

… Said one whose uncommon delicacy of feeling makes it exceedingly difficult to conceive of her ever having sinned against her organization in any manner: "If I had known anything beforehand of the awful processes of childbirth, I should have been effectually deterred from venturing to invoke them prematurely. I expected only a slight variation of the periodical disturbance which any woman, by a proper degree of care and cleanliness, is able to endure without great discomfort or aversion; and more dreadful to bear than even my agonizing suffering, were my fright and my horror when I learned the extent of the catastrophe I had brought about. Let all inexperienced women know that there is not a more solemn scene on earth than the chamber of delivery; and she who is called to occupy that couch of pain needs, even more than natural strength of skillful attendance, the sustaining comfort of a good conscience, in the recollection that the gradual evolutions of Nature, and not the mischiefs of a devilish craft, have appointed the hour of travail!"

Said another: "It would almost seem that this crime, like many another, has its seasons of malignant prevalence; just as diseases, after having long existed in a sporadic form, now and then become epidemic. At the time when I fell a victim to the temptation, I was living in a country place, where all the newly-married women of the neighborhood were discussing the ideas derived from certain pamphlets of the 'Medical Companion' order, that had recently been circulated in that region. These women were unanimous in desiring to postpone pregnancy; and I have reason to think that several besides myself took measures to stop its progress after it had begun. But the generally accepted opinion that we had a right to be the arbiters of our own destiny in this particular, prevented any loss of self-respect on the part of the offenders, as well as of any position in society to which we were otherwise entitled; and it was not until after I had taken up my residence in a city, and through wider knowledge of the world had learned the true relation of the individual to the aggregate of humanity, that I recognized my real condition as a criminal, none the less because undetected and unpunished. And ever since, the thought that I have done something which has rendered me amenable to the law of every civilized country brings the blush of shame to my cheek, and serves as an effectual damper upon whatever degree of pride or satisfaction I might otherwise feel in the more praiseworthy deeds of my career."[108]

… Said a woman who, after many years of despondency, had begun to realize the truth of Madame De Stael's vigorous maxim—*"Repeated penitence wearies the soul—it is a sentiment that can but once regenerate us"*—and to feel that atonement could best be made through diligent and useful endeavor—"From the moment when I began to appreciate my irreparable loss, my thoughts were filled with imaginings as to what might have been the worth of that child's individuality; and, especially, after sufficient time had elapsed to have brought him to maturity, did I busy myself with picturing the responsible posts he might have filled, the honors he might have won, the joy and comfort he might have brought to his suffering fellow-creatures; nor, during the interval, have I read of an accident by land or by water, or of a critical moment in a battle, or of a good cause lost through lack of a brave defender, but my heart has whispered, '*He* might have been there to help and save; *he* might have been able to lead that forlorn hope; *his* word or *his* deed might have brought that wise plan to successful issue!"

… Women know that it is not necessary to wait for eternity to be haunted by "one whom might have come!" A lady writer upon medical subjects, who has had a wide practical experience in the care of chronic female diseases, says, in reference to the agony of intentional abortion and its attendant remorse in causing nervous maladies: "There is a peculiar look in the eye, which I note, and dread the confession of such patients when they come for consultation."

Said one: "I think I was for a long time as near being insane as one can be without really going mad. Although much debilitated through the physical consequences of my sin, I often took long walks, much longer than I could have borne in health; and though going at a rapid pace, and without any pause for rest, I was as unconscious of fatigue as unimpressed by the features of the landscape, or by the persons and objects I passed. I had an idea that I had lost, through that unnatural deed, the normal powers and qualities of a human being. I no longer ate and drank with the old hunger and thirst, nor slept the quiet sleep of innocence; I took no heed of the passage of time, and all that I saw and heard seemed to be the occurrences of a dream, as though life were already finished for me and I was observing it from another state of existence. The first ray of hope that dawned upon me was when, during an illness succeeding to this dangerous excitement, I found that the remedies prescribed for my feverish restlessness and excruciating headache affected me as they would have affected another person. From the moment of that discovery I began to amend in health, and have since recovered sufficient energy to interest myself in the work that seems to belong to me especially to do, though the strange feeling of having set myself apart from the rest of my sex, through that sin against my motherhood, will probably always remain to increase the bitterness of my childless and lonely condition."

Said another: "I envy a mother who goes to weep beside her baby's grave; because she knows where it is laid, and remembers how it looked in life, and is not ashamed to say, *'I have lost a child.'* And when I hear mothers lamenting over such a loss, I pity them indeed; but I feel like saying to them, 'You think you are deeply afflicted, but your trouble is really light, because it is not mingled with remorse, and you are not to blame for the infant's death.' Truly all sorrow that I have ever known or heard of is not to be compared with my sorrow, and that of others who have sinned in like manner!"

Another says: "I go to church in despair, and I hear the minister proclaim free pardon to all sinners through the blood of Christ. Does he know what he is saying? Would he offer me the same comfort if he knew the extent of my guilt; if he knew that I had sinned, presuming upon that very grace which he declared is able to save the uttermost? And yet, if there be any truth in the doctrine, it ought to apply to all kinds of degrees of wickedness. But what avails God's forgiveness if I cannot forgive myself? And what is salvation? Can God heal my self-inflicted wound, and save me from the inevitable result of my evil conduct? Nothing but a child can satisfy the yearnings of maternal love; and I know of no joys of heaven that could make me happy there, unless this craving of my nature be first supplied or the instinct annihilated. Somebody else may have my crown and harp—*I want my baby!*"

—*The Abuse of Maternity*, Philadelphia: J.B. Lippincott, 1875, 37–38, 41–42, 52–53, 65–68, 70–72.

Eliza Bisbee Duffey (d. 1898)

In the nineteenth century, a century that liked words far more than our own does, writing was one of a handful of professions through which women could attain economic autonomy.[109] And Eliza Bisbee Duffey was one of a number of women who succeeded in it while caring for a family. She was a prolific author of etiquette and advice books, into which she worked her spirited arguments for women's rights. Duffey was not shy about taking on the major social controversies of her time. One of these concerned Dr. Edward H. Clarke's book *Sex in Education*, according to which women's biology precluded them from being both successful and physically healthy in a coeducational setting.[110] This treatise, though short, inspired no less than five rebuttals from feminists—including Julia Ward Howe, Dr. Mary Putnam Jacobi, and Eliza Duffey. Duffey's pointed response, *No Sex in Education,* disputed the notion that women were crippled by their physiology instead of by sexism.[111] Rather, Duffey thought, women were impaired by *ignorance* of their physiology—a conviction which prompted her to write her sex education manual *What Women Should Know.*[112] This belief also figured large in her *Relations of the Sexes,* in which she held that sex education and birth control were necessary alternatives to abortion—not inevitably bound up with it as antifeminists charged that they were. Even as she tried to circumvent the technicalities of the Comstock Law, Duffey made a bold case—and one which showed sensitivity to dilemmas like those faced by Evans' interviewees.

The Limitation of Offspring
By Eliza Bisbee Duffey

[The following excerpt from *The Relations of the Sexes* immediately follows the suggestion that readers consult Robert Dale Owen's *Moral Physiology,* an important early birth control treatise. Duffey was not free to describe contraceptive methods herself, as she was writing after the passage of the Comstock Law. She was, however, able to discuss her ethical justifications for pre-conception methods of fertility control, and her reasons for sharply distinguishing them from abortion—a practice which she deplored as much as Comstock did. —Ed.]

I have said, in a previous chapter, that I think women should be left free to accept or reject motherhood. I now say that they should only accept it when their hearts go out towards it, and they feel that it will prove a blessing. They should reject it, when the circumstances which attend it are likely to turn it into a curse in many ways. But the great cry of suffering women is, "How shall we refuse it?" Could this question be answered satisfactorily to them, I *know* that to an overwhelming majority of women life would suddenly be flooded with a light and a beauty that for long years has been absent from it; that a weight of fear and trouble would be lifted from their hearts, that has bowed them down, and made them feel helpless and hopeless. I am not talking at random here; I know just what I am saying. And I know, if they dared to speak, there would come to me as with one voice, the words of hosts upon hosts of women in corroboration of my assertion.

I do not think science has reached its ultimatum in this particular. If scientific men had put out as much effort to make investigations which should be of practical value to humanity, as they have to stifle speech and fetter thought, in obedience to blind prejudice and abominable superstition, the world would be further advanced in morality and happiness than it is to-day. Physicians know, as no other class of persons can do, the need of this knowledge. They know the dreadful effects of ignorance and uncontrolled lust. There is not one of them who has not upon his hands a list of patients, more or less long, the victims of abortion, who might have been saved from crime and invalidism if they had known what it is every woman's right and duty to know. And yet these physicians dare not speak, and say what they know to be the truth, lest a mock morality be offended. That they are not ignorant of the exceeding desirability of this knowledge, I have had from the lips of more than one of them. Still, when they give public utterance to their opinions, they join in the general denunciation of preventives to conception, shrewdly trusting that their readers may receive the necessary knowledge through the very means they take to condemn it.

Sufficient practical means have been discovered to make it possible for a whole nation to modify the size of its families, so that a decrease of forty per cent shall be noted in the census-taker's returns—means sufficiently to be depended upon in their operation to enable the French wife to say with perfect confidence: "My husband and I think we have as many children as we can do justice to, and we do not intend to have any more."

Women should have knowledge of these means in order to save them from the terror and dread which, if they would admit the truth, four out of every five would confess, overcloud and destroy the happiness of all their child-bearing years—embittering affection and killing passion. They should have it, that there may be light, and hope, and love, in their homes—and even conjugal delight; for I cannot conceive that that which is so eminently desirable and honorable in a man, should be valueless and shameful in a woman. They should have it that they may not have offspring forced upon them before they are ready for them; that the little ones may be welcomed with love, and desire, and joyful expectancy.

I know there is a feeling in every woman's heart—a feeling which goes down deeper than prejudice even—which tells her that the constant fear of offspring, and the burden of large families, are more grievous troubles than ought to be thrown upon her. She *knows* I am right in what I have been saying in these chapters, for there is a response—let her try to stifle it as she will—to every word, in her own breast. But she has been taught that she must not harbor this feeling, because she was born to be a mother, and a mother without any limit to her duties. Men have taught her this, though her own nature, while it admitted the former, has rebelled against the latter clause. This might be right, if her capabilities were also limitless. But she knows, alas! too well, that they are not, and there is where I have touched the key-note of her feelings. She is willing to do all she can, poor foolish woman; she counts the sacrifice of her strength and life as nothing, in her tireless efforts to cope with impossibilities. But when it comes to more than she can do—why, she cannot! Women have been held in strict subjection of men in this respect, partly, I think, because it was for men's interests thus to hold them—to make them believe that it was their duty to accept unlimited maternal cares, because their acceptance *implied* unlimited sexual gratification on the part of the men; and partly because men are as ignorant and blinded as women themselves. The women of the present day who feel the heavy drawbacks in this respect under which they are laboring, yet dare not speak one word of the bitterness and reproach which are welling up in their hearts, occupy a position exactly analogous to that of the Mormon women who *feel* polygamy is wrong, yet dare not express that feeling, because they find it irreconcilable with the teachings of their religion which ordains it.

[Duffey then summarizes Isabella Beecher Hooker's arguments from *Womanhood: Its Sanctities and Fidelities,* which are reprinted later in this volume. Duffey does this "not only to show that I am not alone in the view I hold, but to encourage other women to come out and speak boldly the sentiments that are in their hearts." She then takes on one of the common objections to birth control. —Ed.]

… "Children have a right to be born!" … [No one] is justified in interfering with this most sacred and indubitable right, or in any way to lessen the certainty of their being born; which is to say, that if a husband approaches his wife carnally when she is pregnant, and by his approach causes abortion, he is guilty of infanticide, or rather, foeticide. [Birth control opponents] do not mean quite this, I know, but then I do. This is going a little too far for them. But I plant myself firmly on the ground which they have deserted. After a child *is,* no one has a right to tamper with its existence. But, returning to the statement, and considering it in the light in which it is intended to be understood, let us decide whether it can be appropriately applied to the prevention of conception. By what possible twist of imagination can any one suppose something, which is not something at all—which is nothing, because it is nowhere, and has no existence—to be a child? A being which does not exist, has no rights, to be either granted or withheld. If it has, how about those children which numberless married couples might have had, if they had but married a few years earlier, or if the mothers had weaned their babies a few months sooner? How about the might-have-been children of those who never marry? Are there no qualms of conscience about these potential offspring?

When we talk about children having a right to be born, we must understand exactly what we mean by it. *I* mean that no one has a right to jeopardize a life which has already begun ever so brief an existence. *Your* meaning is quite another thing, and if expressed in the most direct words, would not be half so high sounding, or so complimentary to your moral nature. My meaning shuts at once and forever the door of abortion. But before that existence has commenced, we have a right—nay, it is a sacred duty, unmistakably delegated to us by God—to consider whether we shall assume the responsibility of evoking such an existence, and whether we can insure it happy conditions. …

Abortion, intentionally accomplished, is criminal in the first degree, and should be regarded as murder. Yet women have been taught to look lightly on this offence, and to consider it perfectly justifiable up to the period of quickening. "The embryo has no life before that period," they will say in justification of the act. I have even heard a woman, who acknowledged to several successful abortions, accomplished by her own hands upon herself, say, "Why, there is no harm in it, any more than in drowning a blind kitten. It is nothing better than a kitten, before it is born." I was a young girl myself when I heard this, and I accepted the statement as a true one. Nor did I dream of questioning it, until, in later years, I became thoroughly acquainted with sexual physiology, and comprehended the wonderful economy of nature in the generation and development of the human germ.

The act of abortion which I had hitherto regarded as a trivial thing, at once became in my eyes the grossest misdemeanor—nay, the most aggravated crime. Being guided by this experience, I judge that this offence is perpetrated by women who are totally ignorant of the laws of their being. Consequently, the surest preventive against this crime will be a thorough teaching to women, even before marriage, of the physiology, hygiene, duties and obligations of maternity. Men may preach against this act as a sin; but knowing as women do, how one-sided it is possible for men to feel and talk about other matters of a similar nature, in which the sexes are equally concerned, it is not strange that these sermons produce no effect. The strangeness is still further decreased when the sermonizers are not infrequently themselves guilty of the no less heinous offence of forcing motherhood upon a woman against her will. The two offences go together, and neither legal enactment nor social reprobation can ever divorce them. The woman knows instinctively that if her husband is justified in the one, he has no moral right to interfere with her in the accomplishment of the other.

[Duffey then quotes from a Dr. Reeves' address against abortion, which concludes with the following. —Ed.] "Virtuous women should be true to themselves, and thus compel a higher standard of morals among men. Why should the man of easy virtue be honored and welcomed to their parlors, while the poor, ruined outcast and victim of his unbridled passions is denied to rest her weary limbs even within their gates? Let women require it as a condition of respectability and good character that men shall walk upon the same virtuous level, and be pure as they are pure."

… The Doctor, at all events, has seen a direct connection between the characters of the husbands and abortions committed by women. No doubt pure, good men would be more careful than rakes, how their wives were provoked to such deeds, by excesses on their part.

From the moment of conception, the embryo is a living thing, leading a distinct, separate existence from the mother, though closely bound to her. The mother's blood courses through its veins, and she nourishes it, and gives of her physical substance the material for its bones and muscles. From almost the earliest stage, the form of the future being is indicated, and it has its separate heart-beats, distinctly perceptible through the intervening tissues of the mother's body, which cover it. It is a human being to all intents and purposes. The period called quickening is merely a fictitious period, which does not indicate the first motion of the embryo. These first motions are not usually detected—unless the woman is very observant, and knows just what feeling to expect—until they have acquired considerable force.

Nature has put this little creature—this small man or woman, as yet all undeveloped—in a place of seeming security, and has placed every guard around it to keep it safely until the hour shall come when it is fully prepared to make a complete change in its mode of existence. If by intent or accident it is disturbed before that period, the whole of nature's plans are thwarted, and nothing is in readiness. A hundred bleeding wounds remain, when the child, with its accompanying membranes, is torn untimely from the womb of the mother; mouths that would have closed themselves at the appropriate time, but now remain open to bleed away the mother's life. This is the cause of so much flooding in miscarriage, and which renders it so peculiarly dangerous. But this is only one of its many dangers, which I have no space now to enumerate ...

[Abortion] is a crime in the fullest extent of the term, because it is murder, just as much as though the mother took her new-born babe and plunged a knife into its bosom, or cast it away from her, and refused to nourish it. Is there a woman not driven to the last depths of despair by wounded love and impending disgrace, who could do that to the little, soft, helpless thing, that is laid in her bosom so soon after its first cry has appealed to her heart? Yet the abortion-seeker regards with satisfaction the means to kill the little creature that has nestled so confidingly beneath her heart, as if it were the safest place in all the world for it.

But no; I must not be too hard upon these unwomanly women. Their ignorance must be held as responsible for their sins. And men must share the responsibility, too. The husband who has forced an unwelcome motherhood upon his wife, and thus provided her with what seems to her mind as an excuse for this terrible deed, must be judged equally guilty.

I have already said that knowledge among women will do much towards decreasing this crime. Do not be content to tell women it is wrong, and then stop there. Women are impatient of being treated like children, or like unreasoning beings; nor do they like to be dictated to. Tell them the how and the why of the whole matter, and they will discover the wrong themselves, and *feel* the full force of it, far more than they ever can by taking it merely on the say-so of men.

Then the laws which are already upon our statute books should be strictly enforced, not only on the occasion of bursts of indignation, when some unfortunate girl endeavors to get rid of the evidence of her shame; but whenever the fact of a wilful abortion comes to the cognizance of community. And *husbands and seducers should be made to share the punishment as accessories to the crime,* since if they had not forced an undesired motherhood upon the women, there would have been no occasion for the abortion.

Not only every maker, advertiser and seller of patent medicines, warranted to "remove female obstructions," should be subjected to prosecution and punishment, but every publisher who prints an advertisement of this sort should be held equally guilty. Community will not be injured in the least by the suppression of these advertisements; for physicians of every shade of practice will sustain me in declaring that they do harm and harm only to women, no matter how innocent may be the intent of the person using them. But the real intent is for the procurement of abortion, and so everybody knows. If the newspapers which go into families contained nothing of this word, nine tenths of the women who are guilty of attempts to commit abortion, would never think of it.

No; the evils attendant upon large families may be manifold; but they must not be averted by any such criminal means as this; for the remedy is as bad as the disease …

—from *The Relations of the Sexes*, New York: Wood and Holbrook, 1876, Chapter Thirteen.

Sarah F. Norton

S arah F. Norton was a writer and a travelling lecturer in New York. She delivered speeches with such titles as "Woman's Equal Place, Pay, and Opportunity" and "The Rag-Pickers of New York," reflecting her passionate concern with the economic conditions that oppressed women.[113] She stated outright that marriage, practiced as the ownership of women by men, was the prime culprit for all her gender's woes.[114] As a leader of the New York Working Women's Association, she maintained that the relationship of capital to labor was a most appropriate topic for discussion in "any Woman's Rights Convention," despite the efforts of some to dismiss it as irrelevant.[115] Her adventures, including her agitation to expand women's life prospects by having them admitted to Cornell University, are recounted in several letters to *The Revolution* during the spring of 1869.[116]

Foremost among her spirited contributions to the feminist press is the following indictment of abortion. Like Duffey, Norton makes it clear that abortion did not simply involve the exploitation of individual women and children by individual men, isolated completely from powerful social and economic forces. Male exploitation played into that of a callously profit-oriented abortion industry. And the larger society as well had complicity in this "life-destroying trade," despite all the lip service paid to denouncing it.

Tragedy—Social and Domestic
by Sarah F. Norton

Two of those fearful domestic tragedies which occasionally startle society into a sense of its own complicity with what it pleases to call crime have recently occurred—one in New York, the other in a Western city. They were chiefly remarkable for a certain kind of desperate savageness, the result, evidently, of a mania peculiar to parturient women, and also for a striking coincidence in time, in outline, and detail which renders it possible to tell the story of one while rehearsing the circumstances of the other.

Briefly, without prologue and without naming the persons engaged in either of these domestic dramas, the argument runs thus: A young woman, scarcely twenty years of age, of good family, well educated, having amiable manners and enjoying the esteem of a wide circle of friends and acquaintances, alone and unattended, during the gloom of midnight, gives birth in a bath-room to an illegitimate child, which she immediately strangles and throws out of a window into a neighboring yard.

She makes her way as best she can to her own bedroom, and awaits the revelation of the coming dawn. Sick at heart, delirious in mind and exhausted in body, her friends find her in the morning beyond the reach of medical or surgical skill; and, while they are learning the shocking details of that horrible night, her lips are sealed by death, and the secret is told which the sacrifice of two lives could not conceal.

Here are the outlines of a crime at which society shudders, and for a moment stands appalled. In another moment it is put aside with a wave of the hand, after the manner of Podsnap, and the affair is forgotten.

Society would have avenged the murder of the child by making a victim of the unhappy mother, but death prevented that, and now, since the grave hides them both, let the social revel go on.

Sad and tragical as all this is, there is another fact still more sad and tragical, which society utterly ignores.

The woman expiated the murder of her child by her own death; but there is somewhere a *man*, who, if he had been modestly honorable, might have saved both lives, and who, in the last analysis, is responsible for both, if there be personal responsibility for anything whatever.

Who is he? where is he? and what is the name of and penalty for *his* crime. These questions, however pertinent, society does not ask. Its war is against the woman and the child, and as they are both beyond the reach of its revenge, it is entirely willing the man should receive its protection.

In their social aspect it is clearly the use of force that made these murders shocking; for society has made child-murder a fine art, and strangulation, though good enough for a guilty man, is entirely out of place when applied to a babe guilty of being born without the sanction of that law which provides no punishment for the father's share in its conception, holds him to no account for its premature death if it happen, nor to any responsibility for its support and protection, if, perchance it persists in living, despite all efforts to destroy it.

Society has come to believe it an impertinence in children to be born at all. It is even difficult for a family with children to find a home; and throughout the entire city there are few landlords who do not stipulate for childless couples when renting their property. This partiality explains why people in cities might not want children, but is totally inadequate as a reason for the murder of them without a combination of other and greater reasons to lead it; and it cannot be considered at all in relation to the fast increasing crime of foeticide throughout the country, where space is ample, rents low, and provisions comparatively cheap. It is safe to conclude, however, that the prevailing causes are the same in both city and country. What these causes are can only be guessed at by the stray scraps vouchsafed to us through such accidents as this recent one at 94 Chatham Street, [New York,] and which occasionally happen to open the doors of these dens of death and reveal their secrets.

Here we find that a husband had been procuring poison for his wife and prospective offspring! not with any wish to kill the wife perhaps, but as the chances are as five to one against every women who attempts abortion, he could not have failed to realize the danger. Had the scheme been successful in destroying only the life aimed at, what could have been the man's crime—and what should be his punishment if, as accessory to one murder he commits two?

Instead of expressing satisfaction at the non-success of his attempted crime, he writes with a sort of mournful cadence to his infamous coadjutor that "it," "the potion," "had about as much effect as a glass of soda-water. Just as I expected." In this incident we find the proof of two facts: First, that professional child-murders are supported by the married as well as the single; and, second, that the husbands are equally implicated and guilty with their wives.

These, however, are no new facts; for it is generally understood, among women at least, that in such cases the husband approves if he does not instigate. Usually he does the last; as the evidence of weakly wives and their confidential physicians would amply prove, could they be induced or compelled by any means to reveal the truth.

The servants in a house where such cases occur are not to be deceived; and these self-same servants form the greater proportion of the unmarried who patronize such dens as that in Chatham Street. They get an example from their mistress, or if not that, learn from the common gossip in the house about other wives, that child-murder is an easy and every-day affair.

The pernicious effect of all this is to make the seduction of the unmarried an easy matter, and murder an accepted contingency. If the married, to whom maternity is accepted and an honor, have reason to destroy their offspring, how much more reason have they to whom it would be a life-long dishonor; and if the first sets the example, why should not the last follow it?

No returns are made of premature or illegitimate births, and we can only judge of the number by the daily accounts given in the newspapers of some woman dying or dead from the effects of an abortion or premature birth, and newly-born, cast-away infants; and as efforts at concealment are in the main successful, we can very justly determine that the cases which come to notice are mere indications of what remains unknown.

Any business self-supporting enough to become a recognized fact by the people must, of necessity, be on the increase; and the single fact that child murderers practice their profession without let or hindrance, and open infant butcheries unquestioned, establishing themselves with an impunity that is not allowed to the slaughterers of cattle, is, of itself, sufficient to prove that society makes a demand which they alone can supply.

Scores of persons advertise their willingness to commit this form of murder, and with unblushing effrontery announce their names and residences in the daily papers. No one seems to be shocked by the fact; the papers are taken into the family without hesitation, and read by all the members thereof without distinction of age or sex. The subject is discussed almost without restraint; circulars are distributed broadcast, recommending certain pills and potions for the very purpose, and by these means the names of these slayers of infants, and the methods by which they practice their life-destroying trade, have become "familiar in our mouths as household words."

... Is there no remedy for all this ante-natal child murder? Not any, is the reply to the question so frequently asked. Is there, then, no penalty for the crime? None that can be inflicted, for the crime has become an art, and society cannot punish those who serve it so skillfully and well.

Perhaps there will come a time when the man who wantonly kills a woman and her babe will be loathed and scorned as deeply as the woman is now loathed and scorned who becomes his dupe; when the sympathy of society will be with the victim rather than the victimizer; when an unmarried woman will not be despised because of her motherhood; when unchastity in men will be placed on an equality with unchastity in women, and when the right of the unborn to be born will not be denied or interfered with. ...

—*Woodhull and Claflin's Weekly*, November 19, 1870.

Victoria Woodhull (1838–1927) and Tennessee Claflin (1845–1923)

Norton's piece appeared in the newspaper published by two of the most colorful early feminists: Victoria Woodhull and Ten-nessee Claflin. Sisters from a poor and chaotic Ohio family, they became the first female stockbrokers on Wall Street after a stint as Spiritualist mediums. In 1870, Woodhull declared herself a candidate for the presidency—the first woman ever to do so. The next year she presented a speech to the U.S. Congress, giving carefully thought-out legal arguments that women already had the vote under the fourteenth and fifteenth amendments, which had recently enfranchised black men. Radicals such as Susan B. Anthony and Elizabeth Cady Stanton welcomed Woodhull's contributions to their movement, but more conservative suffragists hastily dissociated themselves from her because of the reputation as "bad women" that she and her sister had gained. Stanton, impressed by Woodhull's intelligence, forthrightness, and integrity, retorted: "If Victoria Woodhull must be crucified, let men drive the spikes and plant the crown of thorns."[117]

The sisters' notoriety came from the views they expressed in their speaking tours and in their flamboyant newspaper, whose motto was: "Progress! Free Thought! Untrammeled Lives! Breaking the Way for Future Generations." *Woodhull's and Claflin's Weekly,* published from 1870 to 1876, advocated Spiritualism, alternative medicine, and radical economics. It was the first American periodical to run a translation of the Communist Manifesto. Most outrageously of all, it editorialized in favor of woman suffrage and "free love." "Free lovers," contrary to the accusations of their opponents, did not argue for "promiscuity." They wished, rather, for sexual relationships to be based on personal, mutual choice, respect, and affection, rather than on a legal formality which, they felt, necessarily involved the ownership of the woman by the man. Above all, they vociferously attacked the double standard, especially as practiced by the nineteenth-century counterparts of today's lascivious clerics.

When the eminent Rev. Henry Ward Beecher excoriated them for their views, the sisters published the information that he, a married man, had had an affair with his parishioner Elizabeth Tilton, also married. Never fond of hypocrisy, the sisters accused Beecher of practicing in private the doctrines he denounced from his pulpit. Their "effrontery" incensed anti-vice crusader Anthony Comstock, an adulating member of Beecher's congregation. He arranged for the sisters' arrest on the grounds that they had circulated obscene literature through the mails—an offense against the famous law which bore his name.

Inextricably bound up with the sisters' critique of "Comstockery" or sexual conservatism was their opposition to abortion. Not only did Woodhull and Claflin proclaim that children had rights; these rights began at conception. And it was not the flouting of conventional sexual morality that led to the violation of prenatal children's rights. Rather, abortion was the product of a social system that compelled women to remain ignorant about their bodies, that enabled men to dominate them sexually without taking responsibility for the consequences, that denied women support during and after the resulting pregnancies, and that placed far more value on a child's "legitimacy" than on his or her life and well-being. Like Norton's piece, the following editorials link abortion with societal callousness towards children already born—and towards their mothers.

Press Justice
by Victoria Woodhull and Tennessee Claflin

We have a new sensation of the free lust kind, in the case of Rev. A.B. Carter of the Church of the Holy Saviour. Before we proceed we want it distinctly remembered that we did not bring this social scandal to light, and owe all we know to the pure daily press. The Rev. Holy Parson is accused of seducing a young lady and procuring an abortion, as well as with putting his victim into a house of assignation.

The *Star* asks, which is the sinner? If the charge be true, the man is the greater sinner, because of his age, calling, education, his wife and children; these are arguments against him; it is barely possible she waylaid and seduced him; and if she did, the facts still stand against him. It was his business to save her *soul,* not prostitute her body, ruin her reputation, murder the fruits of their joint act, and send both to hell, if he was not a hypocritical ranter as well as a lecherous divine.

The *Tribune* in harmony with its vulgar and brutal instincts, without hearing evidence further than the charge and denial, at once denounces the woman as attempting to blackmail the innocent *soul maker* as well as *soul saver.* We prefer to wait the hearing of the evidence. The frequent occurrence of those Rev. monogamic *free lust* digressions, as furnished in the columns of the *Tribune,* shows as a class, the per cent of Rev. seducers as very fair; and the inference at first blush against the cloth.

So far as this particular case is developed, the impression is against Mr. Carter. The lady would hardly risk the exposure and loss of standing in the community, where she was thoroughly protected, unless, indeed, there is a necessity for another abortion, which may explain the fact of her desperation and imperative demand for the remaining $30,000.

That he met her in the vestry is conceded. That that was a convenient place to conduct such a transaction, immediately under the droppings of the sanctuary—who will question?

We suspend judgment, and await with patience this piece of pious scandal. We hope the Rev. gentleman will not charge his little misdemeanor to our paper and its doctrines. The *Weekly* was not in existence when this little affair was said to have commenced. Meantime we are curious to know, if it be total depravity or the special depravity of those particular sinners, or monogamic, permanent legal marriage without regard to fitness; or is it a false public opinion begotten of all these.

Here legal motherhood is creditable, hence illegal motherhood begets disgrace, and hence suicide and murder. When the day comes that motherhood is deemed the right of all healthy women, and no disgrace attaches to the manner of it, then murder and abortion will cease, and not until then.

There are countries where this unchristian and unjust distinction does not exist, where an unmarried mother stands as well as a married mother; and there these pests of Christian monogamy do not exist.

We cannot see why an unmarried woman, the mother of a child whose father is physically and morally complete, or of average completeness, should stand below a woman who is a widow, or a woman who prostitutes her body and soul to rearing the offspring of drunken, diseased, and brutal legal *fathers.*

The right of motherhood is founded in nature, and is before, above and beyond all human legislation. There is neither vice nor virtue in it, except as it agrees or disagrees with the natural justice of the case.

In the eyes of the world this woman's confession forever bars her from respectable society. If this man is proven guilty, it will seriously mar his standing—ordinarily it would soon be forgotten.

After marriage, this obligation rests lightly on him, heavily on her. Few men are strictly faithful—few women unfaithful.

The *Times* is as unjust as the *Tribune;* it saddles all the blame on the woman. We think it more reasonable to judge after the evidence; that it is mean, unmanly, and libellous to use the power of the press to manufacture public opinion against either, even if both are guilty, which is just as probable as that the woman *alone* is guilty; and in this case even more so. But the press is willing to accept the denial of the man—but not the affirmation of the woman. The woman loses her social position by her confession—the man retains his and his salary. Let any honest mind compare the cases, and the injustice of the press is apparent. And yet we do wrong to demand justice for women, in the eyes of such creatures!

The fact that the girl is willing to retire, and that the reverend gentleman is inexorable, does not prove her guilt or his innocence. This spirit of persecution is illy in keeping with the life and precepts of the Master; and however innocent he may be of this particular charge, he has proved one thing beyond a doubt—and that is, that he is unfit to be a Christian minister. He cannot endure persecution without resentment—vengeance; and this adds strongly to the suspicion that he is not free from blemish in the affair.

—*Woodhull and Claflin's Weekly,* March 23, 1872.

What Will Become of the Children
by Victoria Woodhull and Tennessee Claflin

… One of the greatest objections that women raise against bearing children, and that one which perhaps more than any other causes so much murder of unborn children, is that to have them is to make a slave of the mother. A woman who conceives and bears children regularly after marriage, and is compelled to have charge of them all, is a slave in reality, at least during the whole term of her child-bearing period; and in this sense every woman who does not turn the care over to some-one, is more or less a slave as she has more or less children. A proper system, which would place those in charge of children who are fitted to have it, would result not only in increased benefit to such children as escape ante-natal death, but it would tend greatly to decrease the desire on the part of wives to commit this class of murders. Even in the small cities in the country it is no uncommon thing for physicians to have a half-dozen applications a day to produce abortions …

This is the danger that threatens American women. And yet these same women cry out, "We don't want the social question discussed"; and the doctors who aid this infamy reiterate this cry, while the preachers and editors do as much more in their lines to stifle discussion on this all-important subject.

In the name of heaven, then, if for nothing else than to relieve the worn-out mothers of the country, let the people adopt some suitable educational system for our rising generation …

—*Woodhull and Claflin's Weekly,* January 24, 1874.

The Slaughter of the Innocents
by Victoria Woodhull and Tennessee Claflin

If there is one fact in modern society more horrible, and at the same time more sorrowful than any other, it is that one which relates to the death-rate among the young from the time of conception up to five years of age. It is one of those things against which almost everybody willfully shuts his eyes and professes to think that it does not exist: and everybody pretends to everybody else that he knows nothing about it; while on every hand—in every household—the young drop off like leaves before the autumn wind. Perhaps many assume this pretended ignorance from the fact that, knowing they can do nothing to remedy the terrible condition, they do not wish to be annoyed with the inevitable, and put it aside as the most consistent thing to be done under the circumstances. But this enforced ignoring of one of the horrible facts of modern society is engendering in society itself a morbid condition of mind regarding children which, if not speedily checked, will prove fatal to civilization itself. The present tendencies cannot continue a score of years longer, increasing in volume and strength as they have for the last score, without wiping at least the American race out of existence, or else eradicating from its conscience all scruples in regard to human life … Such will be the compensation which humanity is preparing for itself in the not distant future.

But it goes on its course rapidly nearing the precipice as if there were no legitimate results to ensue. It is seemingly indifferent to the life or death of the young. Its practices cut them down like grass before the scythe. Parents deposit one-half of their young in the grave-yards before they reach the age of five years. What a commentary this is on the social condition! ... Childhood ought to be the healthiest period of life, but in our condition it has degenerated until it is ten times more fatal than any other period. And yet we talk of the sacredness of human life as if it were so regarded at all! A human life is a human life and equally to be held sacred whether it be a day or century old; and that custom which cuts off one-half of the young almost in infancy, is as virtually murder as would be the same death-rate among adults resulting from compelling them to the use of life-destroying food. Children die because they are not properly cared for. If adults received equally improper treatment as children received, they would die at the same rate; but adults, being capable of judging for themselves as to what is proper and what is improper, by choosing the former, decrease the death-rate ten times below that which obtains among the classes who depend upon others for their treatment ...

But this fact regarding the indifference to life that exists among parents is not perhaps the worst feature of modern society. It is not only a fact that this terrible death-rate persistently continues among children, but that there is still another death method not included in its horrible details, which, if possible, is still more revolting, and which is nonetheless a slaughter of the innocents. ...

Wives deliberately permit themselves to become pregnant of children and then, to prevent becoming mothers, as deliberately murder them while yet in their wombs. Can there be a more demoralized condition than this? ... Why should the birth-rate decrease as the people become more enlightened? ... Simply because with increased knowledge comes increased individuality; and with increased individuality, increased repugnance to submission to the slavery that child-bearing almost necessarily entails in our society as at present organized; and with these also the knowledge that pregnancy can be broken up, sometimes with little present evidence of evil to the, otherwise, mother ... If this practice prevail so widely among wives, who have no need to resort to it "to hide their shame," but merely to prevent an increase in the number of their children, how prevalent it must be among the unmarried class who have social death staring them in the face when they become pregnant without the consent of the canting priest or the drunken squire? ...

We are aware that many women attempt to excuse themselves for procuring abortions, upon the ground that it is not murder. But the fact of resort to so weak an argument only shows the more palpably that they fully realize the enormity of the crime. Is it not equally destroying the would-be future oak, to crush the sprout before it pushes its head above the sod, as it is to cut down the sapling, or cut down the tree? Is it not equally to destroy life, to crush it in its very germ, and to take it when the germ has evolved to any given point in its line of development? Let those who can see any difference regarding the time when life, once begun, is taken, console themselves that they are not murderers having been abortionists.

But horrible and revolting as are the facts of abortion, *per se,* they are as nothing compared to the evil that is wrought in cases where it is attempted without success ... It is safe to assume that four in every five of the children of whom mothers become pregnant are not desired; that is, they would not have exposed themselves could they have helped it and would have known that it would ensue. The more horrible results of abortion than are the facts themselves, are those that fall upon the children. No mother can have a desire spring up in her mind to be rid of the child she carries in her womb without imprinting the thought, the possibility of murder upon its facile mind. ... [118]

We ask the women of this country to consider carefully the subjects thus hastily presented, and see if they do not find in them an unanswerable argument for sexual freedom for themselves, so that they may have control of their maternal functions and thereby be able to bear children only when they desire them, and such as they desire.

... We speak of these things in connection with the subject of child-murder, because originally they are the foundation for it. ... And yet there are still to be found apparently intelligent people who seem honestly to think that the social question ought not to be discussed publicly! ... For our part, so long as the terrible effects of our unnatural sexual system continues to desecrate humanity, there is no other question to be considered in which the health, happiness, and general well-being of the race is so intimately involved.

—*Woodhull and Claflin's Weekly,* June 20, 1874.

Isabella Beecher Hooker (1822–1907)

S uffragist Isabella Beecher Hooker was one of the Reverend Lyman Beecher's several prominent offspring. Her siblings included Harriet Beecher Stowe, best known as the author of *Uncle Tom's Cabin;* Catharine Esther Beecher, a pioneer in the fields of women's education and domestic science; and none other than the Reverend Henry Ward Beecher of the aforementioned Beecher-Tilton scandal.[119] As trying as the scandal was for the whole Beecher clan, Isabella did not allow her relationship with her brother to compromise her commitment to women. She left open the possibility that Henry was guilty as charged. Even more, she defended Victoria Woodhull's right to free speech and right to take on the double standard, despite the fact that Woodhull was widely denounced as "Mrs. Satan."

For this demonstration of integrity, Hooker paid dearly. She was denounced by members of her own family and by more conservative suffragists. Because of her role in the scandal, historians neglected her until quite recently. Yet she was an important and engaging figure in the early feminist movement. Her public career was a natural outgrowth of the many years prior to it that she had devoted exclusively to being a wife and mother.

Before she was married at age nineteen to John Hooker, an abolitionist and esteemed constitutional lawyer, she insisted to him that theirs would continue to be an affectionate, egalitarian relationship. The Hookers had four children together, three of whom lived past infancy. Because this was a small family for its time, and because Isabella later publicly advocated family planning, her most comprehensive biographers have concluded that she and John consciously and jointly decided to limit their reproduction. Although she took a lively interest in public affairs and significantly assisted her husband in his legal and political activities, Isabella's only lengthy respite from domesticity during the antebellum period was a stay at a water-cure resort to alleviate her persistent gynecological ailments. However, she refused the role of delicate invalid which allowed many other homemakers of the period relief from their cares.[120]

Even as she delighted in the unfolding personalities of her children, Isabella chafed at the limitations of domestic life. She envied her sisters' public achievements. Finally, in 1868, when only her youngest child was left at home, she embarked on her career as a suffragist lecturer and writer. Frances Willard and Mary Livermore characterized her career as "one of ceaseless toil, heroic endurance of undeserved abuse, and exalted effort." She began with a tract entitled *A Mother's Letters to a Daughter on Woman Suffrage,* which was, like so many of her works, an attempt to bring the virtues of domesticity into the world at large. As vice-president of the Connecticut chapter of the National Woman Suffrage Association, Hooker delivered many captivating speeches grounded in thorough legal scholarship. In 1878 she spoke before the U.S. Congress, appealing for women's enfranchisement. Before the 1888 International Council of Women, she delivered "a masterly, exhaustive, and unanswerable presentation" of American women's constitutional rights.[121]

In *Womanhood: Its Sanctities and Fidelities,* her only book, Hooker made a masterly, exhaustive, and unanswerable argument on behalf of woman's right to challenge the double standard on all fronts. This book, which was published at the height of the Beecher-Tilton scandal, prompted some of the "undeserved abuse" that Willard and Livermore mention, while at the same time "brought to her many earnest expressions of gratitude from intelligent mothers."[122] In it, Hooker asserted her opposition to legalized prostitution and to cultural strictures that prevented mothers from educating their own children about sexuality. She also objected to men who assailed aborting women without seeing how their own actions and attitudes implicated them in the "crime of foeticide." In her gentle yet compelling way, she specifically took on none other than the Reverend John Todd, a nemesis of nineteenth century feminists.[123] Her refusal to be taken in by his empty rhetoric about exalted womanhood is a striking example of her lifelong fight against oppressive conventions.

Motherhood
by Isabella Beecher Hooker

The subjoined letter, addressed to the Rev. Dr. Todd, was written in April, 1867, under the following circumstances. A very serious and earnest article from his pen appeared in the Boston Congregationalist of April 19th, entitled "Fashionable Murder," in which the crime of foeticide was severely condemned, and the claim made that the chief causes of it were the desire of women to live in ease and fashion, and an unwillingness to undergo the pain of childbirth. It was admitted that a woman's heart naturally longs for children, and yet it was asserted that many more married than unmarried women, in proportion, destroyed the lives of their unborn children; but no other causes for this strange inconsistency were suggested than those above mentioned, while there was a strong opinion expressed that as men usually desire children, and are willing to toil for their support, women must be held chiefly responsible for this criminal suppression of offspring.

The injustice done to women in this article, unintentionally no doubt, and the superficial manner of treating a most profound subject, one which Plato deemed worthy of his deepest thought, and which from his day to our own has not reached a satisfactory solution, drew from me a reply, which was immediately forwarded to the Congregationalist, in which a second article by Rev. Dr. Todd had then appeared upon another phase of the same subject. The editor declined to publish the reply, and soon after these two articles of Dr. Todd were published as a pamphlet, and in that form were largely noticed by the public papers, and had a wide circulation. In the mean time the reply has been privately circulated among the writer's friends, and especially among mothers, with an increasing interest in the subject, and an often-expressed desire for its publication. One of the profoundest thinkers of the day, at the head of one of our most influential secular journals, wrote me as follows after reading it: "Your letter is capital. I think myself, and have long thought, that there is no subject more important, and, as it is surrounded by difficulties, no subject which needs more discussion. I think also that a very large proportion of the ills of humanity, at the present day, comes from the long taught and incessantly repeated dogma that children come, as the rain comes, by the act of Providence; that human will has nothing to do with it, once marriage has taken place ... "

There is a great disinclination on the part of refined and fastidious people to have these subjects spoken of at all, and especially in plain language; but nothing is clearer to me than that the best welfare of our race, both moral and physical, requires that they be understood; and if so, the truths that need to be stated should be stated with delicacy, but in language that can be understood; and language that plainly conveys its meaning is far better in its moral effect than that which deals with its subject in covert and ambiguous expression, and thus suggests concealed indelicacy and stimulates unwholesome curiosity. Every offer of marriage consciously to both parties brings up these sexual relations, and to the joy of both, the thought of their common offspring. If these things may, consistently with purity and delicacy, lie in the mind, and be cherished in the heart, they may certainly be spoken of, where the object is the best welfare of those who are addressed. And if any one, in all the world, should be allowed to speak on these subjects, who so much as we who are mothers and grandmothers, who can speak from our own happy or sad experience, and to whom no unworthy motive can, for a moment, be imputed? In looking upon my own children and grandchildren, I see in them the representative of all humanity, and my heart reaches out in sisterly sympathy to all mothers, and in motherly yearning toward all the children of the earth.

In writing this letter, and deciding to publish it, my only hope has been to contribute something from my own thought and experience that shall throw some helpful light upon this difficult yet profoundly important subject, and perhaps, lead others out of their own perplexities, their successes, and their failures, to bring more effective aid to its discussion. What I ask, then, is the sympathy of parents and of all thoughtful young people, and from the general public such a manner of forbearance in criticism as the purity of my motive and the peril of my task may seem justly to bespeak for me.

April 20, 1867

Rev. John Todd, D.D.

Dear Sir:

I have just read in the Congregationalist of April 19th your impressive words in condemnation of mothers who criminally relieve themselves of unwelcome offspring, and my mother's heart stirs me to immediate reply. I may seem to do this in the haste of the moment, but in reality I shall be giving you the result of many years of observations and reflection upon the subject.

You have spoken of two great laws of our race that came with transgression—excessive labor for man, suffering and subjection for woman; and it is certainly true that mankind are to this day greatly under the power of these laws. It is no less true, however, that both men and women have all along been rightfully striving to ameliorate their condition in these respects, and to come into a condition of perfect liberty of choice, even the liberty wherewith Christ doth make us free.

That some women have mistaken the way to this personal freedom, and been led into deadly sin and into the fearful suffering which inevitably follows the serious transgression of even physical law, is true, perhaps to the extent you have stated, and such need warning; and I, for one, cannot but rejoice when the sin and danger of their evil ways are plainly set before them; but I rejoice also in the whole truth, and the fair statement of a vital question, and in this respect your article seems to me very defective. ...

Is it not time, then, that these vital questions, which do, in fact, underlie all social moralities, were examined and discussed under all the light which science and religion can impart, and be handled by mothers as well as by fathers, and more especially by the former, since they chiefly are the watchful observers and guardians of those young days when right habits and beliefs may be taught to children of both sexes?

And now permit me to say that a great part of the physical and moral deterioration of the present day arises, it seems to me, from the fact that children are not conceived in the desire for them, and out of the pure lives of their fathers, as well as their mothers; and that far worse misfortunes might befall our race than decreasing families, so long as children are born to such an inheritance as too many young men of the present day are likely to transmit. And this I speak, not from a desire to blame them, so much as to call the attention of mothers to their own neglect in the matter of training these faulty sons.

Let us suppose, now, these boys living closely with their mothers in most familiar intimacy up to their very manhood; and how easy for the latter, if only their lips might be unsealed by the removal of all false notions of delicacy, to instruct these sons from whom they hope so much, not only in the physiology of their own bodies, but also in the constitutional differences between themselves and the mothers who bore them, as representatives of all other women?

To my conception, one generation of *instructed* mothers would do more for the renovation of the race than all other agencies combined. ... Under such guidance as this, would there be need, think you, of the warnings of your article? and without it may we ever hope for a truly godly seed to inhabit this earth? Do we not simply lop the branches and leave the sturdy trunk, when we criticize this and that practice of human parents, and overlook their fundamental misconceptions of the nature of their being?

You have spoken of ministers' families illustrating by their size the piety of the parents; but it does seem to me the quality of offspring is far better testimony than the quantity. It may be that, tried by this test also, ministers have done well for their race; but I have sometimes thought that many of them are just as uninstructed in and just as indifferent to the true theory of the relation of husband and wife, and parent and child, as many of those who make no pretensions to godliness or humanity.

At all events I have heard of one New England minister, the father of many children, whose word to his daughter and her approaching marriage was, "You must instruct your husband, my dear, that he do not allow you to have children too often. If I had known what I now know earlier in life, your mother, of blessed memory, might be living to this day. The drain upon her vitality, in giving birth to all those children, and the incessant care of them through many years of poverty and trial, were more than human strength could endure, and disease coming to her at last, she sank under it, with no power to rally." And then he went on to state to her his deep convictions on the general subject, which were in accordance with the views I am urging, and which he had reached, not through the medium of science, but through the promptings of a great and noble heart and a courageous will, which led him to the truth even at the cost of self-condemnation and a great and perpetual sorrow.

By this do I feel encouraged to suggest to all young parents that there is a more excellent way of bringing happiness to their households than by seeking [through abortion] to escape the suffering and care, the toil and privation, that children may bring. You should desire children beyond all mere earthly possessions; they pay their own way, and you cannot afford to live without them; your whole life will be chilled if you wilfully shut out these sunbeams. But you must not invite these little ones to your homes any oftener than you can provide for them in body and in spirit, and for the health and the strength of the mothers who are to bear them; and the call should come to the ear of the Great Father out of pure hearts, reverently desiring his best gift, which you promise humbly to receive and to keep for Him against that day when He shall make up His jewels.

If these words shall bring light and blessing to any such, God be thanked. They come from the depths of a heart that has known only happiness in all these relations, though it has ached sorely and often over the widespread ignorance, which, like vice itself, is dragging hundreds into immeasurable wretchedness.

That these views must prevail I have no more doubt than I have that the kingdom of heaven is at hand. In fact, this is to me one of the open doors to that kingdom, and blessed are they who shall early walk therein. From these faithful souls, made pure by the denials of the flesh, shall come, someday, a happy race of children, who, born to a blessed inheritance of health and purity, shall make their joyous pilgrimage from the cradle to the grave with songs of gratitude on their lips, because of the earthly fathers and mothers who have been to those all the way along fit types of their great Father above; yea, of Him of whom it is said, "He shall feed His flock like a shepherd; He shall gather the lambs with His arms, and carry them in His bosom."

With sincere respect,

A Mother

—Womanhood: Its Sanctities and Fidelities,
Boston: Lee and Shepard, 1874, 7–12, 15–16, 24–27.

Laura Cuppy Smith

Isabella Beecher Hooker was not the only feminist who stood by Victoria Woodhull throughout the Beecher-Tilton scandal. Woodhull was also supported whole-heartedly by her friend Laura Cuppy Smith. Smith is practically unknown today because, as Woodhull's biographer Emanie Sachs has observed, she was "too sincere" and "too faithful" "to win fame or fortune."[124] Smith served as a character witness at Woodhull's trial for violating the Comstock Act.[125] She brought Woodhull food in jail, and defended her on the national lecture circuit.[126]

Smith, the daughter of a British naval officer and "a serious romantic," emigrated by herself to the United States at the tender age of fourteen. She had to fall back on her own resources again when money problems led her first husband to commit suicide. She supported herself and her children by moving to San Francisco and engaging in public speaking and Spiritualist ministry. The *San Francisco Chronicle* proclaimed her "the acknowledged leading champion of Radicalism on the West Coast."[127] She helped to organize suffrage societies in her adopted home state. She was part of the delegation that presented the first woman suffrage petition to the California legislature. The *History of Woman Suffrage* remarked that this "proceeding was without a parallel in the history of the State. The novelty of women addressing the legislature attracted universal attention, and the newspapers were filled with reports of that important meeting."[128] Later Smith took part in labor agitations and, when free lover Ezra Heywood was prosecuted under the Comstock Law, won a pardon for him from the President.[129]

At Woodhull's prompting, Smith revealed what lay behind her commitment to women's rights. Like many of her twentieth century counterparts, Smith was motivated by a personal experience of discrimination: in this case the wrenching dilemmas posed by her single teenage daughter's pregnancy. Their decision against abortion involved a courageous refusal to acquiesce to a judgmental and uncaring society. Smith offers a hopeful message that speaks not only to her own time, but to ours.

How One Woman Entered the Ranks of Social Reform, or, A Mother's Story

by Laura Cuppy Smith

Will a page torn from a woman's heart—a mother's heart—help other women, other mothers, to be strong? If it will, the world shall hear it, come what may. In the year 1865 I found myself a worker on the Pacific coast, a dweller in that sunny land toward which my heart turns ever with wistful longing, not alone because it is the home of my beloved daughter and sons, and the abiding-place of dearly-cherished and fondly-remembered friends, but because to me it will ever seem the land of richest possibilities, holding the germ of grander, freer, more complete lives than can be lived elsewhere. I worked hard, unceasingly, as one who loved work for its own sake. I threw my whole heart and soul into the words I uttered, and found my reward in the knowledge that they penetrated sometimes the armor of custom and conventionalism and reached the inner consciousness of those addressed. But ever, in public and in private, I cherished the dear hope of bringing my little children across the two broad oceans, to a home in the "thousand-masted bay and steepled town" of San Francisco. Every day my heart leaned over the space that divided us, and listened for the echo of my children's voices. My labors were crowned with success. Never did I love gold before; but as with beating heart I touched the shining coin with which I was to pay for my little daughter's passage and I kissed them with almost childish glee. She must come first, as I could not send for all; then my boys should come later. How I watched the aspect of the sky; how in thought, I traversed the ocean till the tardy waves bore my "one little ewe lamb" safely to her place in my heart. At last my boys came; and then, a united family once more, I said: "Now I will shelter my darlings; now no harm can come to the nest over which a mother's watchful love shall brook with ever-waking vigilance and tenderest solicitude." Each day developed my little girl into a woman. The child's somewhat awkward angles rounded into a young maiden's fair proportions and winsome grace. One day I was startled to observe a young man pause, for a second look, at the sunny-haired girl, and to note that her blue eyes drooped and her cheek blushed beneath his ardent gaze, and with a sudden pang such as mothers alone can know, I said: "My child has grown into a woman, she is no longer all my own." Need I tell any mother who reads this page of heart-history what hopes I cherished for my fair young daughter; how I dreamed of a future for her that should realize my dream of a happy and perfected womanhood; and, since I could not keep her a child, sweetly dependent on her mother, pictured her grown into a grand and noble woman, a happy wife and mother, safely shielded from all the storms that had made shipwreck of my peace, in the quiet haven of a perfect home? I suppose all mothers have some such dreams for their beloved. It only remains then for me to relate how infinite wisdom saw fit to thwart these hopes founded on ignorance and weakness and take my child's life into different channels, educating us both for a higher and broader sphere than we otherwise should have occupied by an experience that seemed to us very bitter, very cruel, but for which we now thank God, glad of the thorny pathway that led up to light.

I do not wish to enter into details regarding the events that changed the currents of our lives; suffice it, a mature but young and brilliant man unconsciously, I think, at first, won the heart of this young girl. I warned and counseled; but when did young impassioned love ever listen to the warning and counsels of experience? The interference only estranged the child's heart for a time ... for had I not found flaws in this idol of her dreams? But one day I penetrated the secret of the change that had descended upon the girl's joyous spirit. This young maiden who was not a wife would soon be in the world's sight, as she was now in mine, a mother. I thank God in the bitterness of the revelation that then dawned upon me, nothing save an agony of tenderness filled my heart, a passion of love for my child that revealed depths of devotion unknown, undreamed of in the relations of our past. Strange still, I did not hate her lover; he had not deliberately, wickedly seduced a young and trusting person; circumstances threw in his path a fresh, lovely, girl, who loved him, undisguisedly and engrossingly from the first moment she saw him. Society had made him what he was. I deeply deplored it, but realizing his education, his impulsive, passionate temperament, I dared not judge and condemn him. Circumstances—among them considerations of a complicated nature, into which religious scruples entered that have no place in this relation and belong to him personally—forbade marriage; and my daughter and myself would have proudly rejected the hand that was not spontaneously offered, under any circumstances. What was to be done? was the question pondered over, as I lay on my sick bed, holding to my aching heart my infant daughter only two weeks old, for I had been married a year before. Friends said—well-meaning friends—"There is a way, hide this thing from sight, send her on a journey, destroy this evidence of youthful folly, all may yet be well." I was proud; I loved a good position in society for myself, how much more for my children; my daughter in her youth and grace and beauty, how could I bear that the world should point its finger at her and utter its mocking laugh? how could I save her? should I accept this "one way" suggested? If I wavered—and I might as I wrestled in that Garden of Gethsemane—God knows it was but a second. I made my resolve. I said, "This child of youth and love! this child of my child has a right to live, and *shall live*— has a right to love, and shall have that also; has a mission to its mother and shall perform it. This girl-mother has a right to all tenderness and the society of her lover; while she is solving the divine problem of maternity—learning the sacred lessons which the new life stirring beneath her heart whispers to her awakened nature—and she shall have them (for I think that the children, born of mothers deprived of the sweet and tender magnetism of the father in that fateful period prior to birth, come into the world orphaned in part). No dark secret shall dog my child's footsteps through life; she shall enter no man's home with a lie on her lips. I know that her soul is pure, her heart stainless. Love, not guilt, has made her what she is. If the world calls her 'wicked,' 'outcast,' the world lies, and we will live the lie down." I told my child how I had resolved, and she answered: "Mother, you are right, and I am not afraid since you love me still." And accordingly, we entered upon our future. That we struggled through it alone; that kindest friends shook their heads doubtingly, is not wonderful. I think all souls are alone in their direst extremities. The heart upon which I leaned most, could not indorse so strange a course, could only coldly tolerate it; doors that would have opened to one—gladly to him, and for hire to her—utterly refused to shelter both, and his society I insisted she should enjoy.

A woman of questionable repute, so the world said, opened her door when all respectable people closed theirs, and there I, in time, went also, to welcome my little grandson into existence, a child as bright and fair and pure as if all the priests and bishops in Christendom had given him permission to be born and live and aspire. When his young mother was able to walk out, I took the baby in my arms and we walked the whole length of the principal street, running the gauntlet of curious eyes; then I felt the worst was over, the world could not wound us much after that; we had "grasped the nettle," it could sting us no more.

Some of the purest souls I have ever known gave us their hands at last, our nearest and dearest who had been sorely tried by our unusual course, acknowledged, with tears, the wisdom that sustained us. My daughter came out of the ordeal and took up her new life, a matured woman: girlhood had flown in the trial, but had left a sacred boon in its stead; my hair showed a frost it had not shown before, but my soul had gained strength, my whole nature a divine consecration. My little grandson bears his mother's maiden name, as she does; his father loves and cherishes both mother and child. Quietly and with growing self-reliance and with complete self-respect, she lives her life, and with a smile sad but sweet, meets the averted faces of summer friends. In a recent letter she says: "Mother, when I see how lightly some women who frown on me take the obligations of marriage, I am so thankful my "little mother" helped me live a truer and purer life.

> "And I will strive and still endure
> All storms of pain that time can wreak;
> My flag is white because 'tis pure,
> And not because my soul is weak!"

For myself, do you wonder that my whole life is consecrated to the cause of freedom? that I have sworn that I will never permit myself to brand as outcast, prostitute, or fallen, a sister woman, while men standing erect, knee deep in vice, look God and man unblushingly in the face, and are received into our best society without a protest? Do you wonder that I trample underfoot, in indignation and loathing, that shallow mockery you call, with a reverence born of ignorance, "The Marriage Law," a law obligatory upon woman but ignored by man, and that says to the woman who has gone down into the valley of the shadow of death to win the boon of motherhood, "You have no legal right to the child you have purchased by months of suffering, culminating in mortal agony?"

I have transcribed this page of heart history, not wholly without pain, because I am mortal, and hold my inner life as too sacred for the careless gaze of strangers; but if I can help in any sense some sorrowing mother to be strong, some young girl to be brave, I have not written in vain; I can truly look back on my stormy past and thank God for every agony endured, for every weakness conquered, for every bitter experience that has brought me into closer sympathy with human suffering, and above all for this crowning trial that led me out of the land of bondage and prejudice, through the Red Sea of pain, into the perfect liberty of the children of God. It has been my privilege to stand by the priestess of social reform, Victoria C. Woodhull, in the present crisis, and, while I honored her as one chosen of God, as a leader in this great reform, to possess the dearer right of drawing near to her in the sacred association of close and intimate friendship. She has often urged me to write the above, and now my own soul has prompted me to obey.

—*Woodhull and Claflin's Weekly*, March 1, 1873.

Eleanor Kirk (1831–1908)

In the nineteenth century, as in the twentieth, anti-feminists often complained that expanded rights for women would inevitably cause them to abandon their maternal responsibilities. But the experiences of people like Laura Cuppy Smith and her daughter show that it is an *anti-feminist* society, not a feminist one, that undermines maternal values. The author of the next piece was acutely conscious of how the denial of women's rights harmed children. A resident of New York City, Eleanor "Nellie" Maria Easterbrook Ames supported herself and her children, of whom she spoke with affection, by writing under the pseudonym Eleanor Kirk. Perhaps because of her own life experiences, Kirk became involved in the struggle for women's rights after leaving an abusive marriage. When the American Equal Rights Association held an important celebration in Steinway Hall, she was invited to sit up on the platform with such notables as Ernestine Rose, Matilda Gage, Frederick Douglass, Amelia Bloomer, Paulina Wright Davis, and Lucy Stone.[130] Like Sarah F. Norton, Kirk was a key member of the New York Working Women's Association.[131]

Kirk expressed her profound sympathy for working women in *Up Broadway*, her account of a single mother's victimization by a moralistic society. This young woman, after being turned out of the house by her irate and abusive father, fled to New York City, hoping to make a living for herself and her little girl. When she finally found a job, she rejected it because her employer made it clear that he would sexually exploit her. She then sought work as a chambermaid, but "no one wanted an unrecommended female, with a helpless little one." Finally, seeing no other choice but killing herself and her child, she was drawn into prostitution, at the cost of what little self-respect she had left.[132]

Although she by no means condoned the murderous impulses that poor, overstressed women might harbor towards their offspring, Kirk attacked the dismissive judgmentality they all too often encountered. She remarked sarcastically in the pages of *The Revolution:* "What did you say? tired of taking care of the baby? tired of your offspring? Oh! It is well to qualify a little. Not tired of the child, but so worn out with its screaming and fretting, so exhausted with walking the floor nights; that what? you almost wish it had never been born! You must never, my dear, give utterance to such statements as these. But you are desperate! Tommy hadn't finished teething when this one was born? What of that? Mothers must learn to regard these trifling additions with saint-like equanimity."[133] Not surprisingly, Kirk was at the forefront of the feminist campaign to defend Hester Vaughan. Kirk visited Vaughan in prison and helped to run a large public meeting on her behalf.[134] In the following piece, Kirk discusses how the oppression of women causes the death of unborn as well as already-born children, contrary to the most vociferous objections of anti-feminists.

What Will Become of the Babies
by Eleanor Kirk

From every quarter is wailed this cry—and wherefore? Only because women are waking up to a sense of their position as wives, mothers, and members of society, and insist on their right to have a hand in the management of all public affairs appertaining, however remotely, to their interest, socially and financially. Why is it that a great many cultivated, intelligent men and women, too (that's where the rub comes), persist in ignoring the fact that female equality and suffrage mean more love, more tenderness, an occasion of respect and thoughtfulness for our companions, and better sense in moulding the characters of our children. Said a lady to me yesterday:

"Why should I lift up my voice for this Revolution in social affairs you so strongly advocate? Religiously and politically my husband and myself are one; and our love for each other is such that *his* wish is my law, and vice versa."

Now, just that little sentence caused every nerve in my body to quiver painfully. No true woman can shut herself up in a little Paradise of her own, and never look out into the great thoroughfare of life. Why, woman alive, or woman asleep, where there is one wife happy and contented in the love of a noble man, there are thousands of wretched ones who are driven to feebleness, moral destruction, and the grave. Think a moment. Suppose death, inexorable and strangely exacting, should claim his own; what then? Your husband's salary, which now nicely supports you, you would receive no longer. Your three babies fatherless, and you a widow, educated, refined, and fitted by numberless graces to adorn a little niche in society, undisturbed by want or the necessity of labor; our opinion is, that you would be glad to take into consultation even Revolutionists under such circumstances, and be very happy to welcome any educational or philanthropic movement whereby you could walk out into the world, and demand as an equivalent for your work a comfortable living for yourself and your babies. Then, at the conclusion of that heartless speech, to have her look so sweetly and wisely into our face, and remark:

"But Frank and I have been thinking should women turn to politics and literature entirely, what will become of the babies?"

What will become of *your* babies, madam, should you be suddenly deprived of the means of their support? Have you the courage, stamina, ay, *ability*, to fight the world single-handed? "A fellow-feeling makes us wondrous kind." We have been there, thank you, and know all about it. Every heart-throb, every blush in indignation, every dastardly attempt to change the wages of labor for the wages of sin, we are familiar with; and it makes us *sick* when we see an intelligent female looking at so great a subject through so small a glass, and dirty at that. What will become of the babies? Why don't somebody ask—what *has* become of the babies? Ask Restell and thousands of physicians, male and female, who have been engaged in their work of destruction for years. Physicians who have graduated from our first medical colleges, whose elegant equipages stand in front of Fifth Avenue mansions, who pocket a big fee and a little bundle of flesh at the same time, and nobody's the wiser; not even the *husband* in hosts of instances. What will become of the babies—did you ask—and you? Can you not see that the idea is to educate women that they may be self-reliant, self-sustaining, self-respected? The wheel is a big one, and needs a strong push, and a push all together, giving it an impulse that will keep it constantly revolving, and the first Revolution must be female suffrage. After this, the ponderous affair will move regularly, and perhaps slowly; but education, moral, physical, and intellectually practical, will as surely follow as dawn follows the darkness of night. Then marriages of convenience will not be necessary; men and women will come together, attracted by mutual respect; namby-pamby, doll-faced, wishy-washy, milk-and-water feminine bundles will be unmarketable. God speed the time, for the sake of the babies. Little ones will then be welcome, and mothers will know enough to instruct them sensibly, with a view to the practical side of life. Men, if you desire healthy, intelligent, economical wives, do not oppose this new movement; for in this way *only* can you and yours, and subsequent generations, be saved from degeneracy. Will somebody please tell us why women who pay taxes (we will leave out the rest just at present) should not be allowed a voice in the management of the laws decreeing taxation? Don't be afraid to speak; come out squarely. This is the time for free, earnest discussion on all points of general interest; but please do not take for your final syllogistic premises the foolish idea that women who are self-reliant must necessarily be unlovable. It is no such thing, we assure you, and we know. My dear fellows, this is quite as much for your benefit as for ours. What we propose to do, is so to arrange things that should you ever become sick or poor, we can put our hands to the plough and run the machine, nursing, sympathizing, attending to the finances, and loving you to distraction at the same time. How do you like the picture?

—*The Revolution,* May 28, 1868.

Frances E. Willard (1839–1896) and the Anchorage Mission (founded 1886)

Distorted notions about "strong-minded women" and their agendas have not disappeared from the earth with those Eleanor Kirk took to task. Today, the name of the Women's Christian Temperance Union often calls to mind an image of Bible-wielding, stiffly righteous old biddies who are grimly determined that no one should enjoy the pleasures of the flesh. This image entirely misses the significance of temperance work for those who engaged in it. The unfairness of this stereotype is called into question by the fact that the WCTU was at one time the largest and most effective force for women's rights in the United States. The WCTU reached even conservative church women, women who were utterly put off by the likes of Victoria Woodhull, and moved them to act on a transformed vision of women's power.

The WCTU's crucial role in promoting gender justice does not seem too odd when we understand temperance in its historical context. As noted earlier, many early feminists, including Susan B. Anthony and Matilda Gage, first found their way into politics through their involvement in temperance reform. They connected temperance to women's rights because they saw how frequently alcohol use led men to rape, other domestic violence, child abuse, financial irresponsibility, and abandonment of their families. It was no surprise to anyone that the WCTU came to its heyday through the capable leadership of Frances E. Willard, an unmistakably feminist woman.

Willard initially sought to serve her sex as an educator. In 1871 she became president of the Ladies' College affiliated with Northwestern University in Evanston, Illinois, one of many women's and coeducational colleges springing up around the country at that time. However, discouraged by the many obstacles which male administrators placed in her way, she began looking for a less frustrating way to help women. She then chose to work full-time for the WCTU and rose quickly to a leadership position. While engaged in temperance lecturing and organizing, she toured with evangelist Dwight Moody. She eventually broke with him over his sexist notions of religious orthodoxy—although he considered himself very liberal for allowing a woman to share the pulpit with him. Following her stint as a preacher, she cemented the links between the temperance and suffrage movements through "home protection": the argument that women could best secure their family and domestic interests through the power of the ballot box, an argument which feminists still make today. Seeing the private and public spheres as profoundly interconnected, she eventually became a public advocate for Christian socialism.[135]

Willard's fascinating synthesis of radical and conservative worldviews can be rediscovered through her prolific and influential writings. She authored sentimental biographies of her mother and sister, extolling their feminine virtues. Yet she published *Occupations for Women,* a vocational guidance manual for the rapidly growing number of college-educated women in America, and *Woman of the Century,* a still-valuable source of information about 1400 prominent women. Willard's *Woman in the Pulpit* reinterpreted the Bible to contend that women deserved a place in the ministry and church government. Willard maintained that the qualities which supposedly mandated women's confinement to the home instead provided a rationale for their greater involvement in the world outside.[136]

Activists such as Willard referred to their efforts as "organized Mother-love," i.e., a concerted effort to infuse the nurturant, life-giving virtues central to home life into the world at large: what we in the late twentieth century would call "maternal thinking."[137] The WCTU's Social Purity campaign was a prime example of "organized Mother-love" in action. It grew not so much out of prudery as a deep compassion for the women and children victimized by the parental and sexual irresponsibility and violence of men. It worked for legislation to raise the age at which girls could legally consent to sex; to prosecute rapists and customers of prostitutes; and to fight child abuse. And the campaign opposed involuntary motherhood as staunchly as the free-love movement did. It directly addressed the profound lack of support for single women, especially pregnant ones.

Chicago's Anchorage Mission was one of several Florence Crittenton Rescue Homes endowed by wealthy evangelist Charles Crittenton, named after his deceased three-year-old daughter, and administered by WCTU Social Purity workers across the country.[138] It was founded in 1886 by medical missionary Dr. Kate Bushnell, whom Willard praised as "a woman of great devotion and force of character."[139] The Mission addressed the dilemma of so many young women who came to large cities in search of a living: the lack of economic opportunities other than prostitution. It offered these young women shelter, emotional and spiritual support, and practical training in marketable job skills. Since prostitution and other forms of sexual exploitation were a prime cause of unwanted pregnancies, the Mission, and other facilities like it, could not help but specialize in assisting women who found their motherhood a virtually unbearable crisis.[140] To serve their clients, these facilities had to defy strong public prejudices against single pregnant women who were often presumed to be "bad women" undeserving of aid. The director of a sister agency in Chicago noted that assistance to these women was a life-saving moral imperative: "A large number of those who come to us of their own will, are with child. They come in deep distress, not knowing which way to turn for help. Many have fallen through that which is highest in them … Forsaken by those who should have protected them, shall we receive them? … How can we turn them away? Those suffering ones appeal to our mercy. If we do, suicide or infanticide, a seared conscience and a downward course ending in a whirlpool of despair, is the almost certain result."[141]

For many women and children, the Anchorage Mission broke a cycle of violence, much as battered women's shelters and crisis pregnancy centers do today. Indeed, the Mission's present-day descendant, the Chicago Comprehensive Care Center, continues to assist young impoverished mothers. With Frances E. Willard's blessing, the WCTU instituted an enduring tradition of social service agencies which recognized the victimization of women, yet encouraged them to move beyond their victimization and take responsibility for their own lives and those of their children. This was true, anyway, for clients of most ethnic groups. Although they were often motivated by humanistic impulses, facilities such as the Mission were hardly immune from the racism that pervaded— and still pervades—American culture. Yesterday's social reformers, like today's, sometimes held to an inconsistent ethic of life. The Anchorage Mission holds both positive and negative lessons for contemporary people who want to provide positive alternatives to abortion.

A Plea for the Forgotten
by Frances Willard

To the Union Signal: I have this week visited the Florence Crittenton Anchorage for Girls, on Wabash Avenue, founded some years ago by the Central WCTU.

I found these thirty-five women, some of them pitifully young, and twelve with babes in their arms. It was a sight to make careless hearts thoughtful and steady eyes dim. The poor child who was deceived, betrayed, and robbed a few days ago by the man she trusted, and who tried to take her young life, was there. At last she had found those whom she could trust, and who told her they would do all in their power to help her build her wrecked young life anew on the foundations of industry, purity, and honor.

Some of us talked to these forgotten ones as helpfully and kindly as we could, and then they spoke to us with tears, of their gratitude for a home so friendly and mother-hearts so sheltering as those of Miss Alice Bond, who has stood by the work for years with a heroism that knew no defeat in the darkest hours; Miss Lyman, the matron, who has the love and good will of every person connected with the Anchorage; Mrs. E.P. Vale, whom they term "the mother of us all," and other true and noble women who make this home their special work.

… I make this plea [for funds] because I feel sure that there are a sufficient number of good and true women and men to pay this sum for these deceived and defrauded ones, if only the facts are brought to their knowledge … Let us remember our sisters who are "in bonds, as bound with them … "

—*The Union Signal*, November 28, 1895, the Official Publication of the National Woman's Christian Temperance Union, Evanston, Illinois.

"Women Helping Women"
by the staff of the Anchorage Mission[142]

Another busy year at the Anchorage has passed, the Home has been filled to its utmost capacity during the entire year and we have been unable to care for all who have sought its protection.

As we come to review the work of the year we feel assured that a large measure of success has attended our labors, as we have sought to help those wronged, unfortunate and deserted girls. Many of them have gone into the world again and are making good. They are supporting not only themselves but their little ones, and are living honorable, upright lives.

When these girls come to us in their hour of perplexity and sorrow, their first thought is to find a place of refuge for themselves and when the little ones come to give them away, never thinking it would be possible to keep and care for them. And while the doors of the Home are ever open to all girls in need ... they are taught not to shirk the responsibility of motherhood and are encouraged to keep their babies and care for them.[143]

One of the mothers who is making a brave fight for herself and her little one, writes: "I think we at least owe it to our children to keep them; poor, little innocents! They had nothing to say about coming into the world. My boy has given me a purpose in life and keeps me good." And what is true of this mother is true of many others, the influence of the little ones on their lives to keep them good.

The nursery—the brightest, sunniest room in the Home, filled with little folks, is the center of interest. While this room is in charge of two of the mothers who take turns in day and night duty, each mother is given the care of her child and is instructed how to properly care for it, and is taught that she is the one responsible for its welfare.

As all of these mothers are assigned to various tasks in the Home, they are impressed with the fact that while babies must not be neglected, yet they must so arrange the care of the child and the work, that they will not conflict.

As many of them go to housework with the babies this training is of the greatest value to them.

Several times each week the nursery is visited by a physician to see that all is well ...

During the year ninety-five girls, representing seventeen nationalities have been cared for; among the number one Chinese and two Greek girls.[144] Any intelligent person can imagine some of the difficulties where there is such dissimilarities of birth, education, and character and the difficulty in securing work and homes for them.

Many of those whom we welcome to our Home are in dire poverty, destitute of proper clothing. This need has been most generously supplied by donations from the following groups:

The Needle Work Guild of America, Chicago Branch;
The Needle Work Guild of America, Oak Park Branch;
Ladies' Aid Society, First Baptist Church, Oak Park;
Ladies' Aid Society, Trinity M.E. Church, Chicago;
Ladies' Aid Society, Friends' Church, Chicago;
King's Daughters, Harvard Cong. Church, Oak Park;
Byron Conclave No. 8, Chicago.

One of the most important features of the work the past year has been the prosecution of the men who caused the downfall of the girls in twenty cases. Four of these cases have been continued in court to next year; the remaining sixteen have been settled in favor of the girl. In three of these cases the parties were married.

As we have in our State a law compelling the father of a child born outside of lawful wedlock to provide for the partial support of the child for a period of ten years, by the payment of one hundred dollars the first year and fifty dollars a year for the nine succeeding years, making a total of five hundred and fifty dollars, we urge every mother to prosecute the man who is the father of her child and will assist her in every way with the prosecution. The Court of Domestic Relations provides for the prosecution of these cases without expense to the mother ... [145]

When the time comes for the girls to leave the Home and find their places in the world again, sincere regret is manifested at the thought of leaving, and we hear many expressions such as: "This is like leaving your own home;" and "I never had such a good home as this;" and another says: "I do not know what I would have done if I hadn't heard of this Home."

Those who remain in the city are constant visitors and from those who leave the city we are constantly receiving letters expressing their gratitude for what they received at the Home and for the way in which they had been helped to make a new start in life.

A very large number of girls have been returned to their relatives; some have resumed their former occupations; for others we have found homes with their babies. Eight have been married.

Through a friendly interest in each girl and by various methods employed we have been enabled to keep in touch with seventy per cent of those cared for during the year, and know that the greater number are making good.

—from *Thirtieth Annual Report of the Florence Crittenton Anchorage, 1886-1916*, Chicago: Florence Crittenton Anchorage Mission, 1916, 101-3, Chicago Historical Society.

Dr. Jennie G. Oreman

After the tremendous wave of legislation against abortion in the late 19th century, it declined considerably in both frequency and social visibility. Thus, early twentieth century feminists did not have as much to say about it as their predecessors had. But this was by no means because they had begun in large numbers to reject earlier views on the subject. The idea that abortion was a valid and desirable form of assistance to women in crisis, let alone a liberating act of self-assertion, was still quite alien to feminism. As far as difficult pregnancies were concerned, "women helping women" meant measures such as the work of the Anchorage mission. It did not mean the work of a Madame Restell— as demonstrated by the following piece from the predecessor of the *Journal of the American Medical Women's Association*. Here, Jennie G. Oreman, a Canadian physician, writes that female doctors should be most resolute in refusing requests for abortion, as yielding to such demands does not truly serve women's interests. Dr. Charlotte Denman Lozier probably would not have spoken in Oreman's patronizing tone. Nevertheless, Oreman carries on the very same sense of professional duty that motivated Lozier and her contemporaries.

The Medical Woman's Temptation and How to Meet It
by Dr. Jennie G. Oreman

Women, ignorant of the right way of living, resort to different means of procuring criminal abortion, in order to escape the responsibilities and duties of maternity. For some reason or other they seek the woman physician and beseech her to rid them of their burden, they attempt to play on her sympathy as a woman, they either assume the wheedling tones of the gypsy when desirous of gaining her ends or the imperative tone of one who counts the physician as their obedient servant.

After a little practice, one can guess the woman's errand by the first few words she utters.

If she has come on some "very personal business," or there is considerable hesitancy, the physician may be sure of the errand.

There are a few cases in which they freely, and at once tell their business. In other cases by lie after lie they try to lead the physician to prescribe for a symptom which is sometimes one of pregnancy, but which they assure the doctor must arise from some other cause. A firm determined "no" is the first step in the treatment of these cases. Teach them that sympathies cannot thus be played upon to do wrong. Then make the attempt to put the matter before them in its true light: show them that such an act on their part and on the part of the physician is murder, and nothing else.

We may then tell them that the sexual function is purely physiological and governed by natural laws. In many cases these women are too ignorant to understand, to them our absurdly moral stand. Not much can be done by this method, as we have only the one side of the question.

Education of the young will alone rectify the evil; but by the physician's firm determination not to tolerate abortion, we may control a part of the evil, though by no means banish it. Annihilation of uncleanness must come from a clear understanding of the function and its laws.

Our duty as physicians is to be strong and firm in our "no." Practical moral sympathy is what the world needs, and not a flimsy sensual sympathy which has not altruism in view.

—*The Woman's Medical Journal,* March 1901.

Dr. Mary Ries Melendy

Mary Ries Melendy was yet another physician who brought the feminist women's health agenda, including its condemnation of abortion, into the twentieth century. She received her medical degree and Ph.D. at alternative medical schools and completed her professional training at Chicago's Cook County Hospital, which even today is the primary provider of health care to the city's indigent population. As a lecturer on "Diseases of Women and Children" at the American Health University, and as the author of several popular health manuals, she sought to teach other women "struggling along in grievous suffering and anxiety how to conquer … those ill conditions."[146] Such suffering and anxiety was not the inevitable destiny of female bodies; rather, it resulted from ignorance about them.[147]

Melendy felt that fostering respect for the power of maternity was one of the most important functions of sex education. As one might expect of a woman of her professional achievements, she applauded the gains her sex had made in the public sphere. Yet at the same time, she insisted that "the most divine and sublime mission" of motherhood deserved the utmost reverence.[148] To this end, she approvingly cited Elizabeth Cady Stanton on the inherent healthiness of childbirth, advocated mother's milk over substitute liquids, and asserted that men could and should take responsibility for their offspring and their wives even during pregnancy.[149] She also argued against "compulsory child-bearing,"[150] while maintaining that there was "no apology for abortion," meaning an argument to be offered in its defense. Ironically, many in the present-day women's health movement use these very phrases to argue for an unfettered and unquestioned right to abortion—which was not in the least the meaning that Melendy attached to them. Melendy was quite cognizant of the health risks abortion posed to women, but it never remotely occurred to her that these constituted a reason for legalizing the procedure.

No Apology For Abortion
Dr. Mary Ries Melendy

Children have a right to be born! Alas, that this God-given privilege should ever be called in question! That it is so, however, the testimony of modern physicians, the daily records of the newspapers, the fulminations from the pulpit, the remonstrances of the philanthropists, and the forebodings of philosophers, abundantly prove.

If we examine the history of abortion, we shall find that this crime, so commonly practiced as to demand attention, is of extremely ancient origin, having existed among pagan nations from the earliest times.

If this evil were principally resorted to for the purpose of shielding from open disgrace the victims of dishonored virtue, there might be a faint apology for silence, but with shame for the wives and mothers of our land, who are the chief offenders. This statement may seem strange to the ears of many a devoted wife and mother, but to the physician, who is generally a receiver of family secrets, it is a well-known fact.

Abortion a Murder

Intentional abortion is to all purposes a murder. This is now conceded by all who are informed upon the subject. Among the ancients the distinction was made that before the time of quickening the child had no life, and therefore there was no sin in its destruction. This statement has, however, been proven to be false. The embryo is alive and hence quick from the moment of conception. Modern science has abundantly proven this to be a fact. It follows, then, that this crime is equally as great whether committed in the early weeks of pregnancy or at a more advanced period in the life of the fetus.

The laws of all civilized countries now make abortion a crime, and the punishment severe. All who are accessory to it may be punished with imprisonment, and in some cases even with death.

Danger Attending Abortion

Aside from the crime, however, the maternal instinct of the mother and a sufficient regard for her own health should prevent any and all attempts of this character. The amount of physical suffering that may follow cannot be estimated. Inflammations of the womb and kindred disorders of the generative organs are almost sure to result, and frequently will resist the most skilled treatment. At other times blood poisoning may result from the retention of the placenta and membranes of the fetus. This may produce immediate death, and at best can but end in broken health and lifelong suffering.

—from *The Ideal Woman: A Book Giving Full Information on All the Mysterious and Complex Matters Pertaining to Women*, Chicago: J.R. Peper, 1911.

Estelle Sylvia Pankhurst (1882–1960)

Estelle Sylvia Pankhurst came from an English family known for thorny, complex personalities who threw themselves into reform movements, particularly feminism. Richard, her father, was the highly reputed expert in international law who in the 1860's drafted the first British woman suffrage bill. Sylvia's mother Emmeline and sister Christabel rose to prominence as leaders of the militant, civil-disobedient branch of the suffrage movement, particularly through their work with the Women's Social and Political Union, founded in 1903. Although Sylvia had serious clashes with various members of the family throughout her life, she always shared their passion for political activism, especially activism of the sort that stirred up outrage.[151]

Sylvia began her professional life not as an activist but an artist. Before long, however, she was drawn into the suffragist movement. She donated her talents to it as a designer of banners, posters, cards, and magazine covers—significant means of publicizing the cause. Sylvia eventually broke with the WSPU over power struggles within the organization and between herself and Emmeline and Christabel, especially the latter. Sylvia founded her own feminist organization in the East End of London and gained notoriety for her own resort to such drastic, law-defying tactics as hunger strikes. She worked also for socialist and peace causes, vocally opposing World War I and defining pacifists as people who "rebel against the present organization of society."[152] Among the working class people of the East End, she engaged directly in "social betterment" work. She started a toy factory out of her concern for women's inadequate wages, and "Price-Cost Restaurants" where the hungry could obtain inexpensive meals. She founded "The Mother's Arms" day care center and a Montessori school. She felt it necessary to agitate for birth control and sex education among working women, as their most frequent method of fertility control was self-induced abortion. Her "social work" became a legend in the East End.

In the later decades of her life, she was most known for her crusade on behalf of Ethiopia's attempts to resist imperialist domination. She involved herself so much in this crusade that she moved to Ethiopia, where she was ultimately buried.

As demonstrated by her work in the East End, Sylvia was persistently concerned with the status of motherhood. During her 1921 imprisonment as a "habitual offender," she wrote sympathetic poetry about impoverished pregnant inmates. She insisted that Communist revolution alone would provide these women with occupations other than prostitution and give them the necessary support to raise their children.

In 1927, at the age of forty-five, Sylvia openly and proudly became the mother of a so-called "illegitimate" child. Motivated partly by this experience, in 1930 she published her *Save the Mothers*. In this book she argued that the high rate of maternal, infant, and fetal mortality was all the more reprehensible because it could be prevented. With special attention to the injustices faced by working-class and single mothers, she made the case for a universal, free maternity service. To those who protested the expense, she pointed out the "vast expenditure on armaments" and "urge[d] that the money saved on engines of destruction ... be diverted to the high service of life creation."[153]

Sylvia's agenda would do a contemporary feminist proud. Yet, her biographer Patricia Romero notes with some surprise, "as progressive as she was on health, Sylvia opposed abortion." This opposition was so strong that Romero, discussing a small possibility that Sylvia had gotten pregnant in her twenties, concludes that if this had indeed happened, she must have miscarried in prison. Romero attributes this sentiment primarily to the fact that abortion was illegal in Great Britain at that time, and to sexual puritanism, citing a bit of gossip that "Sylvia engaged in sex only to produce her child."[154] But Sylvia was never one to equate law with morality, nor to accept Victorian notions of sexual propriety. And the following passage from *Save the Mothers* suggests that Pankhurst's anti-abortion position, rather than contradicting the rest of her agenda, was actually completely consistent with it. Sylvia, perhaps, might herself be more surprised that modern prochoice feminists fail to see the correlation between pacifist and prolife philosophies.

Abortion
by Estelle Sylvia Pankhurst

There is undoubtedly a great international tendency towards the limitation of families. Abortion, a terrible and dangerous expedient, is appallingly common amongst married women. Frank Cook of Guy's Hospital says: "The artificial termination of pregnancy, whether therapeutic or criminal, is naturally more prone to fatal or morbid issues than is spontaneous abortion," and even under the best conditions, and with every aseptic precaution, its difficulties and dangers are considerable ...

Numerous indeed are the married women in this country who, under economic pressure and the strain of maintaining the welfare of their families, have attempted abortion, not once but many times. "When I found out I was pregnant again I tried everything!" How often the phrase slips out when a mother is telling her troubles to sympathetic ears! A woman who today is a Borough Councillor, with children already old enough to share her social work, came to me years ago in a pitiable condition; she had doubled and doubled daily doses of Beecham's pills, till she was swallowing thirty-two at a sitting, and had reduced herself to a state in which she was scarcely able to sit in a chair; yet had failed to attain her object.

"What shall I do now?" she wailed, looking to me to find some exit from her dilemma.

"Now we shall have to get you made better to have the baby," I answered. Nemesis-like, perhaps, to her ears; yet the lad has done well; she is proud and glad of him now.

Mothers vehemently defend abortion, declaring that they have resorted to it for the sake of their children. Increasing numbers of people argue that, faced with undesired pregnancy, women will procure abortion by hook or by crook; therefore the law should permit abortion, provided it be done under State supervision, with strict aseptic precautions. Others consider that since even under the best conditions abortion is injurious to the mother, it should be avoided by preventing pregnancy, and that the use of contraceptives should be publicly taught under Government auspices. Both views have received legislative sanction in Soviet Russia, which in this, as in much else, has become a field of experiment in social theories.

It is grievous indeed that the social collectivity should feel itself obliged to assist in so ugly an expedient as abortion in order to mitigate its crudest evils. The true mission of Society is to provide the conditions, legal, moral, economic, and obstetric, which will assure happy and successful motherhood.

—*Save the Mothers*, London: Knopf, 1930, 108–110.

Further Evidence of Prolife Sentiment up to the Present Wave of Feminism

The preceding selections make it abundantly clear that the classi-fication of abortion under the rubric of women's rights, instead of "woman's wrongs," is a relatively recent phenomenon. When exactly did it take place? It did not take place on a wide scale until the 1960's. There were a few pre-"Women's Lib" activists who anticipated modern prochoice arguments—Stella Browne, for example. Browne had an abortion herself in the 1930's. In 1936 she helped to found the British Abortion Law Reform Association. The year before, she had proclaimed: "The woman's right to abortion is an absolute right ... Abortion must be the key to a new world for women, not a bulwark for things as they are, economically and biologically ... It is as much a woman's right as the removal of a dangerously diseased appendix."[155]

No regulations upon it could be enforced without "cross-exam-ining the woman on the most intimate physical details ... installing a dictaphone in every room, a moralist under every bed." She insisted that anti-abortion legislation necessarily was "the ultimate expression of the view of women as vessels for men's use and automatic breeding ma-chines." It subjected them to the mercy of quack abortionists or pun-ished women with unwanted children. *"Why, then,* should abortion not be freely available for all, if and when contraceptives fail? The knowl-edge that a sure second line of defense was available without subterfuge or extortion, would save the wracked nerves of thousands of sensitive men and women, and prevent the shipwreck of much mutual joy and affection. If once the control of reproduction is accepted, the exact method becomes a matter of individual preference and/or expediency, whether by contraception, coital technique, abortion, or voluntary steriliza-tion ..."[156]

Browne not only lumped abortion together with nonlethal meth-ods of fertility control, but stated that it could even be *better* than them in some ways. "Abortion is not only ethically permissible and practically necessary but also erotically preferable to any current and available form of contraception, because any available contraceptive disturbs the essential rhythm, the crescendo, the climax, and diminuendo of the communion of sex ..."[157] Like present-day abortion advocates such as Ellen Willis and Beverly Wildung Harrison, Browne unimaginatively and phallocentrically argued that women absolutely cannot realize their right to sexual pleasure without access to abortion.[158] And like them, Browne made short shrift of the possible claims of fetal life: "Finally, I deny that the right to abortion utterly contravenes any belief in either the possibility of human survival or the mystery of human consciousness and personality."[159] That was about all she had to say on the subject. It did not even occur to her that abortion, even if legal, might have negative meanings or repercussions for not only the fetuses but the *women* involved.

But Browne by no means spoke for all feminists of her time. Even her admiring biographer Sheila Rowbotham notes that Browne was "in a minority" among leftists and feminists and describes the ALRA as "tiny." The Six Points Group, founded by Lady Rhondda to "establish for women equality—economic, legal, moral, social, occupational, and political," furthered a more typical view. It supported a clause in the 1924 Children and Young Person's Protection Bill penalizing abortionists.[160]

In the United States at that time, feminists tended to take the side of the Six Points Group rather that of Browne. Browne mocked Margaret Sanger, who perhaps had more influence than anyone upon public opinion about fertility control, for persistently opposing abortion. It may come as a surprise that anyone would chastise Sanger for assuming such a stand, given the way she is portrayed in the contemporary debate. Prolifers tend to vilify her as a satanic person who is personally responsible for slaughtering millions of unborn babies. Prochoicers tend to uncritically praise her as a pioneering champion of women's reproductive freedom, which, they automatically assume, to Sanger's mind included an unfettered right to abortion. But both camps are adhering to caricatures that slight the complex realities of history. The picture *is* complicated.

So how exactly did Sanger feel about abortion? *The Woman Rebel* and *The Birth Control Review,* journals in which she had a hand, did run some articles defending an individual right to legalized abortion.[161] Sanger, however, did not write these herself, and there are only a few indications that she might have agreed with them. *Family Limitation,* one of her sex education pamphlets from the 1910's, described a technique for inducing abortion as a back-up to contraceptive failure. Here Sanger stated: "It is for each woman to decide this for herself." She added, however, that this right extended only to very early pregnancy, and that many women would understandably recoil from availing themselves of it.[162] Historian Linda Gordon stresses that this defense of abortion was "something [Sanger] was never to do at any later time."[163] Historian James Reed, on the other hand, indicates that Sanger believed in an unqualified right to abortion, on the basis of memos privately circulated during the 1930's at her birth control clinic in New York City.[164] In one of these, Sanger proposes a study of women who come to the clinic with their periods already overdue. She suggests that the clinic locate doctors "who may, in therapeutic cases, give proper attention to those coming under that term." Then as now, "therapeutic abortion" did not include any but medically indicated terminations.[165] According to the minutes of a clinic staff meeting, the clinic decided to provide care for women who suffered complications from abortions obtained elsewhere.[166] And, according to yet another memo, at least one healthy, single patient who tested positive for pregnancy was referred—though apparently not by Sanger herself—to a physician known to sympathize with abortion seekers.[167]

These documents give one pause. At the same time, none of them conclusively establishes that Sanger would whole-heartedly approve of how Planned Parenthood, an organization she founded, lobbies today for abortion "rights." Indeed, the bulk of the available evidence appears to support Gordon's assessment rather than Reed's. Laurence Lader, her biographer and personal friend, wrote: "I would eventually split with Margaret over abortion ... Margaret had always opposed abortion."[168] This is a most telling statement, for Lader is not only the most adulating of Sanger's biographers, but an abortion defender—some would even say *enthusiast*—of truly astounding dogmatism and zealotry. Thus he has nothing to gain by this admission.

In addition, Sanger herself repeatedly articulated a revulsion towards abortion, even legalized abortion. In her first speech to promote *The Woman Rebel,* she spoke of the destruction of fetuses as an unacceptable taking of human life. She lamented the resort of poor people to "the most barbaric methods" of family limitation, namely "the killing of babies—infanticide—abortion."[169] When she opened her first clinic in an immigrant neighborhood of Brooklyn, she circulated handbills that implored in three different languages: "MOTHERS! ... DO NOT KILL,

DO NOT TAKE LIFE, BUT PREVENT."[170] She frequently stated that "nothing short of contraceptives can put an end to the horrors of abortion and infanticide."[171] The denial of birth control compelled women to "undergo an abhorrent operation which kills the tenderness and delicacy of womanhood, even as it may injure or kill the body."[172] Legalization did not make this operation any less abhorrent—not only for fetuses, but pregnant women. She confronted a Soviet abortionist with the following: "Four hundred thousand abortions a year indicate women do not want to have so many children; in my opinion it is a cruel method of dealing with the problem because abortion, no matter how well done, is a terrific nervous and an exhausting physical hardship."[173]

Alice Paul is well known for her formulation of the 1923 Equal Rights Amendment, and for her acts of nonviolent civil disobedience, particularly hunger strikes, to win votes for women. It is not so well known that she condemned abortion, in terms far less open to interpretation than Sanger's. Since she died in 1977, she lived long enough to observe the sea change in most feminists' attitudes toward abortion, and she did not approve of it. She apparently believed that *contraception* was a matter of individual conscience; according to a long-time colleague of hers, as a Quaker she did not "believe in coercion—except in matters of taking life."[174] For Paul, abortion was such a matter.

In the 1960's, Alice Paul puzzled over fellow feminists' increasingly outspoken advocacy of abortion: "How can one protect and help women by killing them as babies?"[175] She termed abortion not only an act of life-taking, but "the ultimate in the exploitation of women."[176] Thus, as Cynthia Harrison notes, Paul "took particular exception to NOW's 1967 endorsement of the movement to repeal abortion laws."[177] Harrison suggests that this was simply because Paul's National Women's Party preferred a single-issue approach to NOW's multi-issue agenda. But it seems that Paul had other reasons for insisting that abortion actually hurt the cause of women, that it "gets the men all mixed up,"[178] and that it "has nothing whatsoever to do with the E.R.A."[179] In an interview a few years before her death, Paul even cited examples of how support for the E.R.A. was eroded by linking it to abortion.[180]

Paul did not stand alone in her objections to the new direction that the women's movement was taking. According to Laurence Lader, the 1967 National Organization for Women convention adopted an abortion plank only after being "dominated by long, strident debate."[181] More than a few of the delegates dissented. Another distinguished dissent of abortion rights advocacy came from Clare Booth Luce, former U.S.

Congressperson, playwright, journalist, and diplomat. Booth Luce went to work for Alice Paul the same year the first Equal Rights Amendment was sent up to Capitol Hill. A continuous supporter of the E.R.A. since its introduction, Booth Luce believed that abortion rights advocacy jeopardized its passage. She felt so strongly on this issue that in February 1978, in response to a letter from the Woman's Lobby soliciting donations for its efforts in defeating select "anti-abortion" legislators in the 1978 elections, Booth Luce withdrew her sponsorship of the Lobby. She states in her letter that she rejects the "extraordinary proposition that women cannot achieve equal rights before the law until all women are given the legal right to empty their wombs at will—and at the expense of the taxpayer" and further states that "if ERA fails to pass, as I now fear it will, a large part of the blame must fall on those misguided feminists who have tried to make the extraneous issue of unrestricted and federally funded abortion the centerpiece of the Equal Rights struggle."[182] The body of Booth Luce's lengthy letter contains a philosophic defense of her position against abortion.

During this same decade, an organization was founded to give people like these dissenters a voice: Feminists for Life. The authenticity of FFL's feminism has been rigorously questioned from the organization's very beginnings. Such questioning comes out of ignorance of women's history. It also stems from a tragic loss of our foremothers' belief that the rights and needs of all human beings are inextricably intertwined— especially those of pregnant women and their fetuses. In an increasingly complicated world, this moral vision of human interconnectedness and interdependence is more relevant than ever. FFL pursues it not to slavishly follow the past, but because it continues to illuminate the plight of women and children in a society that continues to be thoroughly patriarchal. It is vital to realize that the joining of feminism and abortion "rights" is a relatively recent development which can and should be questioned. A growing number of feminists have questioned it.

Part Two

CREATING A FUTURE:
Establishing Life-Affirming Alternatives

Introduction

In Part One we heard the voices of our feminist foremothers telling us that abortion is a violent and unacceptable alternative to the problem of crisis pregnancy. Beyond that, they identified and condemned those societal factors that led women to seek abortion and they demanded and effected some change. These women have handed down to us a vision of a world in which oppression has ceased, violence is rejected as a means of conflict resolution, and women's creative ability is valued and celebrated. The voices of the women in Part Two of this volume share this vision. They, too, consider abortion an unacceptable choice that contradicts those values of nurturing and interconnection that are associated with women, and, like their foremothers, they scrutinize and denounce those patriarchal societal factors that have made abortion an integral part of woman's reality.

There are, however, several differences between the feminist voices of yesterday and the voices of today. Early feminist writings on the issue of abortion differ from ours in that none of our foremothers imagined that abortion would one day be legal and promoted as a "woman's right," and they, therefore, do not address their fellow feminists in their argument: there was consensus among them that abortion was the violent taking of a human life and that its cause could be traced to the oppression of women in a patriarchal society. While the feminists in Part Two of this volume are in complete agreement with the conclusions drawn by their feminist foremothers, they are acutely aware that today they are in the minority among activist feminists, and their writings reflect this consciousness.

Another difference between their writings is that earlier feminists often refer to their religious faith. For many of them, their convictions on social issues were dictated entirely by their Christian faith and so their arguments were often theologically based. In Part Two we will also hear the voices of Christians—Catholics, Protestants, Quakers, Evangelicals—but also of Jews, Buddhists, agnostics, and atheists. In spite of this range of religious beliefs, however, we see few overtly theological arguments. For many of them, abortion is simply not a religious issue; it is a human rights issue that need not involve any discussion of religious faith. But for others, their views on abortion and other forms of violence are inseparable from their faith. And still for others, the current atmosphere of the abortion debate dictates that they de-emphasize their religious convictions. In today's society, one cannot reject abortion simply on the grounds of religion unless she keeps those beliefs to herself and refrains from imposing them on others—anything else is perceived as a violation of church and state. This is ironic in that such an imperative would have negated the works of most eighteenth- and nineteenth-century abolitionists as well as the accomplishments of such women as Lucretia Mott, Sarah and Angelina Grimké, Susan B. Anthony, Matilda Joslyn Gage, and Olympia Brown. In the twentieth century, one would have to dismiss the contributions of dozens of social movements throughout the world that have espoused nonviolent activism based upon their religious faith. Mother Theresa and Bishop Tutu become suspect because they act on the basis of their religious convictions. One wonders if most African-American civil rights activists of the 1950s and 60s would today be dismissed on the basis of their religious convictions (actually, Martin Luther King, Jr. had constant accusations leveled against him for trying to "legislate morality" —the same argument used against prolifers today—but the levelers of his time have since fallen into disrepute).

The diversity of religious views represented in Part Two is also accompanied by a recognition, and celebration, of cultural diversity. Compared to earlier feminists, late twentieth-century prolife feminist writings reflect an increased awareness of cultural diversity and the pervasive forms of discrimination that accompany it. As mentioned in Part One, some of our feminist foremothers espoused or left unchallenged societal prejudices against minorities and immigrants, and a few even held eugenic views about reproduction. Today's prolife feminism is more about inclusion and recognizes the need to seek out and listen to the voices of women from diverse backgrounds. The voices in Part Two speak out not only against sexism, but also against classism and racism as well as discrimination against ethnic minorities and the disabled. In particular, Fannie Lou Hamer, Alison Davis, and Mary Krane Derr write about some of the difficulties they have faced as marginal women in dominant culture; and most of the women in this section write from their extensive experience in social activism against various forms of social oppression. Like those feminist foremothers who were involved in various reform movements, the feminists represented in these essays are also activists in various social justice movements that condemn violence (the anti-war/peace movement and the anti-death-penalty movement) and that promote the rights of various minority groups (including African-Americans, Native Americans, gays and lesbians, and disabled individuals, among others). They also enact their life-affirming beliefs through their work in crisis pregnancy centers, in battered women's shelters and other women's counseling centers, in childbirth classes, in women's studies courses, in churches, in the Two-Thirds World, in their writing and research, in the halls of government, and in their own homes. Some are vegetarians, several are pacifists, most are mothers, and some include among their families so-called "unwanted" children they have adopted. They remind us that the oppression of any group of people strikes at the very foundation of a feminism that is based upon the absolute equality of all humans.

It would seem that there would also be distinct differences between the feminist writings of yesterday and those of today concerning woman's present condition in society—surely the woman's movement has resulted in an amelioration of woman's oppression. Right? While women have certainly made great strides, particularly in areas involving "individual rights," we believe the devaluation of women in society has improved little since the nineteenth century. As will be seen, the articles in this second part of our volume share some remarkable similarities with those in Part One. In particular, feminist prolifers argue that those conditions our feminist foremothers identified as the underlying causes of abortion have, in fact, changed little in this century.

The writings in Part One reflect a belief that as women become more educated about their own physiology, when contraceptives become safe and available, when society learns to appreciate and celebrate woman's reproductive ability, when women gain equal rights and start entering into sexual relationships on an equal basis, abortion will no longer be a problem. Most people in our contemporary society perceive these goals as having been attained: women certainly know more about their bodies than did nineteenth century women; contraceptives are "safe and available"; baby-boomers have brought pregnancy and motherhood back into vogue to some degree; and women are certainly liberated—aren't they? So why have 1.6 million abortions been performed each year in the U.S. since 1973?

While science has provided us with much more information about our bodies, we have failed to effectively pass on this information to young women. Planned Parenthood often cites this lack of knowledge when promoting their sex education programs (although their clients become bastions of reproductive knowledge needing no further education when the subject is informed consent for abortion).[1] Contraceptives, although certainly more available, have never proven to be substantially safer or more reliable than many of the methods available to women of the nineteenth century. Contraceptives in the form of chemicals operate on the principle of interrupting or sabotaging the natural processes of the female body, often with very negative side effects. Barrier methods are relatively safe and available, but surveys reveal that the primary responsibility for their use (and failure) lies with the woman. Our increased knowledge of women's reproductive cycles has thankfully led to a safe, effective, natural method of contraception, but natural family planning works on the premise of equality in the sexual relationship. While pregnancy might be "in" in this latter portion of the century (as long as you limit yourself to two children), there still exists a societal aversion to woman's body and her biological processes—witness the multi-million dollar feminine hygiene industry that bases its profits on the idea that we need constant cleaning and deodorizing. No, we're not liberated—we have only become adept at staking a claim within the structure of the existing patriarchy.

We also see new issues—new degradations of women—that our foremothers did not have to address in the same form. While contemporary popular culture no longer embraces the tenets of nineteenth-century "ideal womanhood," any young woman who turns on the television today or opens a magazine is bombarded with pictures of the ideal woman—skinny body, big breasts, and blond flowing hair—and her resulting feelings of inadequacy and inferiority can drive her to dangerous eating habits, chemicals, and even surgery. These images can perhaps be compared to illustrations in nineteenth-century women's magazines that popularized corsets and other restricting and dangerous fashions; but in today's much more visually oriented culture, the images are more pervasive and destructive. Woman's confidence and self-esteem are constantly attacked as she receives messages of her lack. Who can stand alone against Madison Avenue? In this state of mind, she is assailed with images of woman as sex object and she comes to believe that something must be wrong with her if she does not pursue sexual intercourse at every opportunity. To prove herself "normal," she enters into sexual relationships at an incredibly young age, unprepared and often against her own inclination, and her self-esteem continues to deteriorate. When she ends up pregnant, she receives the clear message from society that career and pregnancy, or more accurately, affluence and pregnancy, don't mix. And the final message she receives is perhaps the most insidious. Faced with her dilemma, she seeks the socially acceptable solution. And what do we offer her? Male-dominated society has a history of attempting to solve its conflicts through violence. Is anyone surprised that women have resorted to abortion? to violence against their own children and their own bodies?

From this vantage point, our feminist foremothers might find it very difficult to comprehend modern prochoice feminists. But as their contemporary sisters, we must attempt to understand them and their motivation. A keen perception of the oppression against women in our society creates an intense desire in women to help other women. Like Laura Cuppy Smith, who recognized that her daughter would make it through her crisis only with much practical and emotional support, women today know that their sisters need them. Unfortunately, these women have also labored under similar oppression and can often offer only those solutions that are expedient within the patriarchy. In addition, because these women are so sympathetic to the plight of their sisters, they reject any stance they might find judgmental, and rightly so. By contrast, prolifers are perceived as sitting in judgment—harsh judgment—upon women who obtain abortions; and while for some this may be a correct characterization, today it is belied by the tens of thousands of prolifers who give of their time, their homes, and their resources to young women facing crisis pregnancies. Little similar aid is offered by prochoice society because pregnancy and childbirth are simply not the desired alternatives.

Part of the problem lies with a lack of imagination or vision. Dominant American culture offers no exemplary construct under which individuals have a greater, or even equal, responsibility to the community (in which all life, including the *in-utero* tenant, is a member) than they do to themselves. Nor does it offer—and this is significant—a paradigm for continuing love and acceptance by the community of one of its members who has betrayed another member. It is assumed that because prolifers condemn abortion, they condemn the women who seek its relief; but women make up the overwhelming majority of membership in prolife organizations in the U.S., and almost all of these women have had personal experiences with abortion—they have either been victimized by abortion themselves or they maintain a relationship with someone who has. Likewise, large proportions of those women who have committed themselves to the prochoice movement have obtained abortions earlier in their lives, and they seek relief from their own grief by "helping" other women in similar situations. The sense of loss and empathy that all of these women feel for their sisters is genuine, and feminists do little for the cause of women by denying this common ground between prochoice and prolife women who are dedicated to helping women.

It is necessary to acknowledge that many prochoice feminists have reached some of these same conclusions concerning the underlying causes of abortion. As mentioned in the introduction to Part One, Adrienne Rich considers abortion a violence inflicted by women first of all upon themselves, and believes that "in a society where women entered sexual intercourse willingly, where adequate contraception was a genuine social priority, there would be no 'abortion issue.'"[2] Germaine Greer echoes Rich when she says:

It is typical of the contradictions that break women's hearts that when they avail themselves of their fragile right to abortion they often, even usually, went with grief and humiliation to carry out a painful duty that was presented to them as a privilege. Abortion is the latest in a long line of non-choices that begin at the very beginning with the time and the place and the manner of lovemaking. ...[3]

Catherine MacKinnon opens the chapter on abortion in her book *The Theory of the State* with Adrienne Rich's statement, quoted above, and makes an excellent case against the privacy argument for abortion upon which *Roe v. Wade* is based.[4] Every feminist should read MacKinnon's argument which reveals much that is wrong with American attitudes toward privacy rights. But MacKinnon imposes a scary alternative upon which to base woman's right to abortion: "The abortion choice should be available and must be women's, but not because the fetus is not a form of life. Why should women not make life-or-death decisions?"[5]

MacKinnon's words, after first sending shock waves through those who absolutely reject violence, contradict her own ensuing argument. She effectively articulates the problem of "privacy"—that while protecting "individual rights," it privatizes woman's sexual oppression; but by endowing women with the right to decide death for an*other*, MacKinnon is suggesting a privatization of the violence against the *in-utero* other.

MacKinnon's concession that the fetus is a "form of life" seems to bear little weight with her. (We wonder what form of life she believes the fetus is. Of course, feminists recall that men have historically had a problem in identifying what kind of life form women are.) The life of the fetus, however, has proven to be more perplexing to other feminist theorists who are reevaluating their views on abortion.

Elizabeth Fox-Genovese, in her book, *Feminism Without Illusions*, cannot take the life of the fetus so lightly.[6] In responding to Carol Gilligan's argument that the appropriate way to approach the issue of abortion is not in terms of the life of the fetus but rather in terms of the woman's perception of responsibility to the quality of life for the mother, her family, and the unborn child, Fox-Genovese argues that the "repudiation of any attempt to define life in the abstract" violates that "highest standard of civilization"—the "respect for human life in all its diversity," a standard, we might add, that reflects maternal values. She further observes that while many view Gilligan's position as one located in the idea of empathy (many people assume that because they would not want to live a life of disability, abuse, poverty or mental impoverishment, neither would anyone else), we all have had experience with abused, deprived, and physically or mentally challenged people who tenaciously hold on to life. (The fetus' fierce struggle for life in the face of the abortionist's instruments has been documented by fetal photography.) Fox-Genovese concludes: "To say, in the face of such evidence, that we have a right to decide which living being would and would not want to live under which conditions is to assume precisely that arrogant disregard for another's subjectivity for which feminists condemn men's attitudes toward women."[7]

It is important to identify the broader context within which Fox-Genovese locates her discomfort with abortion. Like MacKinnon, she sharply criticizes the idea of privacy not only because it privatizes male oppression, but also because it reinforces the male individualistic view of society and "dismisses men's claims and dissolves their responsibilities to the next generation." "Abortion," she comments, "challenges feminists to come to terms with the contradictions in their own thought, notably the contradiction between the commitment to community and nurture and the commitment to individual right." It is within this paradigm that she posits the need for a collective definition of life, a definition based upon respect for the other's subjectivity.

In fairness, it is necessary to point out that Fox-Genovese opposes an outright ban against abortion and has few difficulties with first trimester abortions—before the fetus has demonstrated "signs of life." (We will wait patiently for this distinguished feminist to pick up a fetology text and be introduced to the wonderful, and amazingly active, world of the first trimester fetus.) While we disagree in part with her conclusions, we are delighted and hopeful that women of her intellectual calibre are starting to recognize the inconsistency between abortion ideology and the values of caring, nurturing and community.

Rich, Greer, MacKinnon, and Fox-Genovese also have in common their severe critique of prolifers in general. MacKinnon states that "the problem has been that if the fetus has *any* standing in the debate, it has more weight than women do."[8] Feminist prolifers for years have argued that some conservative abortion opponents have forgotten about the mother, who holds equal value with her child. We have steadfastly criticized our "fellow" prolifers who seem to care more about *in-utero* life than life that has passed through the birth canal; but we also believe that these types of prolifers are on the decline. Prolifers, after all, make no profit from their stand (indeed, the few salaried prolife workers in the U.S. could make better money in just about any other career). Unlike abortionists and playboys (who are among the most liberal contributors to abortion rights organizations), they are not fighting to protect an economic investment or individual rights.

We can also safely attest that few prolifers we know harbor a hidden agenda to increase the population so that someone will be around to pay their social security (although for our sisters and brothers in developing countries, this may be a very real issue). Instead, we have been pleasantly surprised at much of the reaction to our criticism of the conservative prolife movement. Like Jonah, who was astonished at the response of Nineveh to his message of repentance, we have been surprised and (unlike Jonah) delighted at much of the reaction by prolifers to our feminist prolife message. These committed prolifers, who have rarely before been involved in any type of social activism, have become more sensitive to the situation of young women. Hundreds of crisis pregnancy centers throughout the U.S. offering free services to women in need have been funded by these "conservatives," and it has been our further privilege to see many of them become more involved in alleviating the social problems contributing to the high unplanned pregnancy rate.[9] They have joined us in our concern about how women are viewed by society; about how sex is sold to our youth; about how pornography degrades women and promotes violence against them; about how men must take more responsibility for their sexual behavior; and about how employers must make better provision for parents and their children.

We don't claim to have come full circle. There are many abortion opponents out there who are still motivated by little more than a desire to put down the "woman's movement" and whose self-righteous arguments on behalf of the fetus wreak of insincerity and total disregard for the obstacles that mothers with children face in our society.

Our strongest criticism and condemnation is reserved for those abortion opponents who resort to violence to promote their cause. We surmise that many of these zealots have come to believe prochoice feminist rhetoric about the "liberating" qualities of abortion and are so fearful of women's full social equality that they make it their personal mission to restore some kind of misguided notion of womanhood by violently attacking and even murdering abortionists and their clients. Violent prolife activism is a contradiction, insidious and perverse, that we condemn at every level; and despite our differences with some conservative prolife groups, most of them agree with us on this point. Although the media loves to feature inflammatory sound bytes from extremist groups, every mainstream prolife group in the United States has condemned the killings at abortion facilities and has responded by re-emphasizing their organizational policies against any kind of violence.

Feminist prolifers have made significant progress by refusing to discount conservative prolifers simply because they do not share many of our views. Likewise, we refuse to count prochoice feminists as our adversaries, particularly when they work toward mutual goals that will correct those societal conditions that we recognize as having created the perceived need for abortion. Our complaint has been that prochoice feminists have focused so narrowly on abortion rights, tying up the majority of their resources, that they have dropped the ball on those issues that contribute to what so many women perceive as a need for abortion in the first place. We have seen a few signs of recognition of this circumstance, and we have great hope that the realization will continue to grow. We believe that it is only a matter of time before we dance together upon common ground.

The following articles represent what we believe are both echoes of our foremothers—voices passed from mother to daughter—and prophetic voices of our future, when the story becomes reality. A story of how women will come together and work for a world of peace and respect and interdependence among all peoples.

Pat Goltz, Catherine Callaghan and the Founding of Feminists for Life

by Cindy Osborne

In 1971, Pat Goltz and Catherine Callaghan were radical feminists, social activists and members of the National Organization of Women (NOW). As fate would have it, they met in a Judo class and soon realized that they also shared prolife views. Theirs was not a popular position, as NOW was specifically fighting for abortion "rights" as a woman's ticket to sexual and economic freedom. Pat and Catherine saw the demand for abortion as being diametrically opposed to the goals of feminism. In fact, Pat had joined NOW specifically to fight that element.

Pat and Catherine were deeply disturbed because the women's movement was caving in to the demands of the patriarchy by allowing itself to be used by rich industrialists, the population control movement, and the playboy movement. They believed that feminist organizations were failing to provide viable alternatives to abortion for individual women and abandoning them to abortionists and abortion referral services who would exploit their misery. Because the single-minded focus of the movement was on abortion, they were not developing workable solutions to the problems of poor and minority women.

Pat and Catherine teamed up in an effort to change the emphasis on abortion rights in their local NOW chapter in Columbus, Ohio. Catherine met continual challenge by her sisters who questioned how she could call herself a feminist and oppose abortion. Catherine, always cool and logical, returned the challenge with, *"How can I not oppose abortion when half of all abortions kill our sisters?"* Despite Pat and Cathy's patient and consistent arguments, the opposition refused a dialogue on the issue. Pat was ordered by the president of the Columbus chapter not to discuss abortion with any member of NOW at any time or place. Pat was defiant and eventually paid the price.

In April of 1972, Pat and Cathy decided that prolife feminists needed a forum of their own in which to express their views. They set about forming an organization of international scope. One year later, on

April 9, 1973, in Columbus, Ohio, Feminists for Life was born. It immediately took on international proportions when Pat and Cathy were joined
by Jessica Pegis, Martha Crean and Denyse (Handlar) O'Leary of Toronto,
Canada. At the time, Jessica, Martha, and Denyse, along with several
other people, were publishing a monthly journal called *The Uncertified
Human* (later shortened to *The Human*). FFL began publishing a quarterly newsletter, the *Feminists for Life Journal*, which was put together
primarily by Pat with some help from Jessica. Shortly after publication
began, Pat received a letter from Jessica. Instead of closing the correspondence with her usual, "In sisterhood," this time Jessica closed with
the unique, "In sisterlife." The concept behind her closing words was a
perfect frame for the goals and philosophies of Feminists for Life. The
next newsletter went out under the flag *Sisterlife Journal.*

Even after founding FFL, Pat and Catherine refused to give up
on NOW. They continued their outspoken affiliation in hopes that their
words would fall on hearing ears. Catherine continued to work quietly
behind the scenes, and Pat was bold in her criticism of establishment
feminists for promoting abortion as the solution to everything from sexism to poverty. In 1974, NOW of Ohio could take no more; they wanted
Pat out. Benson Wolman, the executive director of the Ohio ACLU, advised NOW Ohio that they had a *legal* right to kick Pat out, but certainly
not a *moral* right. Putting law before morality, the leadership sent out
notification of a hearing scheduled to oust Pat from NOW. Unfortunately, none of these letters reached Pat's supporters in the organization;
NOW leadership claimed some members had been innocently overlooked
during the notification process. At the expulsion hearing, Pat was given
fifteen minutes to defend herself. She chose, instead, to do exactly what
she had been forbidden to do. She spent the entire allotted time vigorously denouncing abortion before a captive audience who was bound,
by rule, to hear her out. With only two votes of support and much fan-
fare, Pat was kicked out of the state chapter for daring to speak against
NOW's "sacred cow," abortion-on-demand.

Unlike the Ohio chapter of NOW, the national organization declined to oust Pat. It is doubtful that they were more tolerant than the
state chapter as much as they were concerned about negative publicity.
Indeed, by that time they had already gotten some nasty press by edito-
rialists who had lambasted them for refusing to tolerate diverse opinions.

Our feminist foremothers of the nineteenth and early twentieth
centuries had spoken out in tireless defense of the powerless within our

society. Besides working for equal rights for women, feminists had been at the forefront of the abolitionist movement, the fight against child labor as well as the effort to stop abortion (this, long before anyone dreamed it would someday be a legally protected "right"). Pat's expulsion illustrates the extent to which the establishment feminists had strayed from their noble roots. Not only was NOW, the alleged voice of the establishment feminist movement, promoting an insidious form of oppression under the guise of reproductive freedom, but in banishing Pat Goltz from their ranks, they made it obvious that they would tolerate no dissent.

Pat's expulsion from NOW punctuates an often ignored point. The prolife movement, often accused of consisting of narrow-minded and intolerant conservatives, eagerly extended hands of acceptance and friendship to Pat and Cathy. They were showered with opportunities to promote the goals and philosophies of prolife feminism. NOW, on the other hand, was promoting itself as the voice for all women, but refused any dialogue with those holding an opposing viewpoint on abortion.

NOW's loss was the prolife movement's gain. Barbara Willke, Chairperson of Right to Life of Greater Cincinnati, remembers, "We welcomed Feminists for Life. Pat and Catherine came from such diverse backgrounds and yet they had reached the same self-evident conclusions. They were way ahead of their time and I think they took the opposition by surprise." In 1974, Feminists for Life was invited to present a workshop at the National Right to Life convention in Washington, D.C. Pat, Catherine, Jessica and Martha made the trek to the Capitol where the four of them camped together on a floor in student housing just one block from the Watergate Hotel. The workshop was a great success. For most of the audience, this was their first exposure to consistent feminism; and many who came in skeptics walked out visibly impressed. Pat has since spoken at hundreds of conferences and other public forums. The National Youth Pro-life Coalition (NYPLC) convention in New York holds a particularly fond spot in Pat's memory. Among the speakers were Connie Redbird Uri, a Cherokee-Choctaw Indian, Jesse Jackson (who has since repudiated his politically incorrect prolife stance), Delores Huerta, and Dick Gregory. Ms. Uri detailed how she considered abortion and sterilization a genocide of Native Americans. Mr. Gregory lightened up the convention with his speech in which he explained his large family. He related that the ZPG (Zero Population Growth) people had told him he should have 2¼ kids. After he and his wife had two, they kept trying for that ¼ kid, but a whole one kept popping out, and that's how he ended up with nine children.

In the travels connected with her many speaking engagements, Pat met people who were interested in starting FFL chapters in their own state or country. State chapters began popping up all over the U.S., and chapters were also formed in Canada, Australia, England, Mexico and New Zealand. Over the years, Catherine took less of an active leadership role because of other commitments. Pat's move to Tucson in 1976 also signaled the end of her prominent role. New leadership was rising up just in time: Pat's workload was quickly becoming unmanageable, and she was fast approaching the point of burn-out. In 1977, the Wisconsin chapter took over the international chapter and became Feminists for Life of America. Maggie Guenther, who had been vice-president since 1974, was elected president, and Wisconsin ran the national organization in parallel with their state chapter. In 1982 and 1983, they held several widely received national seminars on women's issues and prolife feminism. As a result, the mailing list began to swell and continues to grow. Soon there were members in every state as well as the aforementioned international chapters.

FFLA has pulled up roots and moved to new offices several times upon the election of new presidents—from Ohio to Wisconsin to Nebraska to Kansas City, Missouri, in 1984 where it found a home for ten years, and now, finally, to Washington, D.C. While it has taken a while for the national office to find a permanent home, the modern feminist prolife message took root and is rapidly spreading. We are still dismayed that the establishment feminists (who we define as those currently in power of such prominent groups as NOW and mistakenly seen as being the voice for all feminists) continue to promote abortion as the potion for all that ails us. We want equality. We demand liberty. But, as seekers of peace and promoters of justice, we know our road to freedom cannot be littered with the bodies of our own offspring. Having known oppression, we cannot stand by and allow the oppression of an entire class of weaker human beings. Having once been owned by our husbands, we cannot condone a position that says the unborn are owned by their mothers. Remembering a time when our value was determined by whether a man wanted us, we refuse to bow to the patriarchal attitude that says the unborn child's value is determined by whether a woman wants her. Goltz declares that, "Abortion is an attack on the essence of our spirit, our very being." In the original Feminists for Life Declaration, the founding sisters state:

> We pledge ourselves to help the feminist movement correct its failures, purge itself of anti-life sentiments and practices and de-

velop solutions to the problems that we, as women, face. We particularly want to welcome into fellowship Jews, blacks, Chicanas, Indians and Eskimos, Orientals, the aged and the handicapped, for all have suffered at the hand of the patriarchy, even as women have.

The co-founders of FFL are alive and well and living where the air is a little cleaner. Catherine Callaghan is a tenured professor of Linguistics at Ohio State University. She opted out of NOW several years ago because, "they kept adding extraneous planks to their platform that weren't women's issues." When asked how she reached her prolife philosophy, she replies, "Scientists tell us, and I have no reason to doubt them, that life begins at conception … the basis of my belief is on scientific evidence. Science is going to be the only useful, effective way to approach this issue." Because of this conviction, she has a problem with the mainstream prolife movement when they premise so many of their arguments against abortion on religious beliefs, which she finds unnecessary. She continues to actively support FFL of Ohio, predicating her prolife efforts on the basis of human rights.

Pat Goltz, still a maverick, lives in Tucson, Arizona, with her husband, John, and their seven multi-racial children, two of whom are adopted and three of whom were born at home with the assistance of a midwife. She is currently working on a book about the various uses of plants in the Sonoran desert. She also remains active in the feminist prolife movement. In speaking about the current state of the mainstream women's movement, she comments, "They see no problem in trading in the chauvinist in the bedroom for the one on Capitol Hill!" She has a degree in art, has studied law independently, and is an expert on constitutional law and international treaties and declarations, particularly as they relate to abortion and human rights. Complementing her international interests, she has studied 31 languages, 12 of which she reads fluently. She has little patience with international family planning schemes inasmuch as she views extravagant Westerners as remarkably arrogant in the way they order African women to limit their families when it is necessary for them to have at least four children in order for one or two to survive to adulthood and help support them in their old age.

In the mid-seventies, Pat had the honor of meeting Alice Paul, the author of the original Equal Rights Amendment. Ms. Paul, who had known some of our earlier feminist foremothers, made it clear that early feminists were altogether opposed to abortion. Also very much opposed to abortion, she had given her all to getting the ERA into Congress. She was grateful that others were now carrying the torch but was disturbed by the new trend of linking the ERA with abortion. She related to Pat her belief that abortion would destroy feminism if it were not stopped.

In the early years, FFL was very active in promoting the passage of the ill-fated ERA, especially in the home state of Ohio. The abortion issue was a direct contributor to Ohio's failure to ratify the ERA. One Senator who voted to keep the ERA in committee did so primarily because he felt the Supreme Court would be the final arbiter of the ERA. That court, he felt, could not be trusted since they had, in one sweeping decision, ushered in abortion-on-demand. Pat wrote, "As a prolife feminist, it galls me to know that an issue I totally disapprove of, namely abortion, caused the vote to kill the ERA in committee." The following article was written during this period; and, as did Alice Paul and Clare Booth Luce, Pat recognized the detrimental effect of abortion rights advocacy on passage of the ERA.

Equal Rights
by Pat Goltz

One of the goals of feminism is to see to it that women have equal legal protection: that the laws apply to women in the same way as they do to men. There are actually possible ways to do this. We are familiar, in general, with the Equal Rights Amendment, the effect of which would be to give us a legal handle by which class action suits of magnitudes heretofore undreamed of could be brought. The trouble with legislation already existing that purports to undo inequities for women is that there are so many exceptions and that it would cost a fortune in legal fees to cover bringing the exceptions into conformity with the rules. Money for pursuit of problems in court is something women are in short supply of. Whether or not women "own" more money than men, women control less of it. The other effect the Equal Rights Amendment would have is to act as an incentive to get a large number of laws changed at the legislative level with considerably less effort on the part of women.

State equal rights amendments have proved to be of considerable help. The major problem with equal rights amendments on the state level is that they don't apply to the Federal government—the largest agency of discrimination in the country. The Federal Equal Rights Amendment, even if it is eventually unratified, is having a profound effect. In the states where it has been ratified, legislators are busy modifying state laws to conform. Some of this activity is going on in states that have yet to ratify as well. The hope is that even if ERA goes unratified, it will have accomplished much of its purpose already. Perhaps changing laws in one state will exert pressure on the legislators in neighboring states. In any event, the outcome should be a distinct improvement.

Opponents of ERA often cite specific fears about what the ERA would do. Those active opponents I have talked to, to a woman, however, have refused to discuss with me exactly what they hope the laws will eventually be. This head-in-the-sand attitude, along with the small collection of misinformation which is being circulated and recirculated is regarded as nonfunctional by this writer. In a sense, we feminists have to look out for our weaker sisters. They want the right to maintain the traditional female role but don't know how to go about it. The feminist movement, in general, has not been too helpful. If we do not help these women choose the traditional role at their own desire, we have failed them. Much more attention is needed in this area. What we want for women is more options, not a new straitjacket.

One disturbing aspect of the struggle for ratification of the ERA has been the slowdown among states electing to ratify. The big slowdown occurred during this legislative session (1973). It is probably due to two things: most of the states that would readily ratify have already done so, and a combination of gathering momentum on the part of opponents and tactical errors on the part of proponents has made the remaining states cautious. If nothing else, we have the inertia of eons of sexism to overcome.

The tactical errors can be broadly classified into several categories: abortion, lesbianism, and the breakdown of the family. It is known that in Ohio, abortion was a direct contributor to Ohio's failure to ratify this year. One senator who voted to keep the ERA in committee did so primarily because he felt the Supreme Court would be the final arbiter of the ERA and it is not to be trusted since that court legalized abortion-on-request. We talked with that senator, who was open to us because of our prolife stand, and discovered that he actually knows very little about the discrimination women face. He is willing to be educated and has agreed to work on individual legislation to help women. We are quite concerned that Ohio's failure to ratify in 1973 has irreparably harmed the ERA, since Ohio is regarded as a pivotal state by both sides. As prolife feminists, it galls us to know that an issue we totally disapprove of, namely abortion, caused the vote to kill the ERA in committee, after the successful ratification in the house by a comfortable margin of 54 to 40.

Lesbianism has mainly been a problem of timing. It is not a popular issue with the population at large. We at Feminists for Life have not taken a stand on lesbianism because we feel an insufficient case is made for lesbianism being a feminist issue. Open support of the gay movement prior to ratification of the ERA was poor timing. [Today, FFL welcomes gays, lesbians and their friends and shares many members with the Prolife Alliance of Gays and Lesbians. —Ed.]

The breakdown of the family is also attributed to the ERA and the feminist movement by opponents. If opponents think equal rights are causing the breakdown of the family, they are using this as a scapegoat and contributing to the problem! This writer sees the breakdown of the family as due to three causes: breakdown in religious and moral values (religion doesn't have to be sexist), permissive child rearing practices (which, incidentally, make women slaves of their children), and the breakdown of the school system (including the adoption of more ineffective methods of teaching reading and arithmetic, pressure from the teachers for students to conform to the peer group, sensitivity training, and behavior modification, all of which serve to entrench sexism in the young, and will continue to do so as long as the persons in power have sexist attitudes themselves). Although Feminists for Life's stand against abortion and involuntary euthanasia should have tipped people off that we are not a "typical" feminist group, a number of people have assumed that we favor the breakdown of the family. For the record, we support a strong, flexible family structure, and we accept men into membership and active participation on an equal basis with women.

Another way of attacking the problem of establishing equal rights for women is to work to get the Supreme Court to rule that the fourteenth amendment applies equally to women. This method of achieving the goal has been sadly neglected by our movement. We are working on this, also. It may turn out to be our only hope.

Jane Thomas Bailey

Jane Thomas Bailey was an early editor of *Sisterlife*, and with her background in journalism, she helped establish *Sisterlife* as an important voice of the feminist prolife movement. Her early experiences with other prolife groups made obvious their failure to understand the real causes of abortion, and she has continued to offer constructive criticism for those political conservatives who consider themselves prolife. "Feminism 101" was written as a practical help for those prolifers who had little knowledge of feminism and wished to include a concern for women in their struggle for the rights of the unborn, and "Prolifers Too Exclusive" outlines the discomfort many feminist prolifers feel with the mainstream conservative prolife movement.

Ms. Bailey continues her advocacy on behalf of women and the unborn in the midwest where she lives with her husband and children.

Feminism 101: A Primer For Prolife Persons
by Jane Thomas Bailey

Though its committed adherents are a fairly small minority of citizens, feminism may have had more impact on our nation than any other social ideology of our day. Abortion aside, feminist thinking has affected nearly all informed Americans in the way we run our homes, raise our children, expectations we have regarding employment and even in our use of the English language. Many women who would never consider joining the National Organization for Women and who may not be sure just what feminism is have reaped the benefits of better job opportunities, better pay and more respect at home and in church because of the battles feminists have fought.

Any movement or ideology this influential needs to be thoroughly examined and understood, whether we ultimately accept its premises or not. We in the prolife movement must make a special effort to understand and speak to feminists because they are the foremost advocates and guardians of abortion-on-demand.

Some people may dismiss this goal as hopelessly idealistic. "Communicate with THEM?" they say. "We've showed them pictures of unborn children, alive and aborted, for years and they have only pushed us further away." This is true, but it is also true that in our urgency we did not take time to study their language and culture, so our message was incomprehensible to them. People who have advocated and participated in abortion will turn away from our pictures in self-defense because they cannot bear to look at the implications of their own actions. To reach them, we must know how to disarm them and this can only be done gently and in a spirit of love.

Ideological feminism has a much broader vision of life than equal pay for equal work. It will be difficult for many of us who have wept over the carnage of abortion clinics to attempt to listen sympathetically to a feminist vision of justice and peace, but it is necessary for us to do so if we wish to appeal to the highest moral values of feminism itself. And it is wrong for us to snicker at the notion of feminists having morals. Some strains of feminism border on becoming a religion with its own vision of what the millennium will be like.

The feminist ideal posits a world in which everyone, male and female, is treated with equal respect and has a voice in its government. It rejects the oppression of any one group of people by any other group of people. Feminists view the male oppression of women as the central problem of society not because it is worse than whites oppressing blacks or the First World oppressing the Third World, but because it encompasses all the others and represents half the world oppressing the other half.

Though the feminists of the 1960's and 1970's prided themselves on being just as tough and unemotional as men, the neo-feminist movement sees women as having qualities of compassion and understanding that men would do well to cultivate. People who share the feminist vision of the millennium believe that when women receive their full share of power in the world, there will be no more war, no more human rights abuses, no more oppression.

If men appear to be identified as the root of all evil, we ought to note that among committed feminists there is a disproportionately high percentage of women who admit to having been the victims of incest, rape, wife-beating and other torments at the hands of men, while the male-dominated society did little to object and often treated the victim as the guilty party. There are also in the feminist movement many intelligent women who were denied the same educational opportunities as their brothers and women who put their husbands through law or medical school only to be left behind for someone prettier. Add to this single mothers who weren't being paid a living wage for their work, only to be condemned as freeloaders when they decided welfare gave them comparable pay plus more time with their children, plus divorced women whose husbands haven't made a child support payment in years, plus gifted women whose male bosses took valuable ideas from them and passed them off as their own. They embrace feminist ideology because it is appropriate to their experience.

Even prolifers who do not share this vision of the world can find some common ground on which to build bridges to the feminist community. Indeed, if we may be charitable for a moment and set aside the feminist campaign for abortion-on-demand, it is realistic to say that feminists have taken many positions from which unborn children may benefit.

First of all, rights for unborn children necessarily means rights for pregnant women. If a woman loses her means of making a living or is banished from society because she is pregnant, she will have a strong incentive to have an abortion. The feminist movement has campaigned for the right of a pregnant woman to keep working as long as she is physically possible and to be able to keep her job when she takes time off to have a baby. For what they have accomplished we should applaud them and, for what remains to be done on this front, we should join them.

Feminists have targeted campaigns against the medical community in an effort to make childbirth less forbidding and less expensive. In many communities they have led the fight for natural childbirth, where the woman is in control and her family is allowed to be with her to give her emotional support and aid in the delivery of the child. Feminists have also placed great emphasis on re-establishing the role of the midwife. When I was a Birthright director and the local doctors regularly turned away our poverty-stricken clients, I thanked God for the feminist midwives who provided them with competent prenatal care for a fraction of what they would have had to pay a doctor and a hospital.

Shared parenting is another common ground between feminists and prolifers. Feminists believe both children and parents will be happier, healthier people if both parents share in the rearing of the children. Those of us on the street level of the prolife movement have seen that women seek abortions because of lack of help or support from the father of the child, so we should likewise promote parental responsibility among men. Further, many prolifers who would never consider themselves feminists, such as Dr. James Dobson, have urged fathers, according to a biblical mandate, to take a much greater role in the rearing of their children.

With the number of single-parent households still on the rise, we need to think about the care of those children who are not aborted. Feminists have long been advocates of day care. No matter whether it is subsidized through the government, provided by the business that employs the parent, or made available through churches, synagogues and other non-profit organizations, we need to make a commitment to effect responsible child care.

Pregnant women need to eat properly or they risk harm to both their own health and that of their child. And once a child is born it needs to be fed and clothed. Again, in the case of many single mothers and low-income couples, this means providing either adequate public support for the woman who wishes to stay at home with her children or to help her obtain the education and training necessary to provide for her family. These have long been feminist causes; they should be ours as well.

These are just a few of the feminist issues that may provide points of contact with the prolife community, just as opposition to pornography has provided a point of contact between feminists and evangelical Christians. Perhaps some of these feminist goals and ideals sound very much like your own, and you're wondering how a movement with such high ideals could ever have become the leading proponent of abortion. It did not have to be that way.

Feminists of the nineteenth century viewed abortion as an atrocity forced upon women by men who were unwilling to care for the children they had conceived—still an apt analysis. Indeed, the modern demand for abortion did not originate with the modern feminist movement, but with a group of MEN who had formed the National Association for the Repeal of Abortion Laws (now the National Abortion Rights Action League). Bernard Nathanson, a founder of NARAL who is now a prolife activist, writes that this male-dominated group cooked up the ideology of "reproductive freedom" and convinced the fledgling National Organization for Women to take it on as a cause. Some leaders of NOW, apparently including Betty Friedan, argued that it would be a costly mistake to advocate abortion as a cornerstone of women's rights, but were overruled. It is also true that in all movements that are convinced of their own righteousness, it is nearly impossible for members to admit that they are capable of committing evil acts.

The basic argument for abortion-on-demand is that as long as a woman can be tied down with childbearing, responsibility for social decision-making will remain entirely in the hands of men. Therefore, the prolife movement is viewed as a male plot to keep women barefoot and pregnant. The truth is that abortion itself is sexist in nature. The currently accepted feminist argument holds that a woman can be free to take a full role in society only if she can free herself from childbearing. But since women are, by definition, people who can get pregnant, this means that pro-abortionists are not advocating rights for women, but for men. The basic ideal of feminism is a society in which the powerful do not deny the weak their rights, yet abortion is truly patriarchal because it is a prime example of the powerful (women) depriving the weak (unborn children) of their rights, to the point of killing them. The feminist euphemism for abortion is "controlling our own bodies," yet abortion represents a violent example of one person controlling another's body.

Feminists helped pioneer the battle against unnecessary surgery by telling women to stand up to their physicians. Yet abortion is a prime example of unnecessary surgery since the physical "problem" solves itself in nine months. And, while they have argued for women facing other types of surgery to be told of all the options available to them, feminists have argued that women considering abortion should not have to be told about the development of the baby inside them, or about the possibilities of adoption or parenthood.

Abortion does not address the basic inequalities, such as poverty and unequal pay, that make a woman believe she cannot have a baby. It's a cheap fix that leaves the woman as poor and oppressed as she ever was, while the politicians claim to have struck a blow for women's rights and the doctors go home $250 richer.

Finally, abortion perpetuates the image of women as reusable sex objects. If she gets pregnant, all it takes is $250 and she's slender and happy again. If she decides to give birth, the father feels justified in claiming it's not his responsibility to help care for the child since he offered to pay for an abortion. No small surprise that the Playboy Foundation gives generously to NARAL, Catholics for Free Choice, and other groups that lobby to keep abortion-on-demand.

A serious communication problem has developed around our arguments concerning pregnancy from incest or rape. I do not believe abortion is morally justified in such cases, but some prolife arguments I have heard have been inaccurate and so downright insensitive to rape and incest victims that it has made me angry. Yes, it is true that pregnancy resulting from rape is relatively rare, particularly when the victim seeks immediate treatment—which the majority do not. But pregnancy does happen and when it happens it is terribly traumatic for all concerned. Let us not forget that *Roe v. Wade* stemmed from a woman who had become pregnant as the result of gang rape. [This has since been proven false: "Jane Roe" has admitted she constructed the story of the rape to increase her chances of obtaining help. —Ed.] One otherwise helpful prolife brochure states that pregnancy from incest is very rare, if not impossible. Talk to anyone who has done even limited study in the field of incest and they will tell you that not only is incest a great deal more prevalent than we would all like to think, but pregnancies resulting from it are quite common. Our prolife approach should be to stand against social attitudes that condone sexual abuse of any person and to respond to all victims, pregnant or not, with compassion and support. Let our literature reflect this.

Above all, we must realize that when men serve as our spokespersons for the prolife movement, this adds further conviction to the feminist belief that opposition to abortion is a male plot to keep women in a subservient role. It is important that women lead the prolife movement not only to contradict the feminist assumption, but because, legal or illegal, the abortion decision will forever ultimately rest in the hands of women.

Prolifers Too Exclusive
by Jane Thomas-Bailey

I am a faithful participant in our local March for Life each January 22. I feel it's the least I can do to walk a half-mile and listen to a few speeches so that I can be added to the body count that will appear in the next day's newspaper. But I often feel that the people who run the show aren't talking to me. What's worse, they're not talking to a lot of people like me who haven't decided yet what to believe about abortion. Mostly they're talking to themselves.

First of all, they sing a lot of songs about God—and a very Christian God at that. I am not putting them down for being religious. Nor am I saying that faith should be confined to sanctuaries. But I think a lot of people turn off their message as fast as they turn off the TV evangelists who flicker by on the TV dial. Many people do not like to have religion blared at them through loudspeakers in public squares.

The subliminal message from the songs, and from many of the speakers, is that you have to share these religious beliefs before you can become prolife. The Jew, the agnostic, the liberal Protestant, the Unitarian, walk quickly by thinking, "This cause is obviously not for me."

Worst of all, the religious language only reinforces the belief that abortion is "a religious issue," irrevocably linked to school prayer and creches on the courthouse steps. This plays right into the arguments of pro-abortionists who argue that prolifers are religious zealots who are trying to force their arcane beliefs about ensoulment down other people's throats. The prolife cause can be argued brilliantly on scientific and humanitarian grounds that appeal to people of many beliefs, including Christians. If we want to get a broad coalition of people on the side of the unborn, we must base our public arguments on those grounds.

I also feel excluded from much prolife rhetoric because I am a political liberal. I have heard speakers urge me to vote for "godly, conservative candidates." Since when did that become the criteria of the prolife movement? Jimmy Carter was a godly man but, alas, not prolife. Barry Goldwater is unquestionably conservative, but not prolife. You can tell people to vote prolife without invoking either the church or the Republican party. I wonder how many potential prolifers have been turned away because of this ideological confusion?

I have also felt excluded because I am a woman who must work outside my home. Too many of the voices in prolife leadership are male, and I wonder, as they speak, how many of them have ever had to choose between a baby and a promotion? I, and many of my colleagues, have. I chose to delay conception; other women have chosen abortion. Yet I have heard prolife speakers frown on the first and castigate the second as if women were utterly selfish for seeking a bigger paycheck. All too often they are merely trying to keep the rent paid and food on the table. Of course it is wrong to kill an unborn baby in such a situation, but it is also wrong for the prolife movement to ignore the problems that employed women face. If these problems were addressed constructively from the public soapbox, more professional women would pause to listen to our message.

In an odd way, however, men have been excluded from the prolife message, too. I have seen a lot of teenage girls bravely tell of the baby they had, or the abortion they had. I applaud them for their courage in speaking out. I have never seen a boy (or a man) stand up in public to tell of the remorse he feels for impregnating several young women and then for denying responsibility for the babies. That message needs to be heard as much as the message of the woman who had an abortion. Those boys and men are among us, but for some reason we have put only the girls and women on the spot.

The prolife movement needs to address male responsibility for abortion. That must include the personal responsibility of men who don't want children, but impregnate women, and the corporate responsibility of a male-dominated economy that makes few allowances for babies. Then more women, and more men, will begin to take us seriously. But too often these critical issues are on a collision course with the conservative political and religious agendas that I wrote of above. Until all of these ideologies can be sorted out, my fear is that the prolife movement will remain a minority coalition of religious conservatives.

Daphne Clair de Jong

D aphne de Jong authored the following influential articles in 1978 outlining some of the strongest feminist prolife arguments we have come across. These two articles, originally printed in the *New Zealand Listener*, capture the essence of what has become the central tenet of feminist prolife philosophy—that abortion is a symptom of woman's continued subjugation and devaluation by hegemonic culture.

In her first article, de Jong traces the European philosophical tradition that has been used to justify discrimination against women and how that tradition has been appropriated by abortion rights advocates in their arguments against the personhood of the fetus. In the sequel to that article, de Jong argues that if women must be "un-pregnant" at will to gain equality, then they will have attained equality only inasmuch as they are able to overcome their own biology. This point is critical today in the light of arguments by feminists who criticize *Roe v. Wade* on the grounds that abortion rights should be premised not on privacy, but on the basis of equal rights. While we agree that the privacy argument is specious and perpetuates the male idea of the supremacy of individual rights over community responsibility, feminist prolifers also reject the notion that abortion-on-demand is necessary for women to gain equal rights. Under such a construct, women must essentially be able to be wombless, like men, to compete in society. While this may be a practical truth in our society, it should be vigorously challenged rather than endorsed by anyone who considers herself a feminist. In setting up the male as the standard against which one must be measured for equality, we perpetuate phallocentric thinking and values, and we declare the childbearing woman less than equal. We reinforce our status as the "second-sex"—the other that is defined by the male—and devalue our reproductive power.

Ms. de Jong is a full-time writer who has won several literary awards, including a New Zealand PEN award for nonfiction. She continues her work in New Zealand where she lives with her husband and five children, including a Hong Kong orphan adopted at eight years, now an adult.

Feminism and Abortion: The Great Inconsistency
by Daphne Clair de Jong

In the same way that many opponents of slavery and racism have failed to apply their principles to the question of women's rights, so feminist writers have a peculiarly dense blind spot about the unborn. No argument in favour of freely available abortion is tenable in the light of feminist ideals and principles. And all of them bear an alarming resemblance to the arguments used by men to justify discrimination against women.

Principally, the arguments are that the fetus is not human, or is human only in some rudimentary way; that it is a part of its mother and has no rights of its own; that a woman's right to control her body supersedes any rights of the fetus; that those who believe the fetus is a human being with human rights should not impose their beliefs on others through the medium of the law.

Biologically, the fetus is not only human, but an individual human by virtue of its unique genetic inheritance. Six weeks from conception it looks like a very small baby, with a functioning heart, brain and nervous system. The appearance and behavior of very early fetal infants show definite individual patterns. After implantation of the fertilized ovum (and many would say from the first fusion of the parent cells), scientists are unable to pinpoint any stage at which something "sub-human" becomes a human being.

Regardless of arbitrary legal definitions, the concept of a definitive moment when humanity becomes present is simply the ancient religious theory of "ensoulment" rephrased in pseudo-philosophical jargon. Medieval theologians who postulated "ensoulment" at 40 days for boys and 80 days for girls, had only recently decided after much debate that women had souls at all. Even in the nineteenth century, philosopher Otto Weininger wrote: "In such a being as the absolute female there are no logical and ethical phenomena, and therefore the ground for the assumption of a soul is absent ... Women have no existence and no essence; they are not; they are nothing." Weininger described Jews in similar terms. Eva Figes, author of *Patriarchal Attitudes*, comments on those views: "It soon becomes possible to deny such inferiors basic human rights. The implication is that these inferiors are not human at all." Women were not, of course, "nothing" because Weininger believed them to be so; neither is the fetus just a collection of matter because others do not accept its humanity. It is only the latest in a long line of human beings who throughout history have been denied human status because of their "different" appearance. They include blacks, Jews, dwarfs, the handicapped—and women.

Feminist writers clearly see the link between feminism and racism. "It should," Figes says, "teach us a valuable lesson about the dangers of attempting to categorize people on the basis of physique—whether it is a matter of sex or skin color." Perhaps it should also teach us something about categorizing people on the basis of immaturity. Especially since alleged immaturity or "childishness" has been the excuse for sexual discrimination, too. Idealist philosopher Schopenhauer found women "in every respect backward, lacking in reason or true morality ... a kind of middle step between the child and the man, who is the true human being." The unborn, particularly in the embryonic stage, bears little resemblance to the "norm" of adult white male. Feminists ought to be sensitive about arguing the nonhumanity of the fetus on the grounds of its physical appearance or size, or ability to function independently. Jessica Staff, visiting New Zealand to preach abortion on demand, contemptuously characterized the two-months fetus as "a thing the size of a cashew nut." She might have been wise to remember that size has always been a factor in the supposed superiority of the male. Not to mention all those careful measurements of male and female brains. Even now misogynist writers deny women the potential for genius because of "smaller brain capacity." (Fetal brains have similar configuration to adult brains, and EEG tracings have been made at less than six weeks gestation.)

Until this century, the laws of both Britain and America made women a "part of" their husbands. "By marriage, the husband and wife are one person in law ... our law in general considers man and wife one person" (*Blackstone's Commentaries*, 1768). The one person was, of course, the husband, who exerted absolute power over his wife and her property. She had no existence and therefore no protection under the law. The only thing a husband could not do was kill her. The earliest feminist battles were fought against this legal chattel status of women. Many feminists were among those who overturned the U.S. Supreme Court decision of 1857 that considered the black slave "property" and not entitled to the protection of the constitution. Feminism totally rejected the concept of ownership in regard to human beings. Yet when the U. S. Supreme Court ruled in 1973 that the fetus was the property of its mother, and not entitled to the protection of the constitution, "liberated" women danced in the streets.

A fetus, while dependent on its mother, is no more a part of its mother than she is a part of her husband. Biology is constant; not subject to the vagaries of law. The fetus lives its own life, develops according to its own genetic program, sleeps, wakes, moves, according to its own inclinations. The RH negative syndrome which occurs when fetal and maternal blood are incompatible, is one proof of its separate life. That a woman or a doctor does not perceive a fetus or embryo as human is not sufficient reason to put abortion outside the context of morality and law. Most people find babies more attractive than embryos, as most of us prefer kittens to cats, and as Hitler found Aryans more attractive than Jews. But *to define humanity on the basis of one's emotional response is to rationalize prejudice.* To allow any person or group to define that certain human beings are to be regarded as less than fully human is to construct a basis for discrimination and eventual destruction. "Liberated" women who object to being "sex objects" may not care to examine too closely their conviction that embryos and fetuses are expendable objects which become less so as they become more visually attractive.

There have always been "lawful" exceptions to the universal ban on taking human life: notably self-defense and abortion to save the woman's life. The mainstream feminist movement rejects most other exceptions, such as warfare and judicial retribution. Feminism opposes the violent power games of the male establishment, the savage "solutions" imposed by the strong on the powerless.

The feminist claim to equality is based on the equal rights of all human beings. The most fundamental of all is the right to life. If women are to justify taking this right from the unborn, they must contend that their own superiority of size, of power, or of physique or intellect or need, or their own value as a person, transcends any right of the unborn. In the long history of male chauvinism, all these have been seen as good reasons for withholding human rights from women.

The temptation to dominate is the most truly universal, the most irresistible one there is; to surrender the child to its mother, the wife to her husband, is to promote tyranny in the world (Simone de Beauvoir, *The Second Sex*).

To claim that the unique interdependence of the fetus and its mother is sufficient to give her absolute rights over its life, is to claim a right which society in general, and feminists in particular, do not concede to anyone else—the arbitrary right to terminate a human life. Women who will not accept that a woman's value be measured by how far some man wants her body or needs her services, now demand that the unborn be judged by the same standard—to be allowed to live or die on one criterion, its sentimental value to its mother.

A "woman's right to choose" (though more an incantation than an argument) implies that abortion is a matter of private morality. Perhaps because pregnancy is the result of a sexual act, the abortion question is frequently presented as a part of the same moral category as contraception and homosexuality. But questions of human life are always matters of public morality; in the category of war, capital punishment and murder, include abortion. Since Nuremburg, the world has accepted that those who perceive the humanity of groups defined as "sub-human" have not only a right but a duty to protect their human rights. Those who are unconvinced by medical and biological science have a right to try to persuade others to their view. But they must recognize the obligation of those who believe in the human-ness of the fetus, to oppose them. Not to do so would be "truly irresponsible. To abdicate one's own moral understanding, to tolerate crimes against humanity. ..." (Germaine Greer, *The Female Eunuch*). (Greer was writing in general terms. Like other feminist writers, notably de Beauvoir, who was enraged at the callousness of lovers and society toward pregnant women, she fails to see the radical injustice of inflicting abortion on them as a "solution" to their problem.)

How many feminists would defend the right of a man who sincerely believed in the inferiority of women to beat, rape and terrorize "his" woman? Should the law allow him his right to choose who is to be regarded as fully human?

The Feminist Sell-Out
by Daphne Clair de Jong

The women's movement suffers from three classic defense mechanisms associated with minority group status: self-rejection, identification with the dominant group, and displacement.

The demand for abortion at will is a symptom of group self-hatred and total rejection, not of sex role but of sex identity.

The womb is not the be-all and end-all of women's existence. But it is the physical centre of her sexual identity, which is an important aspect of her self-image and personality. To reject its function, or to regard it as a handicap, a danger or a nuisance, is to reject a vital part of her own personhood. Every woman need not be a mother, but unless every women can identify with the potential motherhood of all women, no equality is possible. African-Americans gained nothing by straightening their kinky hair and aping the white middle class. Equality began to become a reality only when they insisted on acceptance of their different qualities—"Black is Beautiful."

Women will gain their rights only when they demand recognition of the fact that they are people who become pregnant and give birth—and not always at infallibly convenient times—and that pregnant people have the same rights as others. To say that in order to be equal with men it must be possible for a pregnant woman to become un-pregnant at will is to say that being a woman precludes her from being a fully functioning person. It concedes the point to those who claim that women who want equality really want to be imitation men.

If women must submit to abortion to preserve their lifestyle or career, their economic or social status, they are pandering to a system devised and run by men for male convenience. The politics of sexism are perpetuated by accommodating to expediential societal structures which decree that pregnancy is incompatible with other activities, and that children are the sole responsibility of their mother. The demand for abortion is a sell-out to male values and a capitulation to male life-styles rather than a radical attempt to renegotiate the terms by which women and men can live in the world as people with equal rights and equal opportunities. Black "Uncle Toms" have their counterparts not only in women who cling to the chains of their kitchen sinks, but also in those who proclaim their own liberation while failing to recognize that they have merely adopted the standards of the oppressor, and fashioned themselves in his image.

Oppressed groups traditionally turn their frustrated vengeance on those even weaker than themselves. The unborn is the natural scapegoat for the repressed anger and hostility of women, which is denied in traditional male-female relationships, and ridiculed when it manifests itself in feminist protest. Even while proclaiming "her" rights over the fetus, much liberationist rhetoric identifies pregnancy with male chauvinist "ownership." The inference is that by implanting "his" seed, the man establishes some claim over a woman's body (keeping her "barefoot and pregnant"). Abortion is almost consciously seen as "getting back at" the male. The truth may well be that the liberationist sees the fetus not as part of her body but as part of his. What escapes most liberationist writers is that legal abortion is neither a remedy nor an atonement for male exploitation of women. It is merely another way in which women are manipulated and degraded for male convenience and male profit. This becomes blatantly obvious in the private abortion industries of both Britain and America, and the support given to the pro-abortion lobby by such exploitative corporations as the Playboy empire.

Of all the things that are done to women to fit them into a society dominated by men, abortion is the most violent invasion of their physical and psychic integrity. It is a deeper and more destructive assault than rape, the culminating act of womb-envy and woman-hatred by the jealous male who resents the creative power of women. Just as the rapist claims to be "giving women what they want," the abortionist affirms his right to provide a service for which there is a feminine demand. Offered the quick expedient of abortion, instead of community support to allow her to experience pregnancy and birth and parenthood with dignity and without surrendering her rights as a person, woman is again the victim, and again a participant in her own destruction.

The way to equality is not to force women into molds designed for men, but to re-examine our basic assumptions about men and women, about child-care and employment, about families and society and design new and more flexible modes for living. Accepting short term solutions like abortion only delays the implementation of real reforms like decent maternity and paternity leave, job protection, high quality child-care, community responsibility for dependent people of all ages, and recognition of the economic contribution of child-minders. Agitation for the imaginative use of glide time, shared jobs, shorter working weeks, good creches [daycare centers —Ed.], part-time education and job training, is more constructive for women—and men—torn between career and children, than agitation for abortion.

Today's women's movement remains rooted in nineteenth-century thinking, blindly accepting patriarchal systems as though they rested on some immutable natural law: processing women through abortion mills to manufacture instant imitation men who will fit into a society made by and for wombless people. Accepting the "necessity" of abortion is accepting that pregnant women and mothers are unable to function as persons in this society. It indicates a willingness to adjust to the *status quo* which is a betrayal of the feminist cause, a loss of the revolutionary vision of a world fit for people to live in.

The movement has never perceived the essential disharmony of its views on sexual oppression and its aspirations to a new social order, and its attitudes to abortion. The accepted feminist prophets of the new age have never brought to bear on the question the analytical power that they display in other directions. Typically, the subject is dismissed in a paragraph or two, the "right" to abortion assumed, without evidence or argument. (De Beauvoir came closest to recognizing the dangers, raging that women were often coerced into abortions they did not truly want— by men or by the circumstances of the pregnancy.) Within the movement, doctors and other men whose attitudes are glaringly chauvinist have been hailed as white knights of women's rights if they espouse abortion on demand, while "sisters" who oppose it are subjected to witchhunts that could teach a thing or two to a Sprenger or a McCarthy.

The reasons for the abortion issue moving to a central position in liberation ideology are partly tactical. It is much easier to fight a statute than to overcome social attitudes. As the suffragette movement became cohesive and powerful by focusing attention on the single issue of the vote, the new feminist wave gained momentum when all its resources were thrown into overturning abortion laws. But the vote was dismissed by some feminists of the 1960's as "the red herring of the revolution." The abortion issue bids fair to be its successor.

The drive to legalize abortion on demand may be not only a red herring, but a tragic mistake which will perpetuate the politics of power and delay equality of rights for decades or even longer. Human rights are not exclusive. Any claim to a superior or exceptional right inevitably infringes on the rights of someone else. To ignore the rights of others in an effort to assert our own is to compound injustice, rather than reduce it.

Rosemary Bottcher

Rosemary Bottcher is a teacher of chemistry at Tallahassee Community College and an environmental chemist specializing in hazardous waste problems. She was a columnist for the Tallahassee Democrat for six years and has contributed essays to three anthologies on bioethics. She lives on a farm in northern Florida (where the waste is not nearly so hazardous) with her husband, an environmental attorney, and her four children, one of whom is adopted. Ms. Bottcher is currently President of Feminists for Life of America (after having served for ten years as Vice President) and has continued over the past seventeen years to spread the feminist prolife message through her writing and speaking.

"Abortion Threatens Women's Equality" is the text of a statement Ms. Bottcher delivered at the Washington Press Club in a joint press conference with the National Right to Life Committee at the Summer 1985 national NOW convention. Her statement addresses the issue of personhood and how it has historically been denied to both women and unborn children, and she draws on the feminist principle that as long as any human beings' rights are threatened, women's equality is at risk.

Her second article, "Free Choice Can Cost Others," originally published by the *Tallahassee Democrat* on August 8, 1982, discusses the semantics, and the repercussions, of "choice."

Abortion Threatens Women's Equality
by Rosemary Bottcher

NOW does not reflect the views and goals of most American women, and it does not reflect the views and goals of all feminists. Support for abortion is not the *sine qua non* of feminism. The term "prolife feminist" is not an oxymoron; rather, it ought to be a redundancy. Feminists for Life of America was established in 1972 by Pat Goltz and Cathy Callaghan after they were excommunicated from NOW for distributing prolife literature at a NOW meeting. NOW, which harshly criticizes the Catholic Church for not tolerating pluralism on the abortion issue, is itself utterly intolerant of heterodoxy on the same issue.

The Catholic Church reprimands, but does not excommunicate, members who disagree with the church's position on abortion, while NOW will not accept prolife feminists as members and will expunge any established member who is foolhardy enough to express wavering faith in the abortion sacrament. It is NOW's policy not to invite a speaker, on any subject, who does not share the major goals of the organization, including, of course, guarding the abortion icon.

Elise Rose is a member of Feminists for Life who attended the recent NOW convention. She attempted to contribute some comments at a workshop, but when it became apparent that she is not pro-abortion, a vote was taken on the spot—and she was not allowed to speak. Supposedly, one of the advantages of being feminist is that we get to do our own thinking; Jerry Falwell doesn't speak for us and neither does Ellie Smeal. Apparently NOW does not agree, at least on its core issues, and while they cannot control the thoughts of renegade feminists, they will try to ensure that unacceptable thoughts will not be expressed.

So the apparent solidarity of feminist thought on the abortion issue is an illusion maintained by NOW's refusal to even acknowledge that dissent exists. The abortion loyalty oath required by NOW is a major reason for its declining membership. Many women who are fervent supporters of equality for women know that they are not welcome at NOW.

Shunned—banished, really—by their pro-abortion sisters, prolife feminists have had to form their own group in order to provide a forum for their vision of feminism, a return to authentic feminism which realizes that feminism is, properly, merely a part of a larger philosophy that respects all human life. The early feminists of the late nineteenth and early twentieth centuries were opposed to abortion because they realized that abortion, and the perceived need for it, reflected the pervasive oppression of women. They understood that abortion is profoundly anti-woman and anti-feminist.

Abortion remains a number one threat to equality for women. There are four major reasons for this.

Defending abortion requires defending the concept of discrimination. By arguing for abortion, feminists are forced to sabotage the philosophical foundations of feminism. It is sheer hypocrisy to argue for equality for themselves and against equality for the unborn. Because of the recent revelations of fetology that let us see, literally see, the complex and delightful unborn child, pro-abortion feminists have been forced to abandon the tumor theory of pregnancy as an excuse for abortion.

Faced with the irrefutable evidence that the unborn child is indeed a living human being, they are reduced to arguing, "Well, yes, but he is not necessarily a person." The irony is excruciating. Establishing the personhood of women has been the ultimate goal of feminism. Gloria Steinem observes that the first 100 years of the women's movement was spent establishing ourselves as persons; before that we were ownable, like cattle or chairs. Or, I might add, like unborn children. In denying the personhood of the unborn child, feminists have borrowed the very same justifications that the patriarchs have used so successfully throughout history to deny full recognition as persons to women.

Abortion threatens women's equality by the very negative image of women that is projected by pro-abortion rhetoric. It makes no sense to argue that women are rational adults capable of reflection, self-direction and self-control, yet claim that unplanned pregnancies are inevitable and that pregnancy is frequently the result of factors beyond a women's control. How can we believe that the same women who will kill themselves, lose their minds, abuse their children, or commit a crime if denied legal abortions, can be trusted to handle distresses of adult responsibility?

Abortion surrenders women to pregnancy discrimination. Those who advocate legal abortion concede that pregnant women are intolerably handicapped; they cannot compete in a male world of wombless efficiency. Rather than changing the world to accommodate the needs of pregnant women and mothers, proabortion feminists encourage women to fit themselves neatly into a society designed by and for men. A society that tolerates 1.6 million abortions a year is under little pressure to make the changes necessary to address the needs of pregnant women and working parents.

NOW's obsession with abortion detracts from constructive feminist goals such as reformation of the work place, democratizing the family, and improving the quality of childcare. Even though NOW admits that fears about abortion helped kill the ERA, it refuses to support an abortion-neutral version of the amendment, which would have a good chance for passage. For NOW, abortion is more important than equality.

Legal abortion has harmed women as a group and has caused enormous harm to women as individuals. The phenomenal growth of Women Exploited by Abortion (WEBA) proves that for many women, abortion has been a wrenching experience. None of the wrenching stories of how illegal abortion can destroy women can match the pathos of WEBA members' accounts of how legal abortion can destroy women. Yet NOW feminists refuse to acknowledge the pain of these women, dismissing them contemptuously as "the guilt-trippers." NOW has not yet realized that any abortion, legal or illegal, harms women and contributes to the oppression of women.

Free Choice Can Cost Others
by Rosemary Bottcher

One of the many innocent bystanders being wounded by the abortion brouhaha is our already beleaguered language. Not since the time of Humpty Dumpty have words been so emancipated from their definitions, so free to mean anything the fancy of their utterer wants them to mean.

A particularly annoying example of this is the corruption of the proper meaning of the concept of "choice." Pro-abortion activists like to call themselves "pro-choice" and prefer to refer to their opponents as "anti-choice." By this cleverly dishonest tactic, they simultaneously divert attention from the real issue, portray themselves as defenders of personal liberty and misrepresent the motives of those who disagree. They also make some amazing assumptions about the moral significance of choices.

The Religious Coalition for Abortion Rights has declared, "Abortion is an individual decision. And therefore your God-given right." Yes, indeed, the modern religious thinking of the theologians of the coalition has concluded that the ability to decide to commit an act is equivalent to the right (God-given, no less) to commit that act.

IT IS THE ACT of deciding that is important, valuable and worth defending; the choice itself doesn't matter much. Therefore, those who decide to abort (or murder, plunder and ravage, I suppose) have an absolute right to do just that.

This argument strikes me as a rather bizarre distortion of traditional Judeo-Christian ethics because it ignores one very important point—namely, that the consequences of choices almost always affect people other than the choice-maker. While it is good to be able to make choices, the fact remains that not all choices are equal; some are foolish, some are stupid, and some are evil.

Sometimes one person's choice results in terrible suffering or injustice for another person; for this reason, a civilized society is justified in limiting the choices of its citizens.

Most people realize this when they stop to think about it; nevertheless, the concept of "freedom of choice" has a long history of successfully blackmailing many people into tolerating situations that their instincts tell them are wrong.

People who objected to slavery on moral grounds were told that they did not have to own slaves if doing so would violate their consciences, but that they must respect the rights of those who did not share their opinion.

Integration was kept at bay for years by people who insisted that they had a right to choose how they managed their communities, ran their businesses and lived their lives.

Eventually the fallacy of these arguments becomes apparent, yet the misunderstanding of free choice continues to make mischief. For example, the liberal community, which prides itself on its championship of the weak and powerless, has offered almost no objection to the spreading practice of infanticide.

The American Civil Liberties Union is so devoted to individual freedom that it has courageously defended even the Nazi Party's right to speech, yet it has never, to my knowledge, offered to defend a handicapped infant's right to life. I suspect that this is because justification for infanticide is almost always couched in terms of the parents' "right to choose" the fate of their own child.

The word "choice" has become a magical incantation; breathe it into a liberal ear and the liberal mind becomes hypnotized. The well-meaning eagerness to be tolerant and open-minded disintegrates into moral paralysis.

Aficionados of handguns, nuclear weapons, drunken driving or baby-seal bashing could probably quash liberal opposition to their causes by patiently explaining their positions in terms of "pro-choice."

This all-purpose argument could be trimmed to fit any situation. For example: "Child abuse is an individual decision. And therefore your God-given right," or, "I am personally opposed to rape, but I believe that every man has a right to control his own body," and, perhaps, "The opinion that women are entitled to the same rights as men is not shared by all. A pluralistic society must respect different opinions; therefore each man can decide for himself if he will discriminate against women."

In the minds of many, these contentions are no more preposterous than the analogous apologies for abortion. Obviously, there must be some limits as to what choices a free society can allow; the disagreement is about the proper extent of those limits.

One of the printable things I am called by my not-always-polite opponents is "intolerant." Actually, I am eager to be tolerant if at all possible. I realize that there is always the possibility (however remote) that I could be wrong. Besides, eccentric ideas—and people—help make life interesting.

My own life is such a fracas that I would really rather not be bothered with having to mind anyone else's business, and few subjects bore me more than other people's sex lives. If I had a choice, I would rather putter than picket, but there is a point at which I feel obliged to obey certain moral imperatives. There is a point at which tolerance becomes irresponsible. The rub is in recognizing that point.

Years ago, when I still suffered from acute idealism and spent most of my waking hours fretting over some injustice or other, my mother counseled me about how to decide if a particular situation was worth all the worry. "Will little children die from it?" she asked. "If not, it's not worth working yourself into such a snit."

I still apply that test when deciding whether an issue is snit-worthy, and the answer to her question is what compels me to be especially intolerant and anti-choice on the issues of child abuse, infanticide and abortion.

Frederica Mathewes-Green

*S*isterlife, the original newsletter for Feminists for Life, reached its peak in quality as well as circulation under the editorship of Frederica Mathewes-Green. Mathewes-Green's articulate and sensitive approach to the abortion issue in her role as Vice President for Communications for Feminists for Life also gained FFL a good deal of respect from the national and local media. Originally an abortion rights advocate in the early seventies, Mathewes-Green changed her position when she read an article describing a second-trimester abortion. As a childbirth educator, her respect for the child in the womb has only increased and convinced her of the violence of abortion that harms the mother as well as the child.

Mathewes-Green's writings have appeared in dozens of journals and publications including *Parenting* magazine, *Policy Review, Human Life Review, Christianity Today, Washington Times, Philadelphia Inquirer, Baltimore Sun, San Francisco Examiner* and the *Phoenix Gazette*. Like so many of our early feminist foremothers, her pen has proved a powerful instrument of inspiration and change and records a maternal voice of compassion and reason. Her first article, "The Bitter Price of 'Choice,'" has appeared in several publications and takes a look at the cruel ramifications of "choice" on both the mother and the child. "Designated Unperson" specifically addresses those arguments against the personhood of the fetus and identifies those chilling similarities to historical arguments against the personhood of women. "The Euthanasia/Abortion Connection" addresses the implications of abortion mentality and abortion rights discourse on those already born.

The Bitter Price of "Choice"
by Frederica Mathewes-Green

When I was in college the bumper sticker on my car read "Don't labor under a misconception—legalize abortion." I was one of a handful of feminists on my campus, back in the days when we were jeered at as "bra-burning women's libbers." As we struggled against a hazy sea of sexism, abortion rights was a visible banner, a concrete, measurable goal.

Though our other foes were elusive, within the fragile boundary of our skin, at least, we would be sovereign. What could be more personal than our reproductive lives? How could any woman oppose it?

I oppose it now. It has been a slow process, my path from a pro-choice to a prolife position, and I know that unintended pregnancy raises devastating problems. But I can no longer avoid the realization that legalizing abortion was the wrong solution; we have let in a Trojan Horse whose hidden betrayal we've just begun to see.

A woman with an unplanned pregnancy faces more than "inconvenience"; many adversities, financial and social, at school, at work, and at home confront her. Our mistake was in looking at these problems and deciding that the fault lay with the woman, that she should be the one to change. We focused on her swelling belly, not the discrimination that had made her so desperate. We advised her, "Go have this operation and you'll fit right in."

What a choice we made for her. She climbs onto a clinic table and endures a violation deeper than rape—the nurse's hand is wet with her tears—then is grateful to pay for it, grateful to be adapted to the social machine that rejected her when pregnant. And the machine grinds on, rejecting her pregnant sisters.

It is a cruel joke to call this a woman's "choice." We may choose to sacrifice our life and career plans, or choose to undergo humiliating invasive surgery and sacrifice our offspring. How fortunate we are—we have a choice! Perhaps it's time to amend the slogan—"Abortion: a woman's right to capitulate."

If we refused to choose, if we insisted on keeping both our lives and our bodies intact, what changes would our communities have to make? What would make abortion unnecessary? Flexible school situations, fairness in hiring, more flex-time, part-time, and home-commute jobs, better access to prenatal and obstetric care, attractive adoption opportunities, a whole garden of safe family planning choices, support in learning how to handle our sex lives responsibly, and help with child care and parenting when we choose to keep our babies: this is a partial list. Yet these changes will never come as long as we're lying down on abortion tables 1,600,000 times a year to ensure the status quo. We've adapted to this surgical substitute, to the point that Justice Blackmun could write in his Webster dissent, "Millions of women have ordered their lives around [abortion]." That we have willingly ordered our lives around a denigrating surgical procedure—accepted it as the price we must pay to keep our life plans intact—is an ominous sign.

For over a hundred years feminists have warned us that abortion is a form of oppression and violence against women and their children. They called it "child-murder" (Susan B. Anthony), "degrading to women" (Elizabeth Cady Stanton), "most barbaric" (Margaret Sanger), and a "disowning [of] feminine values" (Simone de Beauvoir). How have we lost this wisdom?

Abortion has become the accepted way of dealing with unplanned pregnancies, and women who make another choice are viewed as odd, backward, and selfish. Across the nation three thousand crisis pregnancy centers struggle, unfunded and unrecognized, to help these women with housing, clothing, medical care, and job training, before and after pregnancy. These volunteers must battle the assumption that "they're *supposed* to abort"—especially poor women who hear often enough how much we resent our tax dollars going to feed their children. Prochoice rhetoric conjures a dreadful day when women could be forced to have abortions; that day is nearly here.

More insidiously, abortion advocacy has been poisonous to some of the deeper values of feminism. For example, the need to discredit the fetus has led to the use of terms that would be disastrous if applied to women. "It's so small," "It's unwanted," "It might be disabled," "It might be abused." Too often women are small, unwanted, disabled, or abused. Do we really want to say that these factors erase personhood?

A parallel disparaging of pregnancy itself also has an unhealthy ring. Harping on the discomforts of pregnancy treats women as weak, incompetent; yet we are uniquely equipped for this role, and strong enough to do much harder things than this. Every woman need not bear a child, but every woman should feel proud kinship in the earthy, elemental beauty of birth. To hold it in contempt is to reject our distinctive power, "our bodies, ourselves."

There is a last and still more terrible cost to abortion, one that we have not yet faced. We have treated the loss of our fetuses as a theoretical loss, a sad-but-necessary loss, as of civilians in wartime. We have not yet realized that the offspring lost are not the enemy's, nor our neighbor's, but our own. And it is not a loss of inert, amorphous tissue, but of a growing being unique in history. There are no generic zygotes. The one-cell fertilized ovum is a new individual, the present form of a tall blue-eyed girl, for example, with Grandad's red hair and Great-aunt Ida's singing voice. Look at any family, see how the traits and characteristics run down the generations in a stream. Did we really think our own children would be different?

Like the gypsy in Verdi's opera, *Il Trovatore*, our frustration has driven us to desperate acts. Outraged by the Count's cruel injustice, she stole his infant son and, in a crazed act of vengeance, flung him into the fire. Or so she thought. For, in turning around, she discovered the Count's son lay safe on the ground behind her; it was her own son she had thrown into the flames. In our desperate bid for justice we have not yet realized whom we have thrown into the flames; the moment of realization will be as devastating for us as it was for her.

Until that time, legal abortion invites us to go on doing it, 4500 times a day. And, with ruthless efficiency, the machine grinds on.

Designated Unperson
by Frederica Mathewes-Green

The discipline of ethics draws participants from a wide variety of fields, and never more so than when the most basic ethical question is under discussion: what is human personhood, and when does it deserve protection? When is it permissible to kill another human being? If other ethical questions can seem arcane, this one touches common lives and inspires public debate of a deservedly vehement sort. This ancient riddle is being reviewed on many lively fronts today, as public debate targets or defends our wartime enemies, the vicious criminal, those struggling with hopeless disease. Yet the fiercest debate circles around one who is neither an enemy, nor evil, nor ill. The debate concerns our own unborn offspring.

It is certainly a sign of life-out-of-balance that such a debate should arise at all. In a healthy society, new life is welcomed and women's awesome powers of fertility are respected and accommodated. Yet in our nation over a million and a half women each year find that the continuing of a pregnancy would exact such a grievous price that abortion seems comparatively easier to bear. With alternatives so forbidding, abortion must be right; yet how can it be right if it takes the life of one's own child?

It then becomes necessary to demonstrate that the unborn is not a person. It must not be my child that dies in abortion; it must be something else, something less, not really one of us at all. Although one of the greatest lessons of our age is the value of every human life, regardless of race, age, gender, or any other determinant, a grieving sense of necessity drives abortion defenders to insist that their own offspring are not quite human. Thus the depersonalization of the unborn begins.

The unborn is not a person because she is so small. The charge that "every good argument for abortion is a good argument for infanticide" finds confirmation here. Size remains relative throughout human life. The six-week fetus is very small compared to a newborn, but one could just as justly compare the newborn's size with that of Hulk Hogan. The argument from size is a version of one of human society's most durable, least honorable assertions: might makes right. Big people can throw away small people. As most women are smaller than most men, it is a doubtful assertion for us to champion. Too many of us know in our own bodies what violence at stronger hands is like.

The unborn is not a person because he is unwanted. We speak here women's disabling fear: I'm nothing without a man. If no one wants me, I don't exist. If worth depends on someone else's approval, then we may in turn eliminate our own children who do not please us. Worth based on wantedness, that chimerical achievement, is ominous for children, blacks, women, the disabled, and other living things.

The unborn is not a person because she does not have human form. This is in fact untrue; that "glob of tissue" finds order quickly, and every baby aborted has a face, hands, eyes, gender, and a beating heart. But even if a method were available that could strike during that rush to recognizable form, it would be an ominous precedent to embrace. Discrimination against living human beings because they "look funny" has a long and ignoble history. The truth is that even the earliest embryo has a human form, though it may be an unfamiliar one. We are all "globs of tissue" in changing form from conception until death.

The unborn is not a person because he would be disabled. Our disabled friends may well feel a chill; if we'd only caught them before they were born we would have "spared them" their unhappy, unsightly lives. Killing in the name of compassion has had a tenacious appeal for this ruthless and sentimental age. We stand with Scrooge, with the strong and healthy, and locate the "surplus population" in the weak and sick. It is worthwhile to recall that we are each only temporarily able-bodied, each potential candidates for lovingly-administered death.

The unborn is not a person because she could be abused. Prenatal dismemberment is indeed an effective preventative for postnatal abuse, though the net result to the child may not be what she would have preferred. Implicit here is the assumption that the lives of the abused, like the lives of the disabled, are not worth living; that the rape survivor, the battered spouse, should never have been born. When this future abuse is only theoretical, as in the case of an unborn child, we make a devastating affirmation of the abuser's power, and undermine the hope of those who believe the past can be overcome. The hope that abortion would prevent child abuse has been cruelly mocked by statistics which indicate that, though every child in America could have been aborted during the past eighteen years of legality, reported child abuse has in that time increased 500%. The notion of the disposable child persists even after birth.

The unborn is not a person because he is not sentient. Consciousness, self-awareness, is a trait which gradually emerges and then fades during the course of a normal human life, and is by no means fully present in a newborn; the average house cat is capable of more intelligent interaction than a month-old child. Some would choose six months fetal age as the point that the potential for this future awareness is present; however, potential is a slippery concept, as all the potential abilities of a lifetime are present at the moment of fertilization. To attach increasing value to those of increasing awareness is no doubt flattering to the intelligentsia who developed the standard, but a bit worrisome for the rest of us—especially for our mentally disabled friends, who may grow up to star in their own TV shows for all we know. The unborn child is only temporarily lacking in awareness, in consciousness, and daily moving toward its completion. To rush to kill him before he achieves it is as repulsive as rushing to kill a recovering coma victim before she can open her eyes.

The unborn is not a person because she lives inside her mother's body. The unborn is not a part of her mother's body, any more than an astronaut is part of the space ship. The fact that neither is viable without necessary access to oxygen, food, and shelter does not prove that they are not persons. Both the fetus and the astronaut are tenants, though in the case of the unborn it cannot be denied that she can be an uncomfortable and demanding one. Does this give the mother the right to evict her unwanted tenant? The situation may be like that of a sea captain who discovers a stowaway and considers whether to throw him overboard. The missing factor in the analogy is that the unborn did not take up residence in his mother's body under his own will, but was called into being (in virtually all cases) by a consciously-chosen act that the participants were aware could result in pregnancy. For both parents, undertaking to have sexual relations must be accompanied by a responsible recognition that (even with careful contraception) a child may result. That this result disproportionately taxes the woman, that the man can walk out, abandoning his responsibility to her and his child, does not prove that it is right for the woman to do the same. Choices that lead to greater responsibility, greater accountability, are choices that lead to a stronger society for women and their children, and men as well. Choices that feed the cycle of heedless abandonment hurt us all.

This century has already taught us, in too many bloody lessons, that it is a dangerous thing to designate any human life "unperson." Devaluing, rationalizing, renaming, discarding seem to spread outward in concentric rings of expediency. When women so desperately agree to depersonalize their own children, as a condition of full participation in society, a lot more is at risk than those tiny lost lives. Better check your size, your sentience, your wantedness; there's no telling who is next.

The Euthanasia/Abortion Connection
by Frederica Mathewes-Green

On June 4, 1990, Jack Kevorkian attached Alzheimer's patient Janet Adkins to a homemade contraption in his 1968 VW bus, then watched her push the activating button that made her die.

Public reaction was swift and generally negative. Judge Alice Gilbert, in barring Kevorkian from ever again using the device, charged that he "flagrantly violated" all standards of medical practice. She added that through arrogant and self-promoting "bizarre behavior," Kevorkian revealed that "his real goal is self service rather than patient service." Kevorkian's lawyer, Geoffrey Fieger, responded with an admirable non-sequitur: he claimed that Gilbert is "taking up the standard of fanatical anti-abortionists, people who wish to perpetuate suffering." As far as we know, the Kevorkian machine does not perform abortions.

The appearance of prolife activists in the movement against euthanasia has been confusing to many. Opposing euthanasia does not seem to give opportunity for outlawing contraceptives, frowning on sex, keeping women out of jobs, or forced childbearing, goals assumed to be central to the prolife movement. Yet there is a connection. Both abortion and euthanasia make helpless people die. Dying is not, in itself, the activity that prolifers so strenuously oppose. Death naturally occurs along the entire spectrum of life, from the earliest miscarriages to the centenarian's last breath. The objectionable activity is making people die—people who may be small, weak, or disabled, but are not dying; people who cannot defend or speak for themselves. The objection is to the creation of an ever-widening class of unpersons, persons unwanted or imperfect, and imposing on those persons a duty to die.

Consider the following cases. While Nancy Cruzan was dying, the staff at Missouri Rehabilitation center continued to insist that she was no vegetable. They had seen her smile at funny stories, cry when a visitor left, and indicate pain with her menstrual periods. She was not living on machines: a feeding tube had been inserted years before only to replace spoon feeding and make her care easier. An activist present during those days of dying commented, "It was like one of those horror movies where everybody in the town knows something, but nobody can get word out to the outside world." Information about Nancy's true condition was persistently blacked out, while the staff endured the nightmare of watching her die.

In a horrible déja vû, another disabled woman at the Center has been selected for the same fate. Twenty-year-old Christine Busalacchi's condition is improving: she waves, smiles, objects to having her teeth brushed, vocalizes to indicate TV preferences, and very much enjoys visits from young men. This is not enough for her father, who has visited her seldom in the last two years (and then sometimes accompanied by TV cameras) and, we are told, stands to inherit $51,000 from her estate. Pete Busalacchi does not have the "clear and convincing evidence" necessary to have her starved in Missouri, so he is trying to have her moved to Minnesota where the standard is less stringent. [Christine was eventually starved to death. —Ed.]

Dr. Ronald Cranford, the euthanasia advocate who hopes to help Pete Busalacchi take care of Christine when she is brought to Minnesota, had a similar case in 1979. Sgt. David Mack was shot in the line of duty as a policeman, and Cranford diagnosed him as "definitely … in a persistent vegetative state … never [to] regain cognitive, sapient functioning … never [to] be aware of his condition." Twenty months after the shooting Mack woke up, and eventually regained nearly all his mental ability. When asked by a reporter how he felt, he spelled out on his letter board, "Speechless!"

Similar stories recur. Cancer patient Yolanda Blake was hospitalized last November 30 after experiencing severe bleeding. Despite the insistence of her sister and of the friend who held her power of attorney, the hospital refused to leave in a feeding tube or a catheter, and on December 14, the county judge ruled in the hospital's favor that Blake should be allowed to "die with dignity." On December 15, Blake woke up. When asked if she wanted to live, she responded "Of course I do!"

Richard Routh, 42, was hospitalized with head injuries after a motorcycle accident. He had learned to signal "yes" and "no," could smile and laugh at jokes, when his parents and doctors decided to have him starved. A nurse's aide says that as they stood by the bedside discussing the starvation decision, Routh shook his head "no." Though the coroner's report says he died of head injuries, he had lost thirty pounds during the hospitalization. The autopsy showed that he had not been given painkillers to ease the pain of starvation.

Washington State Senator Ray Moore represents more clearly than most the views of those who believe the disabled should want to die. He is supporting that state's Initiative 119, which would allow a doctor to give a poisonous injection to a terminally ill patient requesting it; he believes that his mother would have benefitted from such a service. He says that many people feel medical professionals profit "indecently" by caring for the dying, and we must grant that patience in the face of natural death can have a detrimental financial effect on the estate. But perhaps Moore is most honest when he says, "there is a growing aggravation with the sights and smells of hospitals and nursing homes."

It has been observed that sick and wounded animals do not commit suicide; when they are "put to sleep," it is to ease the pain of their owners. We may be horrified to contemplate life as a paraplegic, or brain-damaged, or unable to chew our own food. Yet once we are there, who is to say that the bits of life we still hold may not be incomparably sweet? The sound of a loved voice filtering through dim consciousness, the sweet breeze when windows are first opened in the spring, a long afternoon in the sun, may become precious tokens, eagerly held. A generation who once pondered the possibility of "alternate states of consciousness" should be especially sensitive here. Rita Greene has been in an unconscious state for forty years; Claire Norton, the nurse who has cared for her throughout those years, speaks of Rita as "a saint" whose life represents "a tremendous amount of mystery." Who can prove her wrong?

Kevorkian's lawyers misunderstand. Prolifers do not wish to perpetuate suffering. We do not wish to prolong dying. But when people aren't dying—when they are only disabled or recovering or even merely old—we want to offer them loving support till the end. It may not make for a neat, tidy society where everyone is productive and attractive. But it does make for the only kind of humane and just society that we can imagine.

Juli Loesch Wiley

Juli Loesch Wiley is considered by many to be the "Grand Mother" of the consistent life ethic movement, and her peace, justice, and prolife activism, writing, and speaking are well known to others within these movements. As a young woman, she organized boycotts for the United Farm Workers, and after studying at Ohio's Antioch College in 1972, she became a founding member of the PAX Center, a Catholic peace and justice community in Pennsylvania. She took her message of justice and nonviolence to schools and churches, and it was through this peace education work that she came to embrace a prolife position concerning abortion. She tells the story of how she was delivering a speech on the effects of radiation on the fetus when a woman in the audience stood and commented that if she thought radiation was harmful to the child in the womb, she should consider the damage abortion wreaks on the fetus. Wiley had to admit that a prochoice stand on abortion was indefensible—totally inconsistent with a life ethic—and in 1979, she founded Prolifers for Survival, an activist organization opposed to abortion and the arms race. Having supplemented her peace efforts to include an advocacy for the rights of fetal children, she has continued to champion the rights of women and other oppressed groups while working toward a world without violence.

In 1987, Prolifers for Survival disbanded in order to invest its resources in the Seamless Garment Network, a coalition of groups that embrace a consistent life ethic including opposition to abortion, euthanasia, war, poverty, capital punishment and the arms race. Wiley served on the board of Justlife and currently sits on the board of the Seamless Garment Network.

Her first article, "Toward a Holistic Ethic of Life," is Part Two of a series published in *Harmony* magazine, Nov/Dec 1987, entitled "Social Feminism: Change the System," in which she articulates her vision of the consistent life ethic philosophy. In her second article, a response to a column written by Ellen Willis in a special 1985 issue of the *Village Voice* devoted to the subject of abortion, she tackles the argument that abortion is necessary for women to live "sexually autonomous" lives.

Toward a Holistic Ethic of Life
by Juli Loesch Wiley

Many of us once looked to feminism as a movement with true change-the-system potential. Disconcertingly, the feminist movement now appears to be composed of a number of strikingly different "teams" all wearing the same jersey. Some feminist factions are actually opponents to each other; others aren't even playing the same game.

For instance: some feminist leaders call the Equal Rights Amendment and abortion the two central goals of the women's movement; on the other hand, Eleanor Roosevelt, credited with having inspired much of the movement, saw abortion as irrelevant to female advancement and opposed the ERA for forty years on the grounds that it would hurt the interests of working women. Some feminists defend the sex-entertainment industry as liberating; Andrea Dworkin of Women Against Pornography denounces it as exploitative. In *The Female Eunuch* (1970), Germaine Greer advocated that women be "deliberately promiscuous" but not have babies; in *Sex and Destiny* (1984), she rejects promiscuity and says the export of contraceptives to the Third World is "evil."

Feminists take such startlingly different stands on economic, sexual and cultural issues that, although there are many different permutations and combinations, it might be said that there are two fundamentally different approaches in the women's movement.

"Assimilationist feminism" insists that men and women be treated identically in law, in the marketplace, and in social relations. Assimilationists oppose special benefits for women as much as they oppose adverse discrimination. Once the differences between women have been eliminated by equal rights legislation plus reproductive freedom (i.e., the freedom not to reproduce), women will achieve power, money, and satisfaction on the same terms as men.

"Social Feminism," on the other hand, holds that it is not primarily legal inequality or normal fertility which traps women in second-class citizenship, but rather the dual burden women carry in the home and in the work force. Social Feminists argue that because women are wives and mothers as well as workers, their mother-status needs extra compensation and support if they are to have equal opportunities in the world beyond the home.

In her brilliant book on women in the work place, *A Lesser Life,* Sylvia Ann Hewlett finds that American feminists' single-minded pursuit of formal equality has trapped millions of women in a very unfavorable situation if they happen to have children.

Pregnant workers are routinely fired. Others are defined as "new-hires" when they come back to work after childbirth, losing accumulated benefits, merit raises, and seniority rights. And large numbers of new mothers, unable to find affordable child care, are forced to take a third or fourth part-time job close to home, or quit the work force altogether.

But most American wage-earning women *have* to work: 75% are either single mothers or are married to low-income men. At some point in their lives, 90% of women have—or want to have—children: the market economy severely penalizes such women *precisely because it treats them like men.*

In every other industrial nation in the world, Social Feminists have pushed successfully for guaranteed job-protection and full or partial income replacement when a woman takes time off to have a baby. Throughout Europe, the *average* maternity leave is five months at full pay. In Sweden, both parents can opt for a six-hour work day until their child is eight years old. In Italy, working women receive two years' credit toward seniority every time they give birth to a child.

But in America, where assimilationists have largely set the feminist agenda, 60% of wage-earning women have no right to any job-protected maternity leave whatsoever. Overall, women lose 20% of their earning power each time they give birth.

The practical effect of assimilationist feminism is to redesign women to fit into a male oriented system. Don't get pregnant—or if you do, don't *stay* pregnant—don't make any demands on the system for child care or flextime or maternity benefits ("preferential treatment"), and you'll be treated just like a man.

The practical effect of Social Feminism, on the other hand, is not to redesign women to fit the work place, but to redesign the work place to fit women.

The same contrast between the Assimilationists and the Social Feminists becomes apparent when they address sexual issues.

For example: a sexual culture which is highly favorable to male-pattern, fast access gratification has contributed to the rapid spread of sexually transmitted diseases and untimely pregnancies, especially among the young.

The Assimilationist approach is to *structurally adapt the women* through gynecological surgery and chemical modification, to conform more easily to the male-pattern system. Thus the goal is short-term damage limitation with notable reliance on the "technical fix": contraception, abortion, and for older-than-teenagers, sterilization.

In contrast, the Social Feminists would see no point in habituating people to sexual patterns which are inherently destructive. They would work instead for behavioral changes in men and women for a more socially constructive, sustainable, and wholesome sexuality. Thus, building self-confidence for adolescent abstinence, resisting date-rape and acquaintance-rape, and promoting fertility awareness are important for Social Feminists. (Interestingly, natural family planning has historically drawn its main support from conservative Catholics and from feminist health advocates.)

Prenatal care, maternity benefits, job-protected parental leave, family allowances, affordable family medical coverage, and more realistic tax deductions for dependents could relieve much of the pressure which tempts even prolife-leaning women to consider abortion. Similarly, strengthening people's ability to resist immature or exploitative sexual encounters would help protect millions from sexually transmitted diseases, callousness, alienation, and abortion. It's exciting to realize that an alliance between traditional prolife and social feminist forces—already begun—could help build a social environment which is much more humane for men and women, and a much safer place for fragile growing children.

Shalom: The Spiritual Ecology

We have considered so far the ordering of society in terms of human good, a society adapted to fit the needs of human beings in all our varied forms, whether we are male or female, pregnant or unpregnant, born or getting ready to be born. However, all these projects—the establishment of rights, peace, and justice within the human race—are not ultimate ends.

Indeed, there exists the awful possibility that "human-right" could be established among us while still ignoring or destroying human dignity in its deepest sense. Such a society could still destroy Creation and mock the Creator. That would make for a well-organized life ending in utter futility, here and hereafter as well.

Who are we? The Contemplatives of Creation. What are we here for? To appreciate it all—every little bit of it—and to praise the one who gave it.

Unless we remember this—who we are, what we're here for, our dignity—then all of our *little justices,* racial and sexual equality, conflict resolution, nonviolent alternatives and the rest, could become components in the making of *one big injustice* toward creation and toward God.

Gender justice can end up simply placing more women in the nuclear chain of command (or its equivalent). While their children in the quality day care centers learn to be materialistic little consumers. While schemes of global economic equality over the next 50 years destroy the water resources needed for the next 5,000 years.

A society ordered *only* in terms of "human rights"—narrowly defined—could still be a society where the inner life is neglected, Creation is degraded, and the Creator is not known. And human hearts, which will not rest until they rest in Him, will play out their restlessness, as they must, in some destructive activism now equally available to men and women alike!

Christ said we must all "become like little children." Maybe he meant we must all become like the unborn. They neither sow nor reap; they are neither producers nor consumers; they don't vote; they aren't even a "constituency"! What good are they?

What Do They Do?

Judging from the findings of modern perinatology: they listen, they savor, they sense. Judging from Psalm 139: they appreciate. They praise.

I think they may be contemplatives.

So the fate of the unborn is the fate of the earth. If we honor our brother the embryo, our sister the fetus, we honor the human being who *just is.*

To love them, is to learn to love the water, the air, the planet—all that is good because it *just is.* But if we devastate them, we have already become the kind of people who could devastate the world.

"Choose life, that you and your children may live"—this is the radical vision of what it means to be prolife.

The Myth of Sexual Autonomy

by Juli Loesch

Late last year the *Village Voice*, a weekly paper serving New York's Greenwich Village, long a mouthpiece for the cultural avant-garde, devoted an entire issue to the question, "Abortion: Where Are We Now?"

The editors were all agog about something they evidently find quite disturbing: the emergence of *left-wing* anti-abortionists who are now challenging the "prochoice" status quo with particular effectiveness.

Most interesting to me was Ellen Willis' pro-abortion piece, which was notable for what it conceded:

That the left and the media tend to be won over by the "seamless garment" approach, which includes opposition to abortion in the context of opposition to other kinds of sanctioned killing.

That prolife feminists have grasped some "essential feminist truths" which make their arguments against abortion more compelling.

Clearly, for Willis, this is no time to engage in peripheral arguments. With the game beginning to go against her, she folds the rest of her hand and slaps her highest card on the table: *sexual autonomy.*

No matter what else happens, says Willis, and no matter what "utopian" changes may come, there will always be the vagaries of sexual passion and the failures of contraception. Thus, come what may, abortion will always be "necessary" if we are to be free to live "sexually autonomous" lives.

Then she hurls the following challenge: "I have yet to hear any right-to-lifers take full responsibility for that fact or deal seriously with its political implications."

On the contrary. I think that it's the advocates of sexual autonomy who have failed to recognize its political implications.

The opposite of sexual autonomy, or independence, is sexual bondedness, or interdependence. What the autonomous wish to enjoy is precisely unbondedness; and one of the bonds to be rejected is a bond to offspring who were conceived without deliberate choice.

To the defenders of such autonomy I would like to post these questions: Is there such a thing as parental obligation? If so, when and how, and for whom, does this obligation arise?

In the past, people assumed that simply by engaging in hetero-sexual relations with each other they acquired parental obligations if and when pregnancy resulted. But now says Willis, this is to be seen as a denial of sexual autonomy. Obligations now arise, not from the decision to have sex, but from the strictly separate decision to bear the child.

But please note: The decision to have sex is a decision made by both partners. The decision to bear the child is made by *only one of them:* namely, the woman.

Thus, the woman's responsibility corresponds to her choice, made at some point during the pregnancy. If she doesn't want to assume any obligation, she can choose abortion and any question of parental responsibility is foreclosed.

But for the man, parental obligation supposedly arises from the woman's choices: her choice to bear the baby, and her choice to name him as the father and even to bring legal action to compel his support, if it comes to that.

The problem here is obvious. You can expect increasingly to hear the sexually autonomous male's just complaint: "How is it that she gets a choice, but I don't? She chose to be a mother. I didn't choose to be a father. I just chose to have sex!"

There will always be men who, at any given moment, want sex but don't want a child; some of these men will get women pregnant. But sexual intercourse now implies for each of them—exactly nothing, no responsibility. It's only the woman's subsequent and separate option that determines everything. That being the case, why should any man feel he's acquired an obligation if the woman decides to give birth? Because he deposited sperm in the woman's vagina? Don't be medieval.

Am I predicting that the elevation of sexual autonomy to the status of a "right," coupled with the availability of abortion, will cut men loose entirely? That paternal responsibility will sink to zero? That men are not only going to take off, but feel justified about it?

Hell, no. I'm not predicting that. I'm *reporting* it. I've done my share of women's shelter work in the last ten years. I see it all the time. A couple has a child. Three years down the line he decides he isn't cut out to be a father.

"But you can't just walk out. This is your child too!"

"Sure, sure. But it was *your choice.*"

Well, the gentleman is right, given that the availability of abortion has made procreation a unilateral female decision.

Most male commitment to the long-term responsibility of child rearing is not obtained through court order. It is obtained voluntarily through a man's sense, bolstered by society, that it's right and fair. Why? Because the choice that obliges both him and the woman is the choice they made together, in the act that made the child.

The vast majority of women and children in this world rely upon webs of interrelation predicated upon a sexually connected man: a man whose sexuality makes him the husband of *this* woman, the father of *this* child. It's sex which binds him, obliges him to another gender and another generation.

If the act of generation loses this weight, this significance—and the abortion culture simply blows it away—then you end up with fathering that never makes a father, mating that never makes a mate, short-circuited sex that dreams of nothing more than being plugged into its own sockets.

Autonomy—in this sense—is as pro-woman as poverty and as pro-sex as an amputation. And abortion—the dismembered offspring—is not only its program, but its most perfect and fitting image.

Fannie Lou Townsend Hamer
(1917–1977)

Fannie Lou Townsend Hamer was one of those contemporary prolife feminists who developed her beliefs through personal experience—in her case the experience of poverty and racism. She was one of twenty children from a sharecropper family in rural Mississippi. Hamer grew up in a distinctively African-American strain of Christianity that celebrated a loving, nurturing, liberating God. Her spirituality provided her the strength to endure and challenge the discrimination she encountered at every turn.

One of the most egregious acts of oppression against her was her involuntary sterilization by a white doctor. Although she and her husband had two adopted daughters (one the child of a single mother and the other handicapped by severe burns), they had still wished to conceive. Like other victims of sterilization abuse or coerced abortion, she was absolutely outraged, yet felt helpless to challenge this violation of her body and her human and civil rights. But not for long. Recognizing that the personal is, indeed, political, she devoted herself to the growing civil rights movement and worked with the voting rights campaign in Mississippi. Her efforts came at tremendous personal risk: she was fired from her job, arrested and severely beaten, and her home was shot at and firebombed. Undaunted, she became secretary for the Student Nonviolent Coordinating Committee and a moving force behind the Mississippi Freedom Democratic Party. At the 1964 presidential convention, Fannie Lou Hamer and the MFDP challenged the timid leadership of the national Democratic Party to embrace African-American participation. Under MFDP auspices, she was one of the first Southern blacks to run for Congress since Reconstruction.

Recognizing the links between racism and other forms of violence, Fannie Lou Hamer campaigned against the Vietnam War. She fought for government programs to improve health care, nutrition, and education for poor Americans of all races, especially children, and she was instrumental in bringing one of her favorite programs, Head Start, to her own community. She spoke out on behalf of single mothers facing personal, political and economic oppression and discrimination, knowing well the difficulties these women faced. Her own daughter, Dorothy Jean, had a child out of wedlock. (Dorothy Jean later died of a medical emergency that local doctors refused to treat—not an uncommon cause of death for rural Southern blacks—and the Hamers adopted her child.)

Hamer acted upon her concern for women's equality and gender justice nationally as well as locally. Fannie Lou Hamer was a co-founder of the National Women's Political Caucus and she supported the presidential candidacy (the first by a black woman) of her friend, U.S. Representative Shirley Chisholm. She worked alongside other women's liberation leaders such as Bella Abzug and Gloria Steinem, gaining their respect and admiration; yet she always maintained an independent spirit and had her points of difference with organized feminism. She could not accept its disregard of racial oppression or its casting of men as "the Enemy," insisting that "we are here to work side by side with [black men] in trying to bring liberation to all people."[10]

Hamer especially questioned a feminism which lethally pitted women against their unborn children. She criticized what she perceived to be the imposition of abortion upon black women by white do-gooders: "If they'd been talking that way when my mother was bearing children, I wouldn't be here now." She argued that if society would only give poor black children a chance, "they might grow up to be Fannie Lou Hamer or something else."[11] As a delegate to the 1969 White House Conference on Food, Nutrition, and Health, she insisted that abortion (whether accomplished through surgery or so-called "contraceptives" which actually work after conception has occurred) was not a humane solution to crisis pregnancy. Rather mothers and children needed more compassionate help from their communities.[12]

Fannie Lou Hamer's public career began and ended in advocacy of what prolife feminists now call "real reproductive rights." In 1973, she retired from public activism because of serious health problems that could be traced back in part to her prison beating in the early 1960's. Her biographer, Kay Mills, tells us that in her final years, Fannie Lou Hamer felt abandoned by her former political colleagues, to whom she had given so much.[13] Sadly, the very social justice movements that so benefitted from her efforts have often shut out her holistic vision of human life and well-being. But a growing number of activists seek to remedy this final indignity and "let her light shine."

In "Is It Too Late?" Fannie Lou Hamer defends the sacredness of all human lives, before and after birth. In the 1971 oration reprinted here (from the copy in the Lillian P. Benbow Room of Special Collections, L. Zenobia Coleman Library, Tougaloo College, Tougaloo, Mississippi), she exhorts her fellow citizens to resist all forms of violence and degradation. The second selection represents an excerpt of Hamer's testimony on behalf of the plaintiffs in the 1973 case of *Katie Mae Andrews and Lestine Rogers v. Drew Separate Municipal School District*, a discrimination suit brought by several young black women against the local segregated school district that had denied them employment on the grounds that they had "illegitimate" children (testimony reprinted in 425 U.S. 559, 1976). Taken in the light of Laura Cuppy Smith's experience over 100 years earlier and the loss of reproductive freedom under slavery, it seems like American society has advanced very little in its treatment of young unmarried, and particularly African-American, mothers. It is significant to note that this case is contemporaneous with the Supreme Court's *Roe v. Wade* decision. The oppressive attitudes and blatant discrimination toward pregnant women and single mothers that Fannie Lou Hamer attacks have no doubt played (and continue to play) a major role in women's perceived need for abortion. While the legal status of the pregnant woman and single mother has improved over the last twenty-five years, anyone working with women facing crisis pregnancies (as we do) will testify that discrimination has only taken on different forms. In this regard, Hamer's testimony speaks to the welfare reform debates of the 1990's, with their vilification of single mothers, especially black single mothers.

"Is It Too Late?"
by Fannie Lou Hamer

I am here tonight to express my views and to attempt to deal with the question and topic of, "Is it too late?"

First, as a black woman, 54 years of age, a mother and a wife, I know some of the suffering and the pain mothers must feel for their children when they have to face a cruel world both at home and abroad.

In the streets of America, my home and land where my fathers died, I have taken a stand for human rights and civil rights not just for my sake but for all mankind.

I was born and raised in a segregated society, beaten for trying to act like all people should have a right to act. Denied access to the ballot until I was 50 years old, but things are a little better now.

God is in the plan; He has sounded the trumpet and have called the march to order. God is on the throne today. He is keeping watch on this nation and marking time.

It's not too late. There is still time for America to change. God have delayed destruction on this nation to test the hearts and consciousness of us all. Believe me, there is still time.

The war in Vietnam must be ended so our men and boys can come home—so mothers can stop crying, wives can feel secure, and children can learn strength ... Women can be strength for men, women can help with the decision-making, but men will ultimately [be the ones in a position to] take the action.

The methods used to take human life, such as abortion, the pill, the ring, etc., amount to genocide. I believe that legal abortion is legal murder and the use of pills and rings to prevent God's will is a great sin.

As I take inventory of the past ten years, I see the many tragedies of this nation: Medgar Evers' death in my state (Mississippi), John Kennedy, Malcolm X, Martin Luther King, Jr., Robert Kennedy, and more recently Jo Etha Collier in Drew Mississippi, and countless of thousands in Vietnam and the streets of our larger cities and towns.[14] For these sins this country should pray. Because we have been spared a little longer. Miles of paper and film cannot record the many injustices this nation has been guilty of. But there is still time.

Maybe if all the ministers in this nation, black and white, would stand up tonight and say, "Come earth's people, it is not too late, God have given us time!" Perhaps we can speed up the day when all men can feel as I do. I am not afraid tonight. Freedom is in my soul and love is in my heart.

While here tonight I have a special message to my black brothers and sisters. As we move forward in our quest for progress and success, we must not be guilty of misleading our people. We must not allow our eagerness to participate lead us to accept second class citizenship, and inferior positions in the name of integration. Too many have given their lives to end this evil ...

"And That's What We Are Talking About"

Mrs. Hamer Wins A Victory For Single Mothers and Their Children

[The Andrews case was first heard before William C. Keady, a United States Circuit Court judge in the district including Fannie Lou Hamer's native Sunflower County. The courage of the plaintiffs is all the more impressive when we understand that the cross-examining attorney for the district, Champ Terney, was not simply a bigot, but a powerful one—the son-in-law of Senator James O. Eastland, that stalwart of Southern white racism. The legal aid attorney for the plaintiffs was Victor McTeer, a colleague of Fannie Lou Hamer. This excerpt begins with Fannie Lou Hamer taking the stand after the plaintiffs have testified. Victor McTeer establishes her credentials as an expert on the moral standards of the plaintiffs' community. —Ed.]

JUDGE KEADY: Are you here today because you feel that you can speak for the entire black community or at least the majority of the black community in Sunflower County?

MRS. HAMER: Yes, I am here because I feel ... the black community would agree, and all of them that I have talked with and, in fact, two rode over here this morning with us because they are concerned too, as we were, that we all agree that these young women are not really on trial. They are trying all of us. Because when you say that we are pulling ourselves up and you tell us to get off of welfare, and when peoples try to go to school to get off of welfare to support theirselves, this is another way of knocking them down. So we are here because we really don't like what is happening.

JUDGE KEADY: You are here because you feel there is a racial question involved?

MRS. HAMER: Yes, I believe it is.

JUDGE KEADY: Well, it is within the reasonable discretion of the court to allow a witness to testify as an expert. I am going to allow Mrs. Hamer to testify. Mrs. Hamer, as you heard yesterday there has been a great deal of talk about the morality of the black community. And I would like to ask you simply at this time how, in your opinion, does the black community feel about unwed mothers?

MRS. HAMER: Well, it's quite a few people, black people in Sunflower County, that have young people that's not married, with children. But these are still our children. And we still love these children. And after these babies are born we are not going to disband these children from their families, because these are other lives, they are—God breathed life into them just like He did into us. And I think these children have a right to live. And I think that these mothers have a right to support them in a decent way.

JUDGE KEADY: You think, then, that the black community has one point of view about children who are the progeny of unwed parents as

opposed to what the white community thinks about the children of
unwed parents. Can you tell me what the difference is, what the white
community thinks about unwed parents as opposed to what the black
community thinks?

MRS. HAMER: Well, being a person who have built from what I would
say the ground, I worked for white people for years, I worked in their
house, I worked in their kitchen, and I know what's going on. And if
justice was really done it wouldn't be only black women in here, it
would be a whole lot of young white folk in here, too. So what I am
saying is I think it is being—the people that's treated unjust—and this
would be almost funny to me if it wasn't so serious.

JUDGE KEADY: Well, how do people in the white community, from
your experience, take care of their unwed children [sic]?

MR. TERNEY: Your Honor, I don't believe she has been qualified as an
expert—

JUDGE KEADY: No, she is qualified, really … In the black community,
is there any morality issue in having an unwed child [sic]? That is the
question.

MRS. HAMER: Well, let me say this, Judge Keady.

JUDGE KEADY: All right.

MRS. HAMER: After a child is born, I don't think that people should be
treated like an outcast.

JUDGE KEADY: No, that is not the question. But in becoming a parent
out of wedlock, is that frowned upon, looked down on, or is it encouraged and approved?

MRS. HAMER: It's not encouraged.

JUDGE KEADY: All right.

MR. MCTEER: What would be the effect, in your opinion, of this rule
upon young black people in the Sunflower County?

MRS. HAMER: Well, it would be quite a few young people lose their
jobs, because I know so many young women that after having one
child go back to school, finish school and yet not marry, but try to
better theirselves by getting a good job so they can support their children without becoming a ward of the welfare. And this is really going
to be a blow to them.

MR. MCTEER: What do you think will be the result when young black
women who have tried to get themselves back through school, suddenly—after having gotten through school, rather, and having gotten
a degree—they find themselves without a job because of the fact that
they have an unwed *child* [sic]? What would be the effect to these

young mothers, in your understanding?

MRS. HAMER: It will be a terrible blow not only to these young women but it will be a terrible blow to all of us, not only in Sunflower County but across the state of Mississippi, across the United States where people are trying to lift theirselves out of certain things and bring theirselves up to a level where they can support theirselves and their child.

MR. MCTEER: What do you think will be the effect upon the child, the children of the unwed mother?

MRS. HAMER: Well, this is saying to the child that it, too, is not fit. And you know, when I think of this—may I say this, Judge Keady? I think about the story of Jesus Christ, I think of what would have happened to Virgin Mary if she walked into Drew Separate School, what would have happened if Christ had been born in that school. What would have happened?

MR. MCTEER: Mrs. Hamer, I know that in your own life this particular question touches very close to home. Could you tell the court about why it touches so close to home in terms of your own life?

MRS. HAMER: Well, for one thing, I will talk about my daughter. I had two children, adopted children, Vergie and Dorothy Jean. And during my traveling around, Dorothy Jean became pregnant. She was 22 years old. And one of my friends, a white friend in California, told me, me traveling, it might affect my reputation for her to have this child at home, and why didn't I send her off. And I told them I would stick as close to her as I could. So I kept her at home. The child was born on the 29th of December in East Bolivar County Hospital, 1965. She died in 1967, my daughter did. And if I had mistreated that child of my child, I would have never forgiven myself. I don't think that we have the authority to forgive man. Only God is that authority. Only God got that power. Man is not to judge man. We don't have that kind of power.

MR. MCTEER: Mrs. Hamer, in your opinion, what do you think the black community thinks about teachers who are unwed mothers teaching their children?

MRS. HAMER: It's nothing wrong with an unwed mother teaching children. Because I'm sure in Sunflower County that we have some unwed mothers teaching some of those kids.

MR. MCTEER: Mrs. Hamer, to your knowledge, what do you think the black community's views are in terms of where values are actually created? Are values created in the home or … in school?

MRS. HAMER: Values are created in the homes. You know, my mother and father of one marriage had 20 children. Six girls and 14 boys. And my mother and father taught me without any formal education about dignity and self-respect from the time that we were very small kids until we were grown. And I—you know, I was surprised yesterday to hear the kind of things, you know, like—that black people don't have any morals and that kind of thing. That's not true. Because they do have. They have moral values. They do care.

MR. MCTEER: Mrs. Hamer, does the black community feel that a woman has a right to her independent life, women like the plaintiffs in this matter?

MRS. HAMER: Yes. The black community feels that a woman, if she is not married and especially with a child have a right to make a decent living. That's why I am here. Because I feel that Miss Andrews and the others have a right to make a decent life for their children. The black community feel that any woman with children or with a child have a right to lift theirselves and fight. One of the people out there that's in the audience now that wanted to further her education after her child was born, we helped her go to Mississippi Valley State College.

MR. MCTEER: Who is that person?

MRS. HAMER: Miss Andrews.

MR. MCTEER: You have known Miss Andrews for quite some time, haven't you?

MRS. HAMER: Yes, I have known her for quite some time. …

MR. MCTEER: Do you know Miss Andrews' reputation within her community for her good moral character?

MRS. HAMER: Yes.

MR. MCTEER: Do you think that Miss Andrews and the other ladies, plaintiffs, etc., who testified today, do you think the black community thinks that their actions are commendable for taking care of their children?

MRS. HAMER: Yes, I think it was good for them to try to do something to take care of their children. And everybody else in the community believe the same thing. That's the reason there's other black mothers here this morning.

MR. TERNEY: [beginning his cross-examination]: Are you aware of the problem at Drew concerning the pregnancies of schoolgirls, unwanted pregnancies?

MRS. HAMER: I'm not aware of how many, no. I'm not aware of how many it is.

MR. TERNEY: Well, as spokesman for the black community and knowing the conditions in the black community, do you see a problem of student-age females becoming pregnant and having to drop out of school? ...

MRS. HAMER: Well, it is a matter of concern if the kids are too young. But the people we are dealing with here this morning are young women.

MR. TERNEY: Well, I realize that. These plaintiffs are over 21. But I am talking about the children 13 to 18 years of age.

MRS. HAMER: Yes.

MR. TERNEY: Now, it is a problem at Drew, isn't it, of school-age girls becoming pregnant?

MRS. HAMER: Well, it's a problem with school age children. That's not only with black children.

MR. TERNEY: No, I realize that.

MRS. HAMER: It's with white children, too.

MR. TERNEY: But it is a problem?

MRS. HAMER: It is a problem with children.

MR. TERNEY: And it is a growing problem?

MRS. HAMER: Yes, with children.

MR. TERNEY: Do you have any idea what the solution to that problem is?

MRS. HAMER: Well, I think maybe more that we should become more active in the schools and visit in the schools, maybe, the parent.

MR. TERNEY: And the school leading them in the right moral conduct?

MRS. HAMER: Well, if he—this prove there's something going wrong if he keep them out and still that many people be pregnant. Then certainly he not doing what he ought to be doing.

MR. TERNEY: Can't you foresee that if he employs people that have illegitimate children that the students will then think that this type of conduct is being condoned and think that it's all right and it may make the problem—probably would make the problem worse? Can't you see that?

MRS. HAMER: I don't believe that. ...

MR. TERNEY: The mere fact that the teacher has engaged in something wrong, whether she says anything about it, the fact that the child, the student, knows that the teacher in front of his or her class has engaged in sex outside of marriage and the product of that is an illegitimate child, can't you see that the child would think that that mother, if that teacher that that child respected engaged in that sort of conduct, that they would infer that it's all right for them to do it?

MRS. HAMER: You know what you have to do if that's what you are going to deal with? When you get back to Drew this evening, lock the doors. There won't be any school.

MR. TERNEY: Why is that?

MRS. HAMER: The moral conduct. Nobody would teach.

MR. TERNEY: All the teachers?

MRS. HAMER: All of them. It might not be two not fall out of the sack, if that's what you call moral. Two. Lock it up.

MR. TERNEY: You don't have much confidence in the faculty?

MRS. HAMER: I'm just calling a spade a spade.

MR. TERNEY: Well, what is your opinion as to whether—

MRS. HAMER: I think people should have a chance, not only—you know that, Mr. Terney? If this was a young white woman with this same problem, I would come here and fight you the same way, because I would fight for her rights as a woman, as a person fighting for her child, just like these young womens are fighting for their right to take care of their child. You always tell us, we go through this thing with the welfare or we have got so many kids on the welfare roll, "Why don't you get up and do something?" And then when we start doing something, "You don't have any business being that high."

MR. TERNEY: You realize this rule is not racially motivated. In other words, it is enforced equally against whites and blacks. You understand that, don't you?

MRS. HAMER: I don't understand that. Because to save my life, is no way that I could believe that every white teacher in Sunflower County is single that a child isn't involved. I don't believe that …

MR. TERNEY: Let me ask your opinion. As spokesman for the black community, do you feel that it's right or wrong for a female student between the ages of 13 and 19 to have sexual intercourse outside of marriage?

MRS. HAMER: I feel like they are too young.

MR. TERNEY: You feel that it is wrong?

MRS. HAMER: I feel that it is wrong.

MR. TERNEY: Do you realize the rule does not condemn the child? It is the conduct of the parent, whether it's the mother or the father, that the rule condemns.

MRS. HAMER: But what I'm saying, if this child, you know—it's wrong, and I'm going to teach this child these things before this happen. But if a child should become pregnant … I wouldn't cast a child out.

MR. TERNEY: The rule doesn't cast the child out. Doesn't ask the child be cast out. It simply says that the parent, whether it is a mother or father, is not qualified to teach in the Drew public schools. Now does that, in your mind, deny that individual that would ordinarily have been teaching in that school system employment anywhere? Couldn't they apply to another school system or in another job?

MRS. HAMER: Well, I just have one question I would like to ask you. Why do they go if they can't work at home? Why do they pick up and go? ...

MR. TERNEY: Does the black community differentiate or draw a distinction between moral conduct of the type of prostitution, that is, voluntary sexual intercourse for pay, as opposed to voluntary sexual intercourse outside of marriage without pay?

MRS. HAMER: See, you know, Attorney Terney, this is ridiculous, to be going with this kind of questions and all that we are talking about, that women should have a right to work in schools if they have got the education to lift theirselves from certain things that are happening in their lifetime, meaning that they have got a kid and ... they have gone to school to get a education to try to support their kids decent. And that's what we are talking about. ...

[Judge Keady, himself an "outsider" because of his poor Irish background and physical handicaps, understood Fannie Lou Hamer's frustration and outrage with the school district's discriminatory policy. His ruling declares: "Human experience refutes the dogmatic attitude inherent in such a policy against unwed parents ... The rule leaves no consideration for the multitudinous circumstances in which illegitimate childbirth may occur and which may have little, if any, bearing on the parent's present moral worth ... While obviously aimed at discouraging premarital sexual relations, the policy's effect is apt to encourage abortion ..." (371 F. Supp. 17, D.C. Miss. 1973). Keady's ruling withstood appeal to the U.S. Supreme Court. —Ed.]

Elizabeth McAlister

Elizabeth McAlister is a dedicated activist who for all of her adult life has been associated with the Catholic resistance and peace making movement. She protested the Vietnam war on the basis of her Christian faith through nonviolent direct actions of resistance such as raids on draft boards. Her protesting extended to the invasion of Cambodia in 1970 and, when the American presence in Indochina came to an end, she continued to speak publicly about the future of the peace movement, advocating the structuring of small communities of resistance. In 1972, as one of the Harrisburg Eight (later the Harrisburg Seven), she was tried on general conspiracy charges associated with raids on draft boards. Although found innocent of the conspiracy charges, McAlister was convicted of smuggling communications in and out of a federal prison.

Elizabeth McAlister and her husband, Philip Berrigan, later formed Jonah House, a Catholic resistance community in Baltimore dedicated to the principles of nonviolence, resistance, community, and contemplation. Their nonviolent direct acts of resistance continued largely in the form of symbolic practices such as pray-ins, sit-ins, and morality plays that protested American foreign policy. One such action occurred in September 1980 when Philip and Daniel Berrigan, along with six others, entered a General Electric plant in Pennsylvania, poured blood on documents, and hammered on the nose cones of nuclear warheads, enacting the biblical prophecy of Isaiah in which swords are beaten into plowshares (Isaiah 2:4). Dozens of such "Plowshares actions" promoting nuclear disarmament have taken place since that time resulting in even longer prison sentences for the activists than those handed down during the Vietnam war era. The price for resistance was going up, and levels of commitment to the peace movement had to increase. McAlister's commitment has never wavered.

In 1983, McAlister and other resisters demonstrated on Griffiss Air Force Base near Rome, New York, and damaged some equipment used for carrying nuclear bombs. McAlister served two years in prison for her actions. It was during this incarceration that McAlister wrote the following letter to Catholics for a Free Choice in response to an ad they ran in the *New York Times.* Her observations are significant not only inasmuch as they criticize what she identifies as an elitist position held by Catholics for a Free Choice, but also as an important reminder that we must not presume to speak for others, but rather, we need to listen to, learn from, and aid those who are offered few real choices in life. McAlister's letter should serve as a challenge to prolifers to support those women who have no family or community from whom to draw encouragement and strength during their pregnancies and to extend our efforts to "protect our endangered human family from *all* that seeks to destroy it." She also challenges our level of commitment by reminding us that "we will accomplish very little unless we are willing to risk everything."

After serving her term, McAlister returned to Jonah House where she lives with her family. McAlister and Berrigan tell their story of forming a resistance community in their book, *The Time's Discipline: The Beatitudes and Nuclear Resistance*, Baltimore, MD: Fortkamp Publishing Co., 1989.

A Letter From A Women's Prison
by Elizabeth McAlister

Dear Friends of Pro-Choice: A friend sent me a copy of your *New York Times* ad, "A Diversity of Opinion Concerning Abortion Exists Among Committed Catholics." I read it with interest and dismay, yet with hope. The hope is that you remain open to questions, to dialogue, to another way.

I read your words, and questions arose. The need to challenge you was intensified as I noted the list of those who signed your ad.

Like many of you, I have been religious; like some of you, I am a parent (mother of three). Like all of you, my life is animated by a struggle for peace, justice, freedom—especially for the freedom of conscience, without which freedom is an illusion.

I have been where you are, read your writings. You have helped me immensely to look hope in the face; I can never forget its physiognomy. In my bumbling way, I have tried to enflesh that hope in my life, as well as in the lives of my children.

Because I had lived 14 years in a religious community, my children were born when I was older. Allow me to write briefly of the experience of my third pregnancy; it was for me an awesome moment of clarity on the issue of abortion.

I was asked to undergo no fewer than 15 tests to determine possible defects in the fetus—our Katy Berrigan. The understanding, the insistence was that "of course one should avail oneself of all these insurances and safeguards that a good healthy baby be born; otherwise, one should abort."

Because I could not consider the abortion of even a damaged child, I refused all tests. (I was also suspicious of the safety of the tests, a suspicion, as I later learned, that was well-founded.) To protect the doctor and midwife from potential lawsuits, I was also required to sign a statement that I had been informed of all dangers, had been advised to undergo the tests and had refused for the following reasons ...

Such an experience is enormously intimidating. I think that, through such pressures, the medical community can pollute Christ's channels of access to us and to one another. And where is the antidote? I was lucky. I had the support of my family and my community to withstand the pressures, to protect Katy Berrigan against these sophisticated gynecological methods. I have also had considerable experience in being regarded as a fool.

Still, I wonder what support other women have against pressures so formidable, assumptions so roundly shared. I wonder, further, whether the religious community does not, in its own way, abandon many women to the radical right, our concern being for something fondly named "pluralism" or "diversity of opinion" or "theological accuracy" or "progressive thinking."

It seems undeniable that millions of parents are being persuaded that abortion is *the* serious, progressive option—the only one, in fact, should complications or surprise or even inconvenience occur in the course of a pregnancy. At the very least, it is constantly insinuated that one is a fool to bear a child without being shored up by all possible insurances that the birth will be normal in every respect. And I reflect on the terrible irony implied in the prayer of Christians, "My life is in your hands, O Lord." The other obsession is to place one's fate in the omnipotent hands of Allstate, Hartford, amniocentesis, sonogram and such.

Let me say it once more: I have been where you are. I have had a small part in your own passion for justice, peace, clarity of conscience. And the search has somehow or other brought me to an entirely different geography. I am now someone whom some choose to call a prisoner of conscience; others, a convicted felon. In any case, a prisoner serving a sentence of three years. The terminology seems irrelevant, given my new life, led at the side of the poor, the marginalized, the down and out—however you or society choose to describe us. I dwell at the Federal Prison for Women, in Alderson, West Virginia, one of more than 600 women prisoners. Probably 80 per cent of the prisoners are mothers; more than 90 per cent are the poor whom you presumably represent in our statement in the *Times*.

But I have a different report, one that has the slight advantage of arising from life lived among the poorest of the poor, the prisoners.

If the Women of Alderson could understand your ad (many are barely literate), they would only be angered by it. I want to tread carefully here. Slowly, I learn that the poor do not speak with one voice. They are neither mass nor class, as one learns who lives their life, eats and sleeps and works with them—and, above all, listens to them. They evade our sociology, which is often a form of scatology, abstract and indecent. The women are individuals, proud, undefeated for the most part—as passionate as ourselves, not to be disposed of or cataloged.

Although these women are my daily bread, my friends and sisters, I hesitate to speak for them in this matter of pro-choice. But of one thing I am certain: they love their children as I love mine; they miss them with the same poignancy and gut-wrenching that afflict me at the thought of Jerry, Freda and Katy. At the hospital here, I have seen women pick up pamphlets on abortion, and invariably cast them down again with the flat phrase, "I don't care what anyone says, I think it's murder."

I have been where you are, in more sense than one. But for now, I feel shut out from your circle of concern and conscience. Your ad strikes me as the statement of a closed club, an elite with its own language, an altogether professional clarity that is at the same time highly questionable.

It is hard for me to write such words; they make me feel childish, even foolish. But I will take the plunge, nonetheless. Your statement excludes me and many others, not only the prisoners of Alderson. We are excluded by the limits you place on your concern for life; by your language; by your exquisite concern, on the other hand, for something you refer to as "job security"; by your presumption that you speak for the poor. Please bear with me as I explain.

I am in prison because I acted in accord with my conscience, doing what I could as spouse, mother, Christian, to reduce the threat of nuclear annihilation. You write on "diversity of opinion" with regard to abortion. Do we walk any common ground? Do we stand together under the biblical mandate to protect and preserve *all* life? If indeed we do, I do not discover it in the way you limit the question of life and its endangerment.

I think you allow the politicians and so-called religious leaders to frame the question for you. But in so narrow a frame, the whole picture can scarcely be seen; one aspect is blown up, all others are shunted literally out of the picture. So we, the conscientious viewers, are divided, even deceived, as to what we see—and what we don't see.

Years ago, many of you taught me about Christ. I learned with you how he grasped the wondrous profundity of the human. He resolved conflicts and reconciled differences, placing an "and" where most of us insist on an "or." Confronted with a narrow image labeled "reality" (an image that was, in fact, inhuman or antihuman), he simply enlarged the frame, insisted on, included, all the variety and verve that is our glory— slave and free, woman and man, gentile and Jew.

There can be no single issue today even so urgent a one as abortion. The human being, the Christian, cannot so speak, or define himself or herself. The issue is, rather: "What is to become of humankind?" Such a question, so put, compels us to welcome and cherish the human in all its likely and unlikely guises and disguises, to protect our endangered human family from all that seeks to destroy it.

Bishop Joseph Bernardin spoke recently of the "seamless garment of life." I think he came closest to the "and" (in contrast to the "or")—an "and" I consider so great a gift of the Lord. The "and" beckons into unity all who struggle against the probability of nuclear annihilation, all who struggle against the mad arms buildup, all who struggle against the oppression of colonial seizures, who struggle against capital punishment, who struggle in behalf of life, for the born *and* unborn—the right of all the living to decent shelter, adequate food and clothing, good education, sensible work, the freedom to follow and form our own consciences.

This larger frame draws us into the human picture, out of sidelines and isolation and single-issue obsessions, into a common human understanding and movement. Or so I think.

Your language, I have said, excludes so many, including myself. What am I to make of, or how shall I explain to the mothers among the prisoners, words such as "polarization," "probabilism," "legitimate Catholic position," "ensoulment," "diversity of opinion"? Such colorless technical terms, such jargon, such signals to the initiated! The terms remind me of those spurious circumlocutions that have made bloodshed, violence and moral evasion such hideous commonplaces. As if "diversity of opinion," rather than sound biblical understanding, should govern conscience.

Years ago, many of you taught me about Christ. I learned from you that he took our deepest longings to heart, that he blessed them, that he hoped for us and with us, and that life might be worth the living.

And I ask myself, What are the longings of humans today, to which we should harken? What is the news we have to offer—that will be both good and new? Is there a word through which our humanity may be healed of its deep hurt? I look in the faces of my sisters in prison, and I rejoice. Christ has made all things new: a new language, an example, our liberation and our hope. Even here, in this demented world.

Let me say, even at risk of odium, I am bemused by the 75 Catholics who agreed with your statement but who were unable to sign it, out of fear for their jobs. Security? The word comes to those in prison as an irony beyond words. We Christians are, then, to hold vigorous convictions, to hold them fast, but inwardly only, *in petto,* a light under a bushel? And was it thus that the world was redeemed, an invisible, interior, pneumatic, "spiritual" crucifixion, *in petto,* the fine resolve of Christ substituting for the unpleasant, untidy public act? I seek instruction in this.

Years ago, you taught me something else. Perhaps my memory is faulty, or illusive; but the lesson remains part of my being. The lesson went something like this: We will accomplish very little unless we are willing to risk everything.

As to speaking for the poor. Because we are more literate (and more affluent), we are tempted in this direction. But I am convinced that our real need, if we but knew it, is rather to listen, to hear from, rather than to speak for others.

Years ago, you taught me that the Lord dwells in the poor and speaks through them. I think I understand why you spoke as you did, in order to provoke and organize, to oppose and question authorities, in both church and state. Many of them seem obsessed today, to prescribe, to lay down law, hard and fast, to foresee and determine everything. And the radical right, the Moral Majority, seizes upon prayer in the schools, right to life, as the godly American way (insinuating that godly *is* American). They would dictate our morality for us (invariably on the personal level only); they would politicize religious issues, would place authority above conscience in every instance.

And a number of our own bishops march in lockstep with the Ronald Reagans and Jerry Falwells in this, narrowing political choices, cherishing the unborn even while they damn the born to the Gehenna of war, violence, social and personal neglect—the expression of utmost contempt for the living.

I think our task implies something more difficult, more imaginative, than merely responding in kind. We must widen the frame. We must stretch our arms and our hearts until we include and cherish every human aspiration, every endangered or despised or expendable life. In such ways, we do great service, both to church and state. We practice in the world the sacrament of sisterhood and brotherhood. We liberate the oppressed consciences that would oppress and enslave others, all, we are told, in a good cause.

Signing these reflections with me are my husband Philip Berrigan, my brother-in-law Father Daniel Berrigan and, I may rightfully infer, the growing number of Plowshares Christians—those in prison, those on appeal, those awaiting trial. As well as those friends searching their hearts, searching the Spirit, wherever they may be led.

Alison Davis

Alison Davis is an outspoken disability rights activist in England who uses a wheelchair because of spinal bifida. In her article, she describes how she came to add the prolife cause to her work for the disabled. She is the organizer of the Handicapped Division of the Society for the Protection of Unborn Children, Great Britain's major prolife organization.

Ms. Davis makes clear the implication of abortion rights on the disabled. If any woman aborts her child because of suspected "deformations" or "abnormalities," she sends a clear message that she believes her child would be better off dead than handicapped. It seems incredible that anyone would doubt that this is, indeed, the message that is conveyed to the handicapped; and that this discourse negatively affects disabled members of our society seems indisputable. The "right" to abortion, says Davis, "is denying our very right to exist."

While we acknowledge that there are perhaps some parents who might not be qualified or prepared to care for children with such special needs, we also know that there are support groups ready to offer practical help to such people, and that there are waiting lists of people who are willing to adopt such infants and take life-long responsibility for their care. These people know something that dominant culture, with its dangerous eugenic tendencies, has missed; they know about the richness of diversity and the valuable contribution handicapped individuals make to our society and our individual lives. If anyone doubts this, they have only to consider the contribution of Ms. Davis.

Women With Disabilities: Abortion and Liberation
by Alison Davis

Ideally the women's movement should provide the perfect vehicle for women with disabilities to discover their potential and it should also provide us with a platform to fight for and protect our rights in the same way as other women from minority groups. However, I will argue that the movement has failed to adequately take account of women with disabilities—in many ways a doubly oppressed minority. By supporting abortion on the grounds of handicap as a "right," the movement denies us an identity as equal human beings worthy of respect, and calls into question the place in society of disabled individuals.

I think it is important to consider the reasons why this is so from several different perspectives, encompassing many different but related issues. We need to look at the relationship between oppressors and oppressed in many differing situations; the historical reasons for the adoption of "abortion rights" as part of the women's liberation "package" and what that means for women today; the attitude of society in general to disability; the attitude of able-bodied women to those with disabilities and how they relate that to the disabled unborn; and finally how the women's movement has managed to reconcile the "right to choose" with the knowledge that that concept includes the right to choose something generally unacceptable to feminists.

Everyone is oppressed in some way, however slight; and because we cannot remove this deeply ingrained system of oppression and achieve true liberation until we confront and understand the mechanisms and emotions that underlie it, I think it is also important to consider the possibility that abortion, far from being an essential part of the liberation "package" sought by the women's movement, may actually be anathema to the whole concept of liberation and freedom.

Abortion on Demand and its Effects

Although in theory abortion is not available on demand in this country [England], in practice it is, and this is not just a claim of "anti-abortionists." Professor Peter Huntingford, a well-known advocate of the right to abortion, and the British Pregnancy Advisory Service, one of the biggest abortion providing charities, both acknowledge that this is so, since it can always be argued that continuing with a pregnancy is more dangerous than an early abortion. My arguments are therefore based on an assumption that we have abortion on demand, that women's "right to choose" is open to the most blatant and oppressive abuse, and that the advent of abortion on demand has resulted in the systematic elimination of people with disabilities.

In the specific case of women with disabilities and the right of handicapped people as a whole, it is becoming ever more obvious that the "right" to abortion is denying us our very right to exist. Whole volumes of cost benefit studies produced by this and past governments testify to the fact that, just as in Nazi Germany, the handicapped are regarded as "economic lumber" and better off dead. Pressure is being put on women to be screened if they are considered to be at high risk of having a handicapped baby, and to abort the baby if it is found to be handicapped. As a result, women with disabilities are beginning to realize that they need to organize a response. A woman in Holland who has cerebral palsy, Yvet den brok-Rouwendal, who has two children, felt increasingly threatened by prenatal diagnosis, believing that it set the handicapped and non-handicapped against each other. She has started a support group for handicapped women which will also monitor developments such as prenatal diagnosis, and encourage discussion on the tendency of society to want only that which is "perfect." In this country, Disabled Women for Life, which I helped to set up, has similar aims and objectives.

Out of Sight, Out of Mind

There are undoubted benefits for oppressors in maintaining the status quo, and this is demonstrated rather well if we consider the oppression suffered by the handicapped.

In many ways, the situation of people with disabilities is very similar to that of women fighting for liberation, since able-bodied society has a vested interest in maintaining a view of us as objects of pity to be shut away, seen on sufferance and generally ignored. Many able-bodied people would rather not be reminded of their own fragility and do not want to face up to the fact that they themselves may one day be less than fully fit, so they subscribe to the "out of sight, out of mind" mentality, and salve their consciences by giving money occasionally to "help the handicapped."

We are all oppressors and oppressed in different situations. We cannot expect to overcome our problems until we confront our own failings and oppressive tendencies, however painful this may be. It involves not only recognizing the situations in which we are oppressed, but also the ones in which we have the upper hand, for instance in the following examples: First World/Third World, white skin/black skin, the west/the east, free abortion on demand/the right to life. Claiming liberation for ourselves involves tolerance of others, and it also involves shouldering more responsibilities and uncomfortable or downright unpleasant confrontations than we may care to. This is what liberation is essentially all about, because if we claim liberation for ourselves at the expense of someone else, we merely create a new system of oppressors and oppressed, which is the trap I think the mainstream women's movement has fallen into.

If we take the issue of the status of handicapped people, if able-bodied society were to accept that those with disabilities are equal human beings with rights, they would also have to abandon the notion that screening and abortion are benefits to society, and that the earlier a handicapped person is killed off the better for all concerned.

A Change of Mind on Abortion

Only a few years have passed since I believed that the only way to achieve equality for women was by identifying with the women's liberation "package" and joining the struggle for equal and full employment rights, equal educational opportunities, equal property rights, free contraception and, of course, abortion on demand. I felt there was no way women could be free and equal until we were able to control our own fertility as easily as men could, and I upheld the right to abortion vehemently for that reason. I am only now beginning to understand how I came to change my mind and separate abortion from the rest of the "package," and why many women, including some women with disabilities, have not yet changed their minds.

Basically I supported the right to abortion because I did not want to be burdened with unwanted children myself. I did not actually know what an abortion involved, neither did I want to know—but I did know I dreaded being unwillingly pregnant more than almost anything else, and did not feel anyone had the right to tell me I could not have an abortion if I wanted one. I breathed a sigh of relief when the Corrie Bill fell, especially since I had just had a pregnancy scare, and I felt a great solidarity with my feminist sisters. We had won, and secured the right to choose about what happened to our bodies. Or so I thought at the time.

And then … I read in the paper an article that was to change my mind. It told the story of a couple who had decided to "allow" their spina bifida baby to die. I read it with a kind of morbid interest, especially the circumstances of her death and the fact that the doctor had encouraged her parents to reach this decision. He had then sedated the baby so she was too sleepy to cry for food, and thus starved to death. He called this "the loving thing to do" because she would have been unable to walk, and doubly incontinent and would, he deemed, have compared herself unfavorably with her able-bodied sisters. She would, in short, have been exactly as disabled as I am myself.

I cut the article out and filed it away. Sometimes I went back and read it again, feeling confused and angry. I wanted to tell the doctor (not the parents who I felt had simply accepted his bad advice) that I was just another human being, and that he had no right to kill this baby because she would have grown up to be like me. Three years later I met the doctor concerned, who expressed sorrow at my disquiet, admitting that I was as human as he was himself, but still defending the parents' right to choose.

It is, I fear, an indication of my slow wit and ability for self-deception that it was another two years before, having read yet another article condoning the killing of the newborn handicapped, I finally did something. I was splutteringly angry, and despite assurances from friends that a letter on such a subject would never be printed, I wrote to *The Guardian*. If nothing else, I thought, it would at least sort out my own anger and confusion, and get it out of my system. How very naive I was.

My letter was printed and almost straight away, I received letters from various prolife groups. I am sure the only thing that saved these anti-abortion letters from an immediate fiery grave was my rather stubborn and compulsive nature which dictated that I actually read every letter I received, and I was somewhat surprised by what I discovered.

These anti-abortion groups, whose views I have always despised, were trying to tell me that the killing of the newborn and abortion were linked and that people with disabilities could not possibly achieve their equality in society until they had first secured their equal right to life. I checked every reference, every subreference, every page, every subject, every author. I did not, you see, want to believe that this was true. So anxious was I that disabled people (i.e., me) should be accorded equal rights, I was advocating that we should have more rights than anyone else. That the unborn handicapped should be protected from abortion but not the unborn able-bodied. A kind of reverse discrimination, if you like, that would not stand up to the slightest examination. The reason for this discrepancy was not difficult to understand, though, because my motive for holding it was not one of mercy for the unborn, but rather of protecting my rights to have an abortion if I wanted one. I believe this feeling underlies the attitude of many women toward abortion. It is not so much that they deny the humanity of the unborn, but because it will so profoundly affect them if they do acknowledge it, they choose (and choice is taken to be a right, remember) to ignore it. In this way, liberation becomes an end in itself, and if it means that women become in turn oppressors of a still more vulnerable group (in this case, their unborn children), then so be it.

The Question of Rights

In my case, the reluctant admission that conception is the scientifically provable start of life meant I had to confront my own inherent oppressive tendencies, which was extremely difficult for me to do. Nevertheless, if I wanted equal rights for me and those like me, I could not in turn deny them to the unborn simply because it was convenient for me to perceive them as less deserving of rights, "inferior" or less "useful." Assuredly, I still do not want to be pregnant until I decide I want children, but I cannot now claim the right to kill my unborn children to protect my right to liberation. If I do, I have no right to deny my children the right to kill me when I get old, inconvenient and unwanted by them.

Abortion as a Liberation Issue

If abortion did not involve the death of a human being, I would, of course, regard it as no more morally contentious than any other surgical procedure. I believe that contraception is the sole concern of individuals exercising control over their own bodies—abortion is different because it concerns a separate human being.

The kind of pressure for handicapped women not to be allowed to reproduce, which could only have come about in the framework of easily available abortion, was made evident by the recent case of a mentally handicapped woman who was "ordered" by a judge to have an abortion. The case hinged upon whether it is acceptable to force an abortion on a woman incapable of dissent because of her handicap. Forced abortion such as this is evidence of yet another erosion of the rights of the handicapped. The "imperfect" unborn lost their right to life with Section Four of the Abortion Act, which made abortion legal on those grounds, and now handicapped women are in danger of being subjected to abortion because someone has claimed the right to decide that they are not fit to be mothers. I wonder if the killing and oppression will only stop when we can be certain that "perfect" women will give birth to "perfect" babies. One would think that the Nazis' attempt at bringing that about was warning enough.

The Abortion Act has not solved social problems, and it has not stopped backstreet abortion. For those with disabilities, born or unborn, it has put the clock back to the Nazi era when the "useless bread gobblers" were killed first under the guise of humanity and later unashamedly for economic reasons. Our own society began the same way with saying as Dr. Garrow did that it was the "loving thing to do" and then backing that up by saying that it was not only loving, but cost effective too.

I believe our present system of abortion on demand should be stopped because it does nothing to help the situation of desperate women, but does conveniently remove problems for those in power, be they abortionists, boyfriends who don't want to support an unplanned child, or those who "care" for handicapped women. I fear more and more that in the wake of the struggle for emancipation, the women's movement has made a crucial wrong turn with the temptation to succumb to the danger of oppressing a still more vulnerable group than ourselves—the unborn—just as we had suffered at the hands of a paternalistic male-dominated society. Perhaps women simply became so accustomed to the idea of one person's rights necessarily conflicting with another's (even though this conflict only really exists if we view the problem in simplistic "winner and loser" terms), that in fighting for our own rights it became natural to eliminate or ignore those with conflicting interests who were too vulnerable to fight back. Rights are, after all, absolute. But power varies—an important distinction to draw—otherwise my power to kill you would become a right to kill you.

The Wider Issue of Abortion and Feminism

A truly feminist approach, I suggest, would be to try to redefine and restructure society in terms different from the widely accepted traditionally oppressive values. The feminist case against abortion is simply that abortionism accepts a view that women are somehow flawed, abnormal, inferior or undesirable when pregnant, which is the time when they are least strong, powerful and oppressive. This is even more true of women with disabilities, who are always weak and powerless, at least in traditional terms. It is also true of the unborn and the disabled unborn in the same way. This view, and radical social reform, which will be necessary if women, and particularly disabled women, are ever to achieve equality, are diametrically opposed, I believe, because abortionism fails to come to grips with the fundamental roots of oppression. We need to fight for the right to be women or to be unashamedly women with disabilities, rather than engaging in a demoralizing and futile struggle to become as like our oppressors as possible.

What I think the feminist movement should be striving towards is the right to be recognized as having the same capacity and opportunity for mixing parenthood and career as men have always been assumed to have. In the same way, able-bodied women should be recognizing that disabled women have rights too, and that being an even more oppressed group, our struggle is still at the stage of establishing the right to have children at all in a society which generally disapproves of us reproducing.

The women's movement claims to support women with disabilities and help them fight against their double oppression, but I do not now believe that it is possible to do so while defending so aggressively the "right" to kill unborn children because they suffer from the same disabilities. Parents of an unborn or newborn handicapped child may ostensibly have a choice about what happens to it, but they generally only have the doctor's estimation of handicapped people upon which to base their judgment.

Some women, as I have shown, are manipulated in their "choice" by husbands who will accept only "perfect" children or by governments who will not accept the economic burden of handicapped children; and some are manipulated by social systems which decree that, in China, women will "choose" to kill firstborn girls, in India, they will "choose" to bear only sons, and in the West, teenage girls will "choose" abortion in preference to a family scandal. Choice is a relative thing, after all, and can only be regarded as a right when it infringes on no one else's rights.

I changed my mind about abortion and its place in the liberation of women because the facts demanded it. If we want true liberation and equality, we cannot allow our selfishness to blind us to reality, even when it is unpalatable. We cannot claim liberation "for me" if it means denying it to others, for eventually the oppression of one group rubs off on us all.

True liberation for all will mean accepting a degree of responsibility for each other which maybe we escape now, but liberation and equality "just for me" inevitably means oppression for someone else—which is unfair, inhumane and, I would maintain, ultimately unworkable.

Jo McGowan

Jo McGowan lives with her family in India and continues to write occasionally for the *National Catholic Reporter.* Her article "All Abortions are Selective" originally appeared in *Indian Express* in 1982, in June 1984 in *Sisterlife,* and later was edited for *Newsweek* magazine.

McGowan brings unique insight to the problem of the devaluation of women and sex-selection abortions based upon her experiences in India. She makes an excellent argument that prochoice feminists cannot have it both ways—if abortion is a matter of choice, they cannot criticize the woman's reasons for abortion—even if she chooses to abort her child because it is female. For many in male-dominated cultures, the female fetus suffers the physical "deficiency" of lacking a penis and has in common with the handicapped fetus an "abnormality" for which reason her life may be terminated. Such specious categorization based upon one's supposed ability to contribute to the parents' (and society's) happiness sets one group of humanity against another—male against female, the able-bodied against the disabled, white against black, the genetically "fit" against the "unfit," those in power against minorities. As McGowan observes, if it is wrong to kill girls, it is wrong to kill anyone.

All Abortions Are Selective
by Jo McGowan

Amniocentesis, a medical procedure by which certain abnormalities in an unborn child can be detected, is fraught with moral dilemmas, the magnitude of which are only now being understood. The standard use of the test has been to provide women in high-risk categories—older women, women with a family history of genetic diseases, women who have contracted German measles in the first trimester of their pregnancies—with information about the well-being of their babies. If the test proves that abnormalities do exist, the options are to abort the child or carry it to term anyway.

The test by itself is not without risk to the child. It involves the precise insertion of a needle into the womb and withdrawing a small quantity of amniotic fluid which is then tested. There is always the chance of the needle going into the placenta or the child, causing severe damage or miscarriage. Women are advised that if they do not intend to have an abortion if the child is found to be defective, they would be better off not having the test at all. As such, it can be termed a "hunt and kill" method.

In the United States, when the first test came out, fears were expressed by many feminists in regard to one of the side aspects of the test: that, in addition to revealing defects, it could also reveal the sex of the child. They were afraid that such information would be used to abort baby girls simply because they were girls and irrespective of their physical and mental health. These fears were brushed aside by most people as unthinkable. Surely, they reasoned, we have gone well beyond the stage where the birth of a girl is a tragedy.

Not so in India. Recent reports in national news magazines tell startling stories of women undergoing the test for the sole purpose of discovering whether the child is a girl. If it is, it is promptly aborted. The reasons given are painfully familiar: the expense of marrying a daughter off, the need for sons to help in the family business and carry on the family name—in short, the age-old preference for boys over girls.

Feminists, naturally, have risen in anger. With morality and justice as their standards, they argue that it is "morally incorrect," to use the words of Dr. Kirpal Kaur who performs abortions at the Guru Tegh Bahadur Medical College in Amritsar, to allow sex to be the determining factor in the decision to abort. In effect, as Manjulika Dubey points out in a recent article in *Mainstream*, using the test in this way affirms what has long been suspected in this country: that to be born female is to be genetically defective.

Both Ms. Dubey and Anjali Deshpande, author of a second article in the same magazine, draw attention to the steadily decreasing ratio of women to men in India (from 1000:972 in 1901 to 1000:935 in 1981). "If amniocentesis is misused on a large scale to weed out female fetuses, the ratio is bound to show a further decline," writes Ms. Deshpande. Ms. Dubey goes on to decry the failures of the feminist movement if it is possible that women could "reject their own kind and … worship and covet power objectified in the male to the point of participating in *atrocities* against their own daughters" (emphasis added).

"Atrocity" is her term for abortion. "Female feticide" is Ms. Deshpande's. And from Vimla Ranadive, secretary of the All India Co-ordination Committee of Working Women: "It is like the Nazi's 'final solution' of exterminating the Jews and it only adds a touch of sophistication to the brutal practice."

"Atrocity," "female feticide," "brutal practice." Apt descriptions of abortion—but they ring a bit hollow coming from people who, in the next breath, assert that abortion rights must be safeguarded so that women can "control their lives."

What are we to make of all this? Without denying in any sense the depravity of killing baby girls simply because they are girls, I submit that the position feminists have taken on this issue is morally bankrupt, without substance of any kind.

Why? Because one cannot have it both ways. Once the abortion of any child, for any reason, is permitted, the abortion of all children becomes acceptable. If it is all right to kill a child because it is handicapped, or because its mother is unmarried, or because it is the third child in a family that only wanted two, why isn't it all right to kill it because it is a girl?

This process of aborting girls when boys are wanted has been termed "selective abortion," but in fact every abortion is a selective one. What changes from case to case are only the values of the parents, determining what they select and what they reject. Parents who only value physically and mentally normal children might reject a child who was retarded or who had hemophilia. Parents who value education and want to be able to provide their children with it might reject a third child if their resources could only educate two. Parents who value their time and freedom might reject *any* children they produced. And parents who value boys might well reject a child known to be a girl.

Feminists who have been so active in assuring women of the "right to choose" can hardly complain when those same women exercise their freedom to choose something with which feminists do not agree. Choice being such a highly personal affair, one can hardly expect everyone to choose the same things. But it is tragically ironic that what has been hailed as the "great liberator" of women may turn out instead to be the means of their destruction—a tool to make them, in Manjulika Dubey's words, an "endangered species."

Perhaps, however, something good may yet emerge from this "female feticide" outrage. Perhaps people, and feminists in particular, will finally realize what is actually at stake in an abortion, any abortion. Perhaps from this undeniable truth that it is wrong to kill girls will emerge the larger truth that it is wrong to kill anyone. Perhaps it will first be necessary for a special interest group to champion the cause of each particular group of children targeted for destruction: feminists for baby girls, disabled activists for handicapped babies, would-be adoptive parents for unwanted babies.

This would certainly be the long way round, but perhaps at the end of it all we would realize that the single unifying factor in all these cases is that the child to be aborted is, first and foremost, a human child and one of us, that to kill her is to kill that which makes us human, bringing us closer to the day when the entire race—male and female—is an endangered species.

Grace Dermody

Grace Dermody graduated from St. Elizabeth's College in New Jersey with a degree in English. With an interest in working for women's rights, Dermody joined NOW in 1975, but her involvement lasted only a short time because of NOW's increasing emphasis on abortion rights. After joining the prolife movement, she read about Feminists for Life and immediately became a member. She formed the New Jersey chapter of Feminists for Life and, along with co-member Judy Novak, has spoken extensively about feminist prolife theory at Universities and other public forums. Her writings have appeared in the *New York Times* and other local publications.

In 1983, the local newspapers and television news teams were covering the trial of a young single mother who had killed her son. Dermody followed the case closely and was impressed with the fact that the psychiatrist testifying on the mother's behalf, Dr. Robert Gould, drew a connection between the traumatization of the abortion she obtained the day before the tragedy and the fatal beating of her son. After the trial, Dermody interviewed Dr. Gould about his testimony and specifically about his opinion concerning the link between abortion and child abuse. He makes clear his conviction that violence begets violence and desensitizes the perpetrator, leading to further devaluation of life in general; yet, despite his strong statements, Dr. Gould still supports a woman's right to choose violence in the form of abortion.

Trial and Trauma in New Jersey
by Grace Dermody

On July 29, 1983, a jury in Newark, New Jersey, convicted twenty-year-old Renée Nicely of the brutal beating murder of her son, Shawn. On the same day, her twenty-one-year-old boyfriend and father of their five children, Alan Bass, was convicted of aggravated murder in the same crime. The subsequent prison sentences were life for Nicely and twenty years for Bass.

Throughout this case, repeated references were made to an abortion Renée Nicely had the day before the crime. Both of her defense lawyers and the defense psychiatrist made a point of connecting it directly to the final act of killing the three-year-old youngster who had been a victim of child abuse most of his life.

Dr. Robert E. Gould, professor of psychiatry at New York University's Medical Center, examined Nicely during two two-hour sessions over a period of four months. In his testimony for the defense he told the jury that the ultimate act—"the stomping death of Shawn"—was prompted by "a very traumatic event," having an abortion the day before Shawn was beaten to death.

I interviewed Dr. Gould in December at his Manhattan brownstone (I had earlier disclosed my prolife leanings in a telephone call), and the results provide some enlightening and surprising second-thoughts from a man whose philosophy, in his own words, "does not coincide with the Right to Life group."

I first asked Dr. Gould why he, specifically, was selected by the defense to examine Renée Nicely, and found that he was a specialist for many years in adolescent and family psychiatry, and was at one time Director of Adolescent Services at N.Y.U. Bellevue. Then we discussed the trial.

DERMODY: Would you say she was a religious person?

GOULD: I didn't pick that up, but it may be an inner feeling. I don't think she was much of a churchgoer, but you can feel very religious anyway. She didn't stress that ever, but made that statement just one time. She expressed guilt and a feeling of great upset.

DERMODY: Did Renée say that the abortion was the reason she killed Shawn?

GOULD: No. She just expressed guilt, guilt and a feeling of great upset. And it was my interpretation then of the events of the next morning that included the abortion very strongly as a trigger.

DERMODY: The *Newark Star Ledger* quoted you as saying during testimony that Renée Nicely would "probably have killed Shawn anyway at some time."

GOULD: See, that's part of the problem with quotations. I would never say with a certainty that she would have killed Shawn no matter what. I'd have to be God to say that. [Here followed a discussion of the confluence of factors necessary to result in suicide or homicide.] … The same in talking about Renée. I am not at all sure, I mean, I couldn't feel any certainty of sureness that she would have killed Shawn had not the abortion been involved. It was the only time in her life she had an abortion. It occurred the day before she killed Shawn. She was very, very upset about it. So I have to think it was linked. It was not purely coincidental.

DERMODY: Sounds as if you were misquoted then.

GOULD: I think so.

DERMODY: Would you say then, without the abortion the day before it's possible she might not have killed him?

GOULD: Yes. That's right. Absolutely. Absolutely.

DERMODY: Dr. Gould, you testified that the ultimate act—the "stomping to death of Shawn"—was prompted by "a very traumatic event," having an abortion the day before Shawn was beaten to death. Will you tell me, if an abortion can cause trauma resulting in murder, as in this case, what other traumatic behavior can result from an abortion?

GOULD: Well, with some people, and I have to emphasize that, it can cause any number of aberrations in one's behavior. I don't think it's stretching a point to say it may make killing easier. If you think that in killing a fetus, you are killing someone human and alive, I think it's fair to say that person who feels that way could then kill someone else more easily.

In spite of this startling conclusion, Dr. Gould defends abortion as the better choice in some cases, and he cites some teenagers for whom the abortion would be "less traumatizing than having a baby ... if they drop out of school, if they have their whole life compromised, if they have to give up the child for adoption and have to wonder all the rest of their lives what this child is doing ..."

He does admit, however, that he has had to change his mind about the number of women who are seriously affected by having an abortion. He told me:

> I do believe that almost every woman is traumatized by an abortion. That is the strongest position I've ever taken. I've felt that a substantial number of women could undergo an abortion as if it were a cold. Let me put it another way. I do think there are some women—I now think it is a minority—I used to think it was a larger number—who can undergo an abortion and not be strongly traumatized. But I used to think it was a much greater number than I now believe.

DERMODY: Is there any way to tell beforehand who will react traumatically to an abortion?

GOULD: Not completely, for sure. Because I think it can trigger responses that the individual was not aware existed. You hear women talk a good deal about what pregnancy means to them which is very different from what they thought before they became pregnant.

But I think there are enough unpredictable reactions that one has to be awfully careful. This is why I am willing to change my idea about it being a relatively simple and emotion-free procedure. But the creation, I guess, is really so unusual, and profound, and strange, that it can have meaning that the individual is not aware of.

DERMODY: Dr. Gould, people, like yourself, who support abortion say that it's necessary to prevent unwanted children to save women's lives—presumedly, make the world a better place. But that's not what I see happening. I see more child abuse, just as many women dying from abortions, and an epidemic of teenage pregnancies and illegitimate births. Is it all worth it?

GOULD: I would reluctantly have to say, yes, we're better off because I place such a high value on an individual's rights. But I do think the larger the national abortion rate, the more it says something is wrong in our society. So I'm on the horns of a dilemma … But one of the reasons I'm in favor of the liberalized position on abortion is that, in the past, abortions were done in two ways that certainly are worse than legalized abortion provides today, that is, in a hospital setting with no criminal implications for having done it. In the past, one did it under dirtier conditions so that the chance of the mother being severely hurt or killed was present. And also, it increased the feeling of guilt that one was doing something wrong … But, on the other hand, the legalization of it and the implied permission, or the lack of it having the kind of importance that I think a pregnancy should have, diminishes one's value about life and makes it easier to become pregnant in a thoughtless way. And I think that has repercussions that are unhealthy.

DERMODY: What do you think the effect of abortion is on the whole society? Do you see a devaluation of human life?

GOULD: I guess I do. I guess I would agree there is devaluation. And it would be so much better not to have the problem at all.

DERMODY: We both agree that a healthy society should put a high value on human life. But in an abortion society, where is that going to come from?

GOULD: I guess it has to come from almost every sector of society, starting, certainly, from your parents—through laws, attitudes towards killing in general, including, for instance, hunting animals. I think there is a devaluation there.

DERMODY: Do you object to hunters shooting animals?

GOULD: I guess I do. I'm saying the more one kills, the less one values life … I would guess killing anything makes it easier to kill in general. But the more—the closer what you kill is to a human, the easier it is to kill a human. So that an insect—a cockroach—if you kill it— would not be so life diminishing as killing a dog, a horse, a monkey. The closer you come to being human in form and thinking, the more, I think, you are conditioning yourself to kill humans.

DERMODY: Thank you, Dr. Gould.

Leslie Keech (1954–1989)

L eslie Keech was Treasurer of Feminists for Life for several years and contributed richly to the organization. She originated, helped write and produce, and participated in a radio spot project; she was President and Public Relations Director of Kansans for Life; and, in the spirit of Elizabeth Cady Stanton, who insisted that the pregnant woman need not be an invalid, Keech was a childbirth instructor dedicated to celebrating woman's reproductive ability and provided practical support and services to young women facing crisis pregnancies. On September 8, 1989, Leslie Keech died unexpectedly as the result of a blood clot following surgery. Her funeral was appropriately held at The Lighthouse, a large Kansas City maternity home, and the overflowing crowd was a testimony to her impact on many lives.

Keech was an articulate speaker, clear thinker, a courageous and witty campaigner as well as a strong and loving friend whose convictions stemmed from her deep Christian faith and feminism. Her loss reminds us that we have far to go; her life reminds us that, with hope, we may arrive.

The following articles are examples of Keech's sharp wit and ability to address even the sober issue of abortion with humor and satire. Both essays represent Keech's responses to articles published in popular magazines. In "Better Living (for men) Through Surgery (for women)," she examines how abortion has facilitated male sexual irresponsibility resulting in woman's "right to be exploited." In "The Sensitive Abortionist," Keech comments on the ironic confessions of an abortion facility nurse who admits to the horrors involved in the profession of killing fetuses. She also notes the nurse's association of abortion with rape, an apparently popular conflation, judging from graffiti we have observed on college campuses stating, "Abortion is Rape with a Price Tag." "The rationalization of abortion," says Keech, is "intellectually dishonest" and underscores the dubious implications of "choice."

Better Living (for men) Through Surgery (for women)
by Leslie Keech

We are all used to it by now: the media establishment portraying prolifers as insensitive, sexist clods, while the noble knights of the proabortion position are the champions of women's rights. But occasionally the hand slips, and even the mass media reveals that the central right abortion grants is the right to be exploited. Two articles that came to my attention recently should cause any thinking person to reexamine just what legal abortion's legacy really is.

In the July issue of *Glamour* magazine an article by Eric Goodman appeared, entitled "Men and Abortion." It is an account of several men's experiences with their partners' abortions. The thread running throughout the article in nearly every instance was that the abortion was *his* idea—and the woman agreed to follow his lead.

For instance, "Walt's" account: Instead of advising her to do what she thought best for her own life, Walt allowed his lover to be guided by her strong desire to "save their relationship." "I said, 'What do you want to do?' She suggested abortion, thinking this would make it possible for me to continue to paint, that that in turn would prolong our relationship … She's my age, thirty-five, and it may have been her last chance to have a child. I believe she would be much happier if she'd had it—but I would be unhappy having a child I never saw and didn't live with. I guess I sound like a real cad. Maybe I was." Gee, Walt, I had a *stronger* word in mind …

Or how about "Christopher," who got the money for the abortion from his mother, then accompanied his girlfriend to a clinic that he likened to an "abortion factory" (front-alley variety). As he waited for the abortion to be completed, he pondered his predicament. "I think I felt more concerned about her than I really was, because I was there with her." Kind of amazing what a little trip to the abortion clinic will do for one's conscience, isn't it?

"Jack's" lover had an abortion while he was in law school. They considered themselves too young to have a child, and they were both in the middle of pursuing careers. They broke up some time after the abortion, and he married a woman who was unable to bear a child. He said, "So it turns out my one chance for a biological child was that aborted pregnancy in law school." The article goes on to admit, "If Jack's wife had been able to have children, it's unlikely he would have given much thought to what happened in law school."

"Jeff" has been involved in two abortions, but it took the second one to make him regret his behavior during the first. "I was afraid of getting snarled up in two kids and a house, so I took the refuge of asking, 'What do you want to do?' She was waiting for me to mention marriage, so she opted for abortion."

The selfish, sexist, irresponsible behavior shown by these and many other men is heightened and encouraged by abortion's easy way out. Our society expects that fathers should pay child support for their children, but at the same time we make it very easy for a man to simply use the woman for his pleasure, and then buy his way out of the deal for a couple hundred dollars! Why should a man pay child support for eighteen years, if he can "get rid of the problem" so neatly?

"Alex" shared his experience: "From the moment she told me, I wanted her to have an abortion. She knew I would. I'm still paying child support for the first three kids, and I don't make that much. The way things fell out, there's been a kid under four in my life for the past ten years. I'm tired of waking up in the middle of the night." Poor "Alex." It *is* important to get your rest—no matter what the cost.

Finally, an interview appeared in *Penthouse* magazine with George Brett, first baseman for the Kansas City Royals baseball team. The interview is extremely enlightening concerning male attitudes towards abortion—and towards women.

George admits to paying for two women to have abortions, and feels that those decisions were the right ones, since he wasn't ready to get married. (Keep in mind that this is a man who could easily afford to raise a child, marriage or no.) George *was* rather pleased about one aspect of the abortions, however. It "proved" that he was indeed the stud he purports to be. He candidly states, "I know I'm fertile. I've got the checkbook to prove it. But getting a couple of girls pregnant gave me a sense that there's no sweat. I can have kids anytime I want. I've had the security of knowing I'm a proven performer."

What a wonderful service to humanity those two women have contributed; by subjecting themselves to surgery, they have assured us that George Brett is not infertile. That's just swell. Did two children really have to die to prove it?

I wonder if the "prochoice" movement really understands how anti-woman abortion really is? It has certainly not brought us forward in establishing equality with men. We need callous, exploitative men to step up to our level, not drag us down to theirs.

The Sensitive Abortionist
by Leslie Keech

One of the most incredible nuances of the pro-abortion movement is the ambivalence that occasionally leaks out of it. This was epitomized in the pro-abortion book, *In Necessity and Sorrow*.

Possibly the all-time best example of this philosophy, however, is an article which appeared in the October 1987 issue of *Harper's* magazine entitled, "We Do Abortions Here," by Sallie Tisdale. It is written by a registered nurse in an abortion clinic, and is as graphic in its description of an abortion as anything I have ever read from the prolife movement. Her conclusions, however, about the need to continue this practice are quite disturbing.

The article must be read in its entirety to completely appreciate the mental gymnastics one must perform in order to work in a place such as she describes, but there are several points crying out for comment.

It seems as if the pro-aborts have decided to admit to hand-wringing, agonizing and having second thoughts about abortion—this apparently makes them "sensitive." Their conclusions, however, are predictable. You may have second thoughts as long as the *second* one is that abortion is acceptable and right, agonizing though it may be.

Ms. Tisdale reaches this conclusion, even though she admits, "I have fetus dreams, we all do here: dreams of abortions one after the other; of buckets of blood splashed on the walls; trees full of crawling fetuses." I'd be willing to bet that other nurses performing legitimate medical procedures don't have similar dreams about tonsils and appendixes.

The abortionists are even ambivalent—"For one physician the 'boundary' is a particular week of gestation; for another, it is a certain number of repeated abortions. But these boundaries can be fluid, too ..." Why all this wishy-washiness if this is so acceptable and necessary?

The pro-abortion movement has long maintained that abortion is simply a "removal of the contents of the uterus," an allegedly safe procedure with no long-term side effects. Ms. Tisdale explains, "Abortion is so routine that one expects it to be quick, cheap and painless." Why then do we hear her admission, "Abortion is the narrowest edge between kindness and cruelty. Done as well as it can be, it is still violence—merciful violence ..." This is painless? For who? The abortionist?

Feminists have long pointed out that violence against weaker members of the human race by stronger ones only perpetuates society's inability to deal with social problems. The chauvinism of men "owning" their wives and children has long contributed to this problem. Abortion is the continuation of this violence by those who should know better—women, who brutalize their own children (property) in the name of gaining control over their own lives. At whose expense? Does this really liberate us, or lower us to the level of the original perpetrators of the violence?

And has the exercise of this "right" improved women's options in life? Apparently not. Tisdale states, "Women who have the fewest choices of all exercise their right to an abortion the most."

Feminists for Life has said all along that abortion takes away real, affirming choices and replaces them with women who have abortions because they feel they have no choice.

Abortion has always seemed to me very much like a rape in reverse. The doctor (usually a male), for a fee, undoes what has already been done. Interestingly, Tisdale relates a dream she has had: "I dreamed that two men grabbed me and began to drag me away. 'Let's do an abortion,' they said with a sickening leer, and I began to scream, plunged into a vision of sucking, scraping pain, of being spread and torn by impartial instruments that only do what they are bidden." I am both fascinated and repulsed by the revelation that even to nurses in the clinics, this supposedly safe, allegedly necessary procedure is subconsciously perceived to be a male-on-female rape.

The rationalization of abortion as a necessary evil, if only you are sensitive enough and wring your hands enough, is where the pro-abortion movement has finally landed. It is an intellectually dishonest position, especially after looking at the facts as Ms. Tisdale obviously has.

"We talk glibly about choice," she admits, "but the choice for what?" We've been telling you, but you haven't been listening, Ms. Tisdale—the choice to kill.

Rachel MacNair

Rachel MacNair, President of Feminists for Life from 1984 to 1994, graduated with honors in 1978 from Earlham College in Richmond, Indiana, with a degree in Peace and Conflict Studies. Her Quaker heritage places her activism in the tradition of Lucretia Mott and Susan B. Anthony, and her agitating for social justice extends back to the McGovern Campaign and the Vietnam antiwar movement when she was only thirteen years old. She has vigorously protested the production of nuclear weapons, the use of nuclear energy, and U.S. military interventions; and she has long been committed to the feminist and prolife movements.

MacNair was introduced to the prolife movement by Juli Loesch Wiley and her group, Prolifers for Survival. She has served on the boards of the Seamless Garment Network (a network of groups that embrace a consistent life ethic that includes opposition to abortion, euthanasia, war, poverty, capital punishment and the arms race) and the Civilian Based Defense Association which explores alternative (nonviolent) defense strategies. Her work with Feminists for Life has included writing (she contributed to the amicus curiae brief on behalf of FFL in the case of *Webster v. Reproductive Health Services* and has written several articles that have appeared in *Sisterlife* and other feminist and prolife publications), radio and television talk show appearances, and extensive public speaking.

In the tradition of Sylvia Pankhurst, MacNair has been arrested for her activities 17 times. Most of her arrests resulted from protests at nuclear weapons and nuclear energy sites, and five resulted from distributing literature at abortion clinics (she observes that the legal establishment has dealt much more harshly with her for her prolife activities than her peace activities). Although she has not served as much time in jail as her English feminist foremother (a record none of us really want to see her break), MacNair's civil disobedience bespeaks her deep convictions and commitment to life issues. MacNair continues her politically incorrect activities in Kansas City, Missouri, where she lives with her son.

In MacNair's first article, she addresses probably the most fundamental case made for abortion "choice"—the back-alley butcher argument. While fully acknowledging the tragedy of women who, in desperation and terror, sought illegal abortions and lost their lives in the process, MacNair points out that "safe and legal" abortion is not the panacea abortion rights advocates would have us believe. Women are still placing their lives in the hands of men of questionable qualifications and motivation. Providing these women with "cleaner knives" (in the words of Anne Maloney) instead of working to change the conditions that lead women to the desperate act of seeking out an abortionist to kill their *in-utero* children may be the easier answer, but it is not the right answer for them, their children or society.

In "Parallel Cages" MacNair discusses the effects of abortion on men. Always working toward inclusiveness, MacNair addresses what much feminist dialogue on the abortion issue has ignored: that male domination hurts everyone, including men, and that in condemning male oppression we must not condemn men in general. She makes a case for relations in which the partnership continues beyond the sex act. In her last article, "Schools of Thought," MacNair continues her theme of inclusiveness as she explores the value of diversity in the prolife movement and social movements in general. Here we see her functioning in her best role—that of peacemaker.

Would Illegalizing Abortion Set Loose the Back-Alley Butchers? No—Legalizing Abortion Did That

by Rachel MacNair

Many people now understand the harm abortion does to women but still think making it illegal will cause more problems than it solves. We need to make it clear why it's in women's interests that abortion be illegal.

It used to be that when abortions were botched, the woman at least had the option of turning her abortionist in. On those few occasions when the woman actually died, at least then the prosecutor would pay attention and maybe put the abortionists out of business. But now, we can cite several instances where women died of legal abortion and the abortionist had only to put up with the irritant of a malpractice suit. We do not protect women by telling back alley butchers they are free to advertise in the Yellow Pages.

For example, when Richard Mucie was convicted of a woman's death by abortion in 1968, his license was revoked. When *Roe v. Wade* came down, he used it to go to court and get his license back. He is back in business.

In 1983 and 1984, the state of California reported no abortion deaths—but we documented with our amicus brief in the Webster case the incontrovertible evidence that at least four women died in Los Angeles County alone in those two years. California has not corrected its records. The mother of one of the young women wrote, "I cry every day when I think how horrible her death was. She was slashed by them and then she bled to death ... I know that other young black women are now dead after abortion at that address ... Where is [the abortionist] now? Has he been stopped? Has anything happened to him because of what he did to my Belinda? ... People tell me nothing has happened, that nothing ever happens to white abortionists who leave young black women dead."

We should not be allowing the government to participate in the deception of women. Abortion kills a living human being and mutilates another. Surgery done on a healthy body is mutilation, and such surgery done without adequately informed consent is a battery. Legalized abortion without even minimal informed consent is widespread, epidemic battering of women. Women deserve a straightforward acknowledgement by government of this fact.

Many women wouldn't consider abortion if it were illegal. Others would find many of the unfair pressures for abortion lifted if their families and friends knew this was not a quick way out. Nonviolent solutions to the problem become more attractive when the violent solution is less expedient.

Illegalization would cause the number of abortions to go down dramatically. When Medicaid funding was cut off, studies contrasting one year with funding to the next year without funding found that the number of abortions went down dramatically—and the number of childbirths went down slightly. The abortions that didn't happen weren't replaced by childbirth. They were replaced by greater responsibility in avoiding pregnancy.

Illegalization would cause the number of services to pregnant women to increase dramatically. Not only would the emotional support of friends and family improve in many cases, but volunteers working on alternative services would have more time and resources. Already, crisis pregnancy centers outnumber abortion clinics. More is needed.

Finally, it is the abortionists who will try to get prosecutions of women, not the prolifers; if the abortionist can make her an accomplice, her testimony is less credible and she is less likely to turn the abortionist in.

Let me underscore this point: in practical terms, abortion laws will be enforced by the women who have had abortions.

Women should no longer be denied this power.

Parallel Cages: The Oppression of Men
by Rachel MacNair

Abortion defenders say that women must have access to abortion in order to have equality with men. The prolife feminist responds that there is no other oppressed group that requires surgery in order to become unoppressed. Abortion defenders suggest that we now have technology available to fix the inherent biological handicap of women. Prolife feminists believe that Nature was never the source of the idea that our bodies are inferior due to their innate abilities.

We apply that reasoning on a biological basis, and should apply it on a social basis as well. Oppression has not been confined to one sex. For instance, we complain about the playboy mentality that treats a woman's body as a recreational object. Under traditional role constraints, there is also a female parallel: the woman who regards a man as a walking wallet. The gold digger is like the playboy; for each their prey is seen as an object rather than as a real person.

There is also a common strain popular in current anti-feminist rhetoric, which holds that men are basically predators, always on the prowl, and require the virtuous woman to "civilize" them.

This is a breathtaking put-down of men.

We complain of the hysterical image of the woman who "finds herself pregnant" and needs her abortion paid for by "the one who did this to you," as if the idea that she is responsible for herself, or in control of her life, were impossible. The predator image of men suggests that a man is not responsible for himself or in control of his life either, but subject to irresistible impulses.

It is striking to set the stereotype of feminist man-haters against this man-hating anti-feminist rhetoric. Likewise, just as some women organized against suffrage, the Equal Rights Amendment and other matters of benefit to women, men are expounding on this anti-male theme with vigor.

One way this insulting predator image hurts women as well as men is the role assigned to the virtuous woman: to keep men in line. If she fails to do so, if she makes herself sexually available—indeed, if she fails to make herself emphatically sexually unavailable—then she has not done her job. *His* bad behavior becomes *her* fault. This becomes an example of an air-tight blame-the-victim strategy.

As this gender theory of man-as-predator gets worked out, a striking paradox emerges. It would seem to be a forceful argument against any form of male domination; she should rather take control of disciplining that conscienceless brute. It's therefore puzzling to see proponents of the theory upholding female submissiveness as virtuous. The philosophy that has women being submissive to husbands—or potential husbands—is in internal conflict with the philosophy that sees women's role as taming the prowling male.

In my frequent radio talk-show interviews on prolife feminism, the subject of male irresponsibility for their own children comes up constantly. It's one of the major causes of abortion, and comes clearly under the heading of abortion as a male-dominated society's oppression of women. But whenever I make this point, I follow up by adding that men are entitled to be nurturing of their children—not just the wallet and spanking paddle of the family, not nurturing confined to an occasional storybook or baseball game, but involved in the whole spectrum of childrearing, just as women are expected to be.

Abortion, then, has another negative effect on the development of healthy, responsible roles for male adulthood. While it rewards rotten fathers by letting them off the hook, making it easier to use women and walk away, abortion can also punish men who would be good, sensitive fathers by telling them to chill their emotions until birth and don't begin bonding: they have no right to care about that "tissue."

Men who engage in exploitative behavior are indeed one of the root causes of abortion, and we should cry that from the roof-tops. But it is not properly sensitive to oppression, not really feminist or egalitarian, if we leave it there. Just as you can't help the unborn child without helping the mother, and you can't hurt that child without hurting the mother, it's also true that the very same things that hurt women worst also hurt men.

Equality goes both ways—women becoming equal to men, men becoming equal to women. If it doesn't go both ways, then we are accepting the model of "natural" male superiority at the same time that we rebel against it.

Men get post-abortion syndrome. Men usually have a strong desire, not merely to protect, but to be strongly involved in the raising of their children. Thoroughly right-wing men will often become more sympathetic to feminism when they understand that we value and support such male interests as these.

Making this connection is crucial, because otherwise anger at oppression leads merely to different forms of oppression. If feminism is about dispensing with oppression, all of it, we must identify "The Oppressor" not as a set of individuals, but as the attitudes and philosophies that confine both women and men.

Schools of Thought
by Rachel MacNair

Every large movement has internal disagreements. Hostile outsiders call these factions. If the movement accepts that designation, the opposition succeeds in making it a divided movement. If they are regarded as schools of thought rather than factions, the movement is strengthened by its diversity.

Among divisions common to every movement:

1. The "purists" vs. the "pragmatists." Purists say compromise is immoral and detrimental in the long run. Pragmatists argue for an "all or something" approach. In the prolife movement, American Life League (ALL) is the largest purist group, and split from the National Right to Life Committee (NRL), the pragmatists, over that point. Among abortion defenders, the National Organization for Women (NOW) springs to mind as purist, and has come under fire from pragmatist groups for it. (Someone in the National Women's Political Caucus was quoted as saying she'd like to take out a contract on Molly Yard for proposing a third political party.) In Feminists for Life, both schools of thought live side by side remarkably well.

2. The "straight" people vs. the "street" people. Nonviolent "street" people argue that it's immoral to wait for normal legal channels rather than taking direct action immediately, versus "straight" people who believe respectability is important, and being outside the system is harmful to the cause. In the prolife movement, of course, nonviolent rescuers are "street" people, and NRL emphasizes respectability. This isn't a

strict division, of course; both schools of thought are represented in normal legal demonstrations, and large numbers of people will engage in both kinds of activities. NOW tries hard to essentially do both. Still, there are tensions between the points of view.

3. "Single Issue" vs. "Everything's Connected." In prolife circles, the latter school of thought may be the seamless garment or consistent life ethic position, or alternatively the pro-family blanket of issues typically espoused by the right. That shows immediately what people see of value in the single issue approach—people of widely divergent views can still work together on a single problem.

Feminists for Life has many members who argue that we should have a broad platform that includes a large number of issues. Feminism is, after all, a philosophy that is multi-issue in nature. As any reader of [*Sisterlife's*] Letters to the Editor column knows, there is a countervailing viewpoint that we ought to focus only on what makes us unique, not dilute our efforts or lose members who disagree on side issues. Broaden the platform, narrow the membership; narrow the platform, broaden the membership.

I would argue that, on all the above points, both schools of thought are correct and add strength to the movement.

1. If the entire movement stands ready to compromise, the final goal could get lost, and there is value in the strategy of pursuing the fullest expression of the movement's goal. If you convince people that killing the child is wrong and hurts the mother even in cases of rape and incest, then you've settled the question on just about everything else as well.

On the other hand, an all-or-nothing approach will probably end up achieving too much nothing. Compromise can save lives, and moves us closer to the goal than we were before.

In short, let the pragmatists push and the purists pull, and between the two of us, we'll get there faster than either one of us alone.

2. Concerning "street" people vs. "straight" people, I recall an instance in which I was attending my state NOW convention. Outside the conference of 50 people, there were 400 prolifers yelling "Stop the Killing Now!" They were regarded as crazy, of course, but an interesting phenomenon occurred: several of the NOW women attending turned to me as the reasonable person to whom they could come and explain their sincerity, that they really weren't advocating mass murder of children, etc. I enjoyed some of the most productive dialogue that I have ever had at such a convention. If I had not been

there, the prolife view would have been entirely dismissed as crazy. If the picketers had not been there, I would have had little opportunity for the matter to come up. In our movement, as in any other, a good balance of respectable people wringing their hands over the tactics, while the people in the street keep the issue hot, results in good progress. That's how women finally got the vote.

3.   Finally, the single-issue vs. multi-issue question gets FFL the most passion. We try to strike a balance by being single-issue, broadly defined. That gets us into related issues like equal male responsibility for children, family leave, child care, rape, childbirth choice, but keeps us out of issues like religion and the military.

Our more thoroughgoing single-issue members must understand that we are constantly accused of using the word "feminist" as a gimmick, so we cannot leave unstated our genuine beliefs on related feminist issues. We are then able to work in coalition with other groups concerned with these matters; this does not dilute, but strengthens our ability to work on the single issue.

Our multi-issue members should understand that we must avoid the loss of members that occurs every time we add another issue. Our resources are not great, and we must leave some matters to other groups who can do them just as well. Nor can we afford to spend scarce media time arguing other points which are not central.

When we published our list of resolutions a few issues back, for every letter of complaint that we received, we got another praising them. Among the complainers, it was an even split between those who thought we had too few resolutions, and those who thought we had too many!

Balancing these different schools of thought is not easy, since all are valid and all have something to contribute. On the other hand, we are a remarkably large group to have made it this long without splitting into factions, aren't we?

Mary Krane Derr

Mary Krane Derr is a psychotherapist, poet and nonfiction writer. Her works have appeared in such publications as the *Utne Reader, Chicago Sun-Times, Journal of Poetry Therapy,* and the women's spirituality journals *Daughters of Sarah* and *Mother's Underground.* She earned a bachelor's degree in biology at Bryn Mawr, a women's college founded in the nineteenth century. There she first recognized herself as the beneficiary of a movement with a long but little-appreciated history: feminism. She later earned a master's degree in social work from the University of Chicago. She has worked principally in the field of reproductive counseling.

Derr is also the mother of a miniature "strong-minded woman" born in 1987. In the following article, Derr recounts the difficulties that she and her fiancé, now husband, experienced bringing their daughter into the world. This story reminds us that crisis pregnancies must never be taken lightly. It is mere rhetoric to speak either of "saving babies' lives" or "giving women a choice" unless we as individuals and as a society are willing to offer practical and emotional support for *all* the humans involved in untimely pregnancies, before and after delivery. The thousands of pregnancy centers throughout the country established, funded, and staffed by prolifers are an important legacy of the prolife movement, but we cannot assume that they are enough. We must change those societal conditions and attitudes that make abortion a seemingly easier alternative than facing an unplanned pregnancy; and we must help effect the healing of those who, thinking they had no other choice, were unable to choose life for their children.

Pregnancy is No Mere Inconvenience, Abortion is No Solution
by Mary Krane Derr

During my very crisis-ridden pregnancy, a conservative male abortion opponent of my acquaintance surveyed my huge belly with smug knowingness. "Don't have that baby," he joked. "It'll ruin your life." What could I say to this person who so proudly declared himself to be "prolife" and yet so blithely overlooked the very real hardships that had come with this most untimely pregnancy? Wasn't *my* life as worthy of reverence as my unborn child's? This fetus was not simply floating around in the air somewhere. This child was growing inside another equally human being, a woman whose surprise transition to motherhood marked a cataclysmic and irreversible change in her own body, her own life story.

Despite conscientious use of family planning, my fiancé and I had become parents years before we really wanted to. We were not planning to be married, or even live in the same part of the country, for at least another year. We had both hoped to finish our educations before starting a family. Because we were both in school, our financial resources were very limited. How to afford maternity clothes—much less years of raising a child? And how was I going to pursue my long-held hopes of completing graduate school and having a rewarding and productive work life? For so many years I had worked minimum wage jobs and struggled to land scholarships—to high school, college, and then graduate school. Would all this painful struggle turn out to be in vain? And what of my boyfriend's own plan to establish himself in a profession that requires years of schooling?

These considerations were daunting enough, but there was also the factor of my health. I had long suffered from several medical problems, most notably juvenile diabetes. The baby and I faced numerous perils: a high risk of miscarriage, toxemia, complicated labor, and fetal handicap, among other things. I had to have weekly visits with a specialist in high-risk pregnancy and several hospitalizations. Luckily the student health insurance had a maternity rider. But would the policy be canceled while I took the necessary leave of absence from school? Diabetic pregnancies are extremely expensive; mine came out to over $20,000 (and that was in 1986-87).

And then—worst of all—there was tremendous emotional pain to bear. Although I was desperately in need of support, certain relatives ostracized me for this very public evidence that I had been sexually active outside of marriage—the very people who had always vociferously declared "abortion is murder!" Didn't they see what it took for a woman in a situation like this NOT to have an abortion? Didn't they have any inkling that a woman might be so desperate and so frightened that she might abort rather than risk facing such hostility and judgment?

Was I going to take out the pain of being rejected and unwanted on this child? While growing up, I had been physically, emotionally, and sexually abused. Did abused children really all grow up to be child abusers? What sort of a mother would I make? I had a lot of experience caring for children, and enjoyed their company very much. But could this demanding, absorbing, sacred task be entrusted to the likes of *me* for years and years to come? At the same time, I was pretty sure from the start that adoption was not the right choice for me, even though it is for many women. I had had too, too many losses and traumas and disappointments over the course of a lifetime. Intuitively I sensed that healing lay ultimately in parenting rather than placing this child—though for other mothers, the opposite may be true. And, because of my medical problems, this might be my only chance to bear and nurse a child—experiences I had longed for, though I'd certainly wished to have them much later in life.

But HOW was I going to make it all work? I became especially scared the one time I felt a flicker of resentment towards my developing baby: *how dare you presume to take over!* I immediately recognized this as the victim-blaming turn of mind that any tired, frustrated, overstressed parent can easily slip into. I also knew that I could refrain from acting on it, before or after this child was born.

But who was going to help me begin the monumental task of breaking the cycle of violence? At the university women's health clinic, it was assumed that of course I wanted an abortion. When my pregnancy test came back positive, the nurse automatically offered to refer me for a "termination." She didn't even stop to ask me what I wanted, let alone bring up what that would mean for the baby. She only knew that I was a student, diabetic, and not married. The nurse was quite astonished when I did not gratefully seize the opportunity to abort. She seemed quite unprepared to offer any encouragement or concrete advice about how I might have this child, other than, with an incredulous silence, referring me to an OB-GYN specialist.

A few weeks later, a doctor at the same medical center patronizingly informed me—again without first bothering to consult my feelings and my preferences—that I should "consider termination, because the fetus may be defective." At that moment, I recognized a more appropriate target for my anger and frustration than the baby. I angrily responded that "defective" people weren't the problem—I knew that from being one myself—but rather attitudes like his. "Uh, well, it's your choice," he stammered, drawing back and leaving the room as fast as he could.

This pregnancy was certainly no minor inconvenience. But the problems, complex and confounding as they were, did not amount to a rationale for lethal violence against this new life within my body—and myself at the same time. Yet they were problems all the same. Thank God for the people who understood their gravity and who were willing to help me find alternatives other than the non-choice of abortion versus a hell-on-earth upbringing for this child.

Despite the disruption in his career plans, despite his own lack of funds, despite everything, the baby's father made good on his earlier promise to marry me in the unlikely event of a pregnancy (a choice that was right for us, though it may not be for other couples). He held my head and cleaned up the mess when I repeatedly vomited up the meals he had carefully planned and cooked. He patted the baby and talked to her *in utero*. He stayed with us through all the hospital stays and through a complicated 52-hour labor that ended in a Caesarian section. At the moment of her birth, she quieted immediately when she heard the already familiar sound of his voice. Before the delivery, even before the marriage, his family immediately accepted me as one of their own. Not all my biological relatives were hostile; some of them gladly joined my new in-laws in providing moral support, financial help, maternity and baby clothes. Somehow I was able to sustain the health insurance just long enough to cover all the obstetrical expenses. My employer, a well-known prolife attorney, was understanding about the leaves I needed during the pregnancy and invited me to return to work after the birth whenever I felt up to it.

Despite the rejection and judgmentalism we had encountered, the baby and I were miraculously surrounded by others who wanted to sustain us. Their loving attention helped reassure me that I could find the wherewithal to be both a good mother and, someday, an accomplished professional.

I often contemplate the compassion I felt for both Sarah and for myself from the time I first incredulously sensed her existence, even before missing a period. I had felt a sudden change deep in my body: I somehow knew a fragile yet tenacious little presence had taken up residence there. I sensed that this little being, just like me, had a unique life-plan which deserved to unfold. Venerable Khenpo Karthar Rinpoche, a beloved teacher of Tibetan Buddhism, has written: "Once a child is conceived, it is a being. This means abortion is destroying the life of a being, and one reaps the negative karma of having taken a life. It does not matter what size the being is. Even a small seed can develop into a flower." (Ven. Khenpo Karthar Rinpoche, *Dharma Paths,* Ithaca, NY: Snow Lion Publications, 1992, 75.) Abortion, I felt, would have simultaneously cut my daughter off from this realm of existence and pushed me down deeper into the very patterns of suffering I wanted to escape. Violence always generates more suffering than it promises to resolve. Incredibly, against all the odds, the desire to nurture both of us was being realized. I began to see that it could be realized for a lifetime.

Thus a difficult pregnancy was made bearable. But what of the countless women and girls who cannot see any answer but abortion? Who don't have health insurance? Who can't get Medicaid because of the latest budget cuts? Whose employers fire them, or refuse to hire them in the first place? Whose schools expel them? Whose churches will hound them as paragons of immorality if they do not in secret destroy the evidence of their unsanctioned libido? Whose boyfriends beat them, or walk out on them (even though *they* were the ones who refused to use condoms, or to ask permission for sex in the first place)? Whose parents really will throw them out into the street? Who can't find food or clothing or shelter? Who honestly feel that giving a child life necessarily means the horrible kind of life they had growing up? Who fear that the adoption system always dehumanizes birth parents? Who have internalized societal prejudices against disabled persons? Who have been taught nothing about their bodies but to loathe them? Who never learned their unborn children are not insensate clumps of tissue? Who never learned that *women* are not insensate clumps of tissue? Who do not know how to challenge the pressures that health care providers, relatives, friends, and others may put on them to abort, because they have been undermined and violated and trampled on since their own infancies?

I often wonder why some abortion opponents casually toss out the phrase "convenience abortion." This phrase insinuates that aborting women are by definition wicked, frivolous pleasure-seekers. If this is the case, then one need not bother even trying to empathize with a beleaguered woman—let alone lift a finger to *help* her. ("Hey, she made her own bed. Let her lie in it!") This trivializing of women's sufferings is as harmful and self-defeating as the dogma that the merest hint of concern for unborn humans, or even for women's wounds from abortion, is by definition virulent misogyny. Are our hearts so closed down, our moral imagination so restricted, our attachment to rigid and inhuman ideologies so staunch that we cannot enfold both pregnant women and their babies, both the born and the unborn, in our compassion? Can we do it any other way? Isn't "an injury to one an injury to all" after all?

When we recognize that childbearing is an arduous achievement, especially in a male-dominated society that makes it much harder than it has to be, we strengthen our ability to name and fight the injustices that pressure so many women into having abortions, that cause so many children to die. It is when we acknowledge and remedy the problems of a crisis pregnancy that we really help women choose life.

When my acquaintance made his flippant remark about my crisis pregnancy, I did not know quite how to articulate this point. But the ordeals and pleasures of being a mother have made me a stronger woman, and I can say it now. How can I keep silent? Sarah owes her life, and I my bodily, psychic, and spiritual integrity largely to people who did not write off our troubles as "mere inconveniences."

The positive karma of their actions is evident on a daily basis. Sarah is now an exuberant, imaginative, long-legged, tangle-haired eight-year-old who revels in making up stories, reading, doing math, jumping double-Dutch, and braiding hair and laughing with her friends. Sometimes she likes to "sit still and think about infinity" or "sit still and just let life happen to me!" Being her mother has certainly inspired me to finish school, and to find not one but two rewarding professions in which my deepest hurts have proven my most valuable resource. Most of all, I am finally coming out of the depression that has burdened most of my life. How much heavier it would have become if Sarah had not been born—especially considering that she was the only child we ever conceived before my total hysterectomy at age thirty (to relieve severe pain from endometriosis). She is living a happier life than I ever imagined was possible when I was her age. For I have learned in a very powerful, enduring way that genuinely caring people do exist, and I can treat my daughter the way they treat me. And every other person blessed by Sarah's presence in the world has their own story to tell.

All this positive karma may have even rubbed off on the man whose flippant remark once called forth all the hurts of my crisis pregnancy. Rumor has it that he has become considerably more familiar with women's reproductive dilemmas, and that he has actually become quite involved in providing abortion alternatives. Ironic, but might not this say something, too, about the innate potential for growth that should be honored in every person?

Abortion and Women's Sexual Liberation
by Mary Krane Derr

Extremist "prolifers" sometimes portray aborting women as "sluts" who wantonly kill innocent babies for the sake of their own sinful gratification. Extremist "prochoicers" echo this stereotype when they proclaim that women absolutely cannot realize their right to sexual pleasure without abortion, and when they insist that abortion opponents are motivated exclusively by a desire to punish women uppity enough to enjoy sex. Both camps reinforce an underlying premise of patriarchy, one that finds its clearest, most hideously honest expression in pornography: the belief that sex is necessarily fused with violence, that fulfilled women are murderous, devouring monstrosities. Contrary to popular belief, abortion causes, and is caused by, the undermining of women and their sexual powers.

Abortion cheats women of the intense pleasures natural to gestation, delivery, and breastfeeding. And often it leads not to sexual bliss but dysfunction—from a phobic avoidance of intercourse to inhibited orgasm to compulsive, self-punitive sex with multiple, inappropriate partners. According to sex therapist Margo Anand, the deepest part of the vagina, the part around the cervix, stores up the pain of rape, traumatic childbirth (often caused by undue medical interference in labor and delivery), and abortion. This pain must be released and resolved before a woman can attain the satisfaction she deserves.[15]

A growing number of women have courageously spoken out about this pain—psychologist Sue Nathanson, for example. She experienced a suicidal depression and physical numbness after her husband pressured her into an abortion. "Instead of feeling free, sensuous, sexual, I feel like a 'thing,' a piece of meat, existing only for the pleasure of my husband and deadened to any possibility of pleasure for myself."[16] An even more horrifying story is that of Sappho Durrell, the daughter of English novelist Laurence Durrell. Her silence was broken too late, not until the posthumous publication of her journals. Not surprisingly for someone who inflicted such a sexually loaded name on a baby girl, Sappho's father may have sexually molested her. Later, in one of his novels, he created a character supposedly inspired by his daughter—a rapaciously lustful monstrosity of a woman who ultimately hangs herself. As an adult, Sappho described herself as "attracted to anyone who's really traumatized by sexuality as I am." Her relationships resulted in a series of painful pregnancy terminations. She also struggled with "a hypochondriac obsession that I will die early and that [my father] wants me to die before him." She wrote away to Exit, the British counterpart of the Hemlock Society, to request their suicide manual. At age thirty-four, following a fifth abortion, Sappho hanged herself, several years before Laurence himself died. Countless women have, tragically, followed a script such as the one Sappho Durrell's father wrote for her.[17]

The root causes of abortion help explain these crippling, even lethal, effects on women and their impulses towards life and wholeness. Vicki Thorne, founder of Project Rachel, a Roman Catholic post-abortion counseling effort, estimates that at least 75% of post-abortion clients have a history of sexual abuse.[18] A deep reverence for one's embodied self is essential to life-affirming, freely chosen sexual expression. Abused women often do not develop this reverence. So their adult relationships recapitulate their childhood traumas. And their wholly appropriate rage at their recurrent victimization is allowed no healing expression. Their rage may implode in the self- and other-destructive act of abortion, whose hurt they may hold deep inside—even if it literally kills them in the end.

Fortunately, some have seen through the rhetoric that covers over this cycle of violence, like this group of Italian women who refused to participate in an abortion "rights" march:

Abortion for the masses ... does not represent a conquest for civilization, because it is a violent and death-dealing answer to the problems of pregnancy, which, moreover, further culpablizes the woman's body. ... We cannot be complicit with this false consciousness. ... Surgical violence on women's bodies is none other than the dramatization of sexual violence ... To ask for free abortion on demand together with men is to recognize concretely the violence which is done to us in these relationships of power with masculine sexuality, by making ourselves complicit with it, and consenting to it ...[19]

Abortion must be named as the product and perpetrator of a culture which thwarts women's unique capacities for bodily pleasure at every turn, in both biological motherhood and sexual activity. This is NOT to imply that women must either be celibate or have sex only to conceive, regardless of where their own consciences lead them. Certainly women have the right to choose, in accordance with their personal beliefs and preferences, nonviolent family planning methods, or sexual practices which involve no possibility of conception. Women have a right to choose their preferred methods of childbirth and infant feeding. They have a right to choose whatever combination of work inside and outside the home serves their particular needs best. If women do not become biological mothers, whether through infertility or personal decision, they must not be denounced or pitied as unwomanly "failures" whose sexuality is either grotesque or nonexistent. They deserve honor for whatever other, equally sacred ways of giving life they find: adoptive or foster parenting, nonprocreative partnerships, service work, artistic expression, or something else.

Narrow, oppressive scripts for women's sexuality, whether from detractors or supporters of abortion, are the leading cause of abortion. Abortion will be with us until women secure authentic sexual and reproductive self-determination. "Life and let live": this is the healing truth that emerges from the tragic stories of women who have experienced the most hidden oppression of their gender.

Mary Jean Doe

But what about cases of rape and incest? Every prolifer must frequently deal with this issue, and few aspects of the abortion debate ignite more emotion. This is because rape and incest are so tragic and unspeakable that few can see past the initial repulsion to seriously consider the repercussions of resulting pregnancy. This repulsion also explains why even the most dedicated prolifer might capitulate on the abortion issue in the instances of rape and incest. Mary Jane Doe, who has asked to remain anonymous, relates here her personal experience with molestation and incest, and she cites the shortcomings of both sides of the argument in the debate. While she rejects the abortion alternative, refusing the notion that the child should pay for the sins of her father, she argues that most prolifers need to open their eyes to the frequency of these crimes against girls and women.

We as feminists must make society aware of how the female enters into sexual relationships on an unequal basis. The young girl has no choice and is violently robbed of her innocence; and for many women, the circumstances differ very little. Sexual relations are usually entered into on the male's terms with the female bearing the primary responsibility for birth control and shouldering the additional burden of having to defend her decision *not* to have sexual intercourse when she so chooses. Abortion is merely a band-aid solution to this oppressive situation and serves to perpetuate it by hiding the trespasses of the male.

Mary Jean Doe currently lives in the midwest with her husband and three children. We would like to thank her for sharing her story, and it is our sincere hope that she will experience full healing from her early traumas.

Incest and the Abortion Clinic
by Mary Jean Doe

Now that the "rape and incest" exceptions to laws against abortion are once again making headlines, my own experience sheds what I believe to be desperately needed light on the subject. I am a victim of child sexual abuse—both incest, and the family friend variety. I write this story in the hope that in the reading of it, both sides of this terrible debate will pause to think long and hard about their position.

Just before I was thirteen years old, I was sexually abused by an older brother, and by a college-age friend of the family. I was never assaulted by the two together, but each knew of the other's involvement—the older brother gave me "tips" for sexual acts on the family friend.

About three or four months after the abuse began, I was late for a period. I told my brother this, and he informed me that I "should have made that guy wear a rubber, you idiot." I did not know what a "rubber" was, or where it was worn, or why. All I knew was that if you did not have periods, you were pregnant. And if you were pregnant, you were in trouble.

I turned to my Sunday School teacher for help. When I told her I thought I might be pregnant (at twelve years old) she didn't even blink. She gave me a hug and said I should go to Planned Parenthood for a "rabbit test," that I should get one of my older brothers to take me and not tell my parents. She never asked who the male partner was, or why I was sexually active at my age.

So my older brother took me to Planned Parenthood.

I had never been to a doctor without my mother, and I had never had a gynecological exam. The whole visit was terrifying. No one explained anything. I was examined, gave urine and blood samples, and was shown a chart of an egg going around a big circle marked by days of the month. I was asked questions like "frequency of intercourse?" and "method of birth control preferred?" I did not know what intercourse meant, so I just said "a lot," and I had no idea what birth control methods existed. No one asked who my "partner" was, no one expressed any dismay, concern, or even interest that a twelve-year-old girl needed a pregnancy test.

I heard a lot about "being responsible" and "taking control of my body." Someone gave me a handful of condoms on the way out, and made a joke about it being an assortment—red, blue, and yellow. The yellow ones were called Tinglers. I stuffed them in my purse, and threw them away later.

My older brother maintained a strong silence throughout the entire time—no one asked him a single question.

Two days later I received a phone call telling me the test was positive, and to come in the following Saturday morning with a sanitary napkin and a friend who could drive. The caller never used the word "pregnant" or "abortion." I did not keep that appointment; my period started that evening.

The sexual abuse ended a couple of months later, as the family friend moved away, and my older brother began to abuse two younger neighbor children instead.

It was not until three years later that I discovered, in a high school biology class, that you cannot get pregnant from *oral* sexual contact. I also found out what intercourse was, and that I'd never had it.

I remember the feeling of horror that came over me as I realized that I had been scheduled for an abortion. I remember trying to figure out who would have paid the bill (it must have been my brother), and wondering why I was such a horrible person that those people thought I should have an abortion. Obviously, the worst thing that could ever happen to anyone must have happened to me, so what kind of person did that make me? Bad enough to have to kill a baby, according to what I'd just learned in my biology class. I thank God that my period started when it did.

Over the years, I have found that my story is *very* common in two aspects, neither of which will be good news for either side in the abortion debate. The first is the fact that my experience with Planned Parenthood was not an aberration. The sexual attitude often championed by Planned Parenthood is a serious factor in preventing the discovery of sexual abuse of young people. Had *anyone* shown even the least bit of disapproval or concern, I would have divulged the truth and begged for help. Everyone around me seemed to accept as normal that a 12-year-old girl could and should be sexually active (so long as she is responsible—remember the "rubber rainbow"!). And remember, too, who took me to Planned Parenthood—an older brother with an urgent interest in my being aborted! Abortion on demand, no questions asked, makes it *easier* for incest and child abuse to continue. Abortion for incest victims sounds compassionate, but in practice it is simply another violent and deceptive tool in the hand of the abuser.

The other unhappy aspect of this situation is that incest, rape and child abuse are far more common than most prolifers want to admit. Pamphlets, speeches, and articles regularly claim that pregnancies from incest are so rare as to be negligible. My experience with other victims is that sexual abuse of children, incestuous and otherwise, is *very* real, *very* common, and terribly underreported.

Both sides in the abortion debate have a lot to learn. Abortion defenders need to realize that while abortion may keep one of the results of incest and sexual abuse from seeing the light of day, it does absolutely nothing to protect a young girl from continued abuse, and, in fact, aids the abuser in his crime. Furthermore, birth control counselling and abortion often indirectly contribute to the victim's sense of shame, guilt, and blame for what is happening, since she is told to "take control" and "be responsible" for her "sexual activity," implying that this situation is, indeed, within her power to control. On the other hand, prolifers need to realize that incest, rape, and child abuse *do* happen, frequently and often with devastating results. In the assembly-line process of abortion on demand, incest-related abortions are seriously underreported.

Anne M. Maloney

Anne M. Maloney graduated from Mount Mary College in Milwaukee, Wisconsin, in 1980 and obtained her Ph.D. at Marquette University in 1987. She is currently a (very popular) professor of feminist philosophy at the College of St. Catherine in St. Paul, Minnesota, Vice President of Feminists for Life of Minnesota, and resides in St. Paul with her husband and three children.

In "Cassandra's Fate," Maloney eloquently describes the plight of the feminist who recognizes abortion as a form of violence that exacts its price not only from the child, but from the wounded mother as well. Being censored, silenced, dismissed, and misunderstood become commonplace to the vocal feminist who opposes abortion, but understanding this does little to mitigate its dismaying effect. This fact was chillingly illustrated in Professor Maloney's experience at the 1992 Democratic National Convention in New York City. Eager to represent those who elected her as a delegate to the Convention, Maloney took the money she had saved for a family vacation and headed for Madison Square Garden with some like-minded fellow delegates. She knew that her anti-abortion position would be unpopular, but she nevertheless believed that the party she and her family had supported all their lives would listen to dissenting views. Instead, she was screamed at, shoved, pushed, and verbally harassed by other Democratic delegates. She saw fellow prolife Democrats hit with signs, kicked, and shoved out of their seats so that their signs could not be seen, and she saw security guards watch the whole process without making any effort to intervene or remove the aggressors. Not only were the prolife dissenters silenced, the media covering the convention failed to report any of the violence captured by their cameras.

The Democratic National Convention proved to be the most violent censorship Professor Maloney has experienced, but it was certainly not her first such encounter. On February 25, 1991, she was scheduled to testify before the Senate Health and Human Services Committee of the Minnesota legislature. At the last minute, the hearing time was cut and testimony was discontinued shortly before Professor Maloney was to have been called. The following is a condensed version of her intended testimony.

To the Minnesota Senate Health and Human Services Committee
by Professor Anne M. Maloney

Thank you for giving me this opportunity to speak with you. I come here this evening to offer you what I believe to be the feminist view of abortion.

Women, as I tell my students in my Feminist Philosophy class, should be on the same list as the spotted owl. We are an endangered species. To be a woman in the United States today is to be the potential victim of battering and rape. Pornography eroticizes our victimization and screams it from every newsstand. The majority of families living below the poverty level are headed by women. Women are used as medical guinea pigs, subjected time after time to untested drugs and procedures. Witness DES, the IUD, the early form of the Pill—now acknowledged to be a hormone bomb—and silicone breast implants. When abortions are performed for sex selection purposes—and they are performed for that reason—it is female fetuses who are killed.

Women are 51% of the U.S. population. We are beaten, raped, starved, experimented on, and killed because of our gender. I'm not even going into the rest of the world, where women are routinely sterilized, have their clitorises excised, and are killed as infants in a ritual called "giving the baby a bath" because their lives just aren't valuable enough.

Is abortion any solution to these brute facts of a woman's life? Indeed not. Abortion further victimizes women by giving society an "easy out," a cheap fix for deep, real problems, problems that abortion exacerbates rather than solves. Were you raped? Well, it isn't a safe world for women. But here, it's OK. Have an abortion. Are you the victim of incest? Too bad. Men are powerful, aren't they? But hey, it's OK, have an abortion. Too many kids? Are you in poverty? Trying to finish school or hang on to your job? Being pregnant won't do. Don't expect society to change or help you. But hey, it's OK, have an abortion. This, ironically, is called "choice." In reality, abortion is no choice at all.

Some people will argue that if abortion is not legal, women will be desperate enough to resort to knitting needles and coat hangers. The solution these "prochoice" people offer is *not* to address the cause of such desperation, *not* to root out and destroy the viruses inherent in a society that forces women to such measures. Oh, no. To the woman so beaten down by society's callousness that she resorts to killing her own offspring, they offer not food, or a job, or education, or help. They offer her a cleaner knife to abort with, the so-called "safe" legal abortion. ...

Feminists for Life stands for a different version, a society where women are valued and where their power to give and nurture life is valued. As long as abortion exists as a cheap and easy solution, this society will remain a dream. Abortion exists because it's a man's world. If men got pregnant, they would demand health care, living wages, family leave, child care. They would demand that society value their ability to give and sustain life. But abortion? Having one's body forcibly violated, being told that the price of success is such constant violation? Forget it. Men would never stand for it. It's time for women to stop standing for it, too.

I hope that none of you will stand for it, either.

Cassandra's Fate: Why Feminists Ought to be Prolife

by Professor Anne M. Maloney

In ancient Greek mythology, Cassandra, a daughter of Priam, was so loved by Apollo that he gave her a great gift: the gift of prophecy. Cassandra did not return Apollo's love, however, and the spurned god was enraged. No gift, once given by the gods, can ever be taken back, and so Apollo could not take away Cassandra's vision of the future. Instead, he cruelly twisted it: yes, Cassandra would always have knowledge of what was inevitably to come, but whenever she might try to share this knowledge with fellow human beings, they would disbelieve her. With all of her foresight, Cassandra would be impotent, spurned and laughed at by the very people she would desperately try to save.

In the late twentieth century, we find ourselves in the frustrating and even terrifying situation of Cassandra—seeing so clearly the disastrous consequences of the current abortion ethic, consequences not disastrous just for the unborn women, who are aborted in far greater numbers than men, not just for the women who abort, but consequences disastrous for all of society: all women, all children, all men. When we try to point out what awaits us ahead, we are usually ignored, sometimes laughed at, while our feminist credentials are questioned.

The term "feminist" refers to anyone who is dedicated to the ideal that men and women, although possessed of different sexual natures (and thus, as we shall see, of differing ways of relating to reality), have equally valuable and valid contributions to make to the world, and therefore ought to have equality of opportunity. Furthermore, to be a feminist is to be wholly committed to making this world into one wherein both women and men are equally valued and respected.

The term "prolife" refers to the position that human life is intrinsically valuable; in other words, human life ought to "count" in society, regardless of whether it is useful, convenient or pleasant.

Some women's rights advocates react with incredulity, even anger, when prolife people dare to call themselves feminists. At a "woman-to-woman" conference in Milwaukee, Wisconsin, fifteen years ago, Letty Cottin Pogrebin, co-editor at the time of *Ms.* magazine, told the organizers of a Feminists for Life booth to pack up and go home because they did not belong at a convention dedicated to helping women. What is sorely needed in such situations is an explanation of why anyone would be both prolife and feminist—of why, in fact, a correct understanding of feminism demands that we be both.

Abortion advocates such as Carol Gilligan and Beverly Harrison argue on two basic fronts: First, they claim that women have an absolute, fundamental right to abortion because they have a basic right to control their reproductive lives. Without such control, these authors argue, there can never be social equality for women. On the other front, they argue that abortion is proscribed only because we still inhabit a patriarchal society which seeks to elevate men at the expense of women, and anyone who opposes abortion is either a perpetrator or a victim of this patriarchal ideal. Witness the following: "Many women who espouse the prolife position do so, at least in part, because they have internalized patriarchal values and depend on the sense of identity and worth that comes from having accepted 'women's place' in society."

Entwined in the discussion of these points is usually the conviction (a correct one, I think) that men and women approach reality from two different ethical perspectives: that men tend to focus on the principles involved in making choices, where women tend to view such choices in terms of the persons involved.

I believe (1) that the demand for abortion rights as a necessary prerequisite for a woman's reproductive freedom, for a woman's control over her own body, betrays a decidedly patriarchal, rather than feminist, understanding of both "freedom" and "control"; (2) that, whereas our society is, in many ways, constructed on a model that erects and sustains patriarchal values at the expense of feminine values, the solution to this patriarchal bias does not lie in an abortion ethic, and in fact, an abortion ethic feeds, rather than destroys, this bias; and finally (3) that while men and women do approach reality from different ethical perspectives, one focused on principles and the other on persons, these are not always conflicting perspectives, and an abortion ethic destroys both of them.

In calling for abortion rights as the ultimate guarantee that women can control their own bodies, abortion advocates are viewing a woman's body as a kind of territory to be subdued, interfered with, dominated. This is not a feminist perspective, regardless of how many people maintain that it is.

Abortion, if it is an act of control, is a violent act of control. When a woman is pregnant, be it six days or six months, her body has become inextricably wedded to the body of another living being; the only way out of that relationship for a woman who does not want to be pregnant is a violent one, an act that destroys the fetus and invades the body (and often the mind) of his or her mother. Traditionally, it has always been women who have realized that violence solves nothing and usually begets more violence, that violent solutions often wound the perpetrator as well as the victim. That is why women have historically been opposed to war, to capital punishment, to the rape and destruction of the environment. Why should women's traditional (and quite wise) abhorrence of violence stop at the threshold of their own bodies?

In the male-dominated world we have all inhabited for the last 2500 years, unfortunately power (thus, "control") has been accorded only to those strong enough to seize it, or at least demand it. Furthermore, it has historically been those in power who have set the standard for who gets to "count" as persons. For far too many of those 2500 years, it has been men who have been in power and women who have not been "counted." It is, therefore, particularly chilling to read arguments such as those of theologian Marjorie Reiley Maguire, who says that in order for a fetus to count as valuable, the pregnant woman must confer value upon it; as she puts it: "The personhood (of the fetus) begins when the bearer of life, the mother, makes a covenant of love with the developing life within her to bring it to birth. ... The moment when personhood begins, then, is the moment when the mother accepts the pregnancy."

The fetus, according to such argumentation, is a person if and only if the pregnant woman decides to invest her with value. How, we ask, does this differ from the long entrenched patriarchal ideal that it is the powerful who determine the value of other human life?

The notions of control and power at work in the abortion ethic, then, are ones that surely ought to give any feminist pause. It is indeed unconscionable that women have, for so many thousands of years, been dominated and victimized by men, whose hold on power was reinforced by the patriarchal structure of society. Thus, it is especially disorienting to hear the argument that the only road away from such victimization is to victimize, in turn, another group of human beings—their completely powerless and voiceless offspring. Their very powerlessness makes them the ideal victims: the question which all women must ask themselves is whether the path away from victimization really lies in joining the victimizers, whether the road to freedom must really be littered with the dead bodies of their unborn children.

In the "March on Washington" in the spring of 1989, women of all colors and walks of life forcefully proclaimed their commitment to the tenet that women will never be truly free or equal to men until they can walk away from their sexual encounters just as men have always been able to do. The feminists who were not marching that day wonder whether the March on Washington was not a march down the wrong road, a road fraught with danger.

Men and women are different, not just in their biological characteristics, but in their sexual natures as well. There are exceptions, of course, but throughout history men have traditionally approached sex differently than women have. No one can deny that women have always had a higher biological investment in sexual union; abortion seeks to undo that tie. Is the ideal to be pursued a world wherein sex can (and often will be) commitment-free? Leaving abortion aside for just a moment, even most forms of contraception invade the woman's body, not the man's—and in more cases than we want to admit, scar and irrevocably damage those bodies. (Even condoms, the one "male" form of contraception, usually ends up being the woman's responsibility—survey after survey shows that it is invariably women, not men, who are responsible for purchasing condoms.)

One of the points on which all feminists agree is that women need to build their self-confidence and self-esteem. In a sexist culture, this can be hard to do. As Carol Heilbrun pointed out in a talk given to the Modern Language Association, a man's traditional experience of selfhood can be summed up in a line from the poet Walt Whitman: "I celebrate myself and sing myself, and what I assume you shall assume," whereas poet Emily Dickinson best sums up how women have, for too long, experienced selfhood: "I'm nobody." Does abortion build a woman's self-esteem? The point is to question whether abortion on demand can ever bring about the condition wherein the feminine perspective is valued as much as the male, or whether, in fact, abortion ultimately robs women of their self-confidence and self-esteem.

Those who acquiesce to the conviction that pregnancy is a form of enslavement and childbearing a burden are adding weight to, not destroying, the yoke of patriarchy. They are letting men be the arbiters of what is valuable and fighting hard for the "right" to have their own bodies invaded and their own children destroyed so that they can get it.

What feminists, all feminists, should be doing is working to achieve a world in which the power to bear children is viewed as a gift to be protected rather than a burden of which to be relieved. That means working for fundamental changes in the structure of society, including, but not limited to, far greater flexibility in the work place for both mothers and fathers, better pre- and postnatal care for impoverished women, and much more stringent enforcement of male responsibility for child support. Such changes would be a true feminization of society. They will occur only when we insist upon them, however, and abortion on demand precludes such insistence. When abortion is easily accessible, society no longer has to take pregnancy seriously. Once a woman decides to continue her pregnancy, society is under no obligation to help her: it is, after all, her choice, her responsibility.

In militating for the right to abortion on demand, abortion advocates are trying to win their game on the same old game board—the patriarchal world view that denigrates what is unique to women as unimportant, trivial, not to be taken seriously.

They are embracing a kind of freedom that uses the female body as an object to be invaded and, if need be, subdued. Feminists who are prolife see that this can lead only to disaster for women and for their unborn children—yet our voices still go unheard and unheeded.

Cassandra's fate was to see the future.

And be disbelieved.

Alice Louise Dietz

A lice Louise Dietz served as an intern with Feminists for Life in the spring of 1991. At the time she was a student at Antioch College and experienced the dilemma of being "politically incorrect" at a terribly "politically correct" institution. Her essay articulates the irony of the censorship being practiced by our institutions of higher learning headed by the "free-thinkers" of the sixties.

Tie-Dyed Tyrants
by Alice Louise Dietz

I am a student and community member of Antioch College.

I am an agnostic.

I am a pacifist.

I am a vegetarian.

I am a feminist.

I tend to poke fun at conservatives and the "radical right."

I am an avid supporter of the Feminists for Life movement.

Antioch College is a community which theoretically encourages diversity and individual empowerment. However, I recently have discovered the Antioch reality: diversity at Antioch is encouraged only when it conforms to the Antiochian "politically correct" elitist definition of diversity. Recent experience has taught me that my prolife brand of diversity has less "merit" than that of the Antiochian status quo.

My experience is this: I wanted to exercise my right as a community member to bring a speaker to Antioch—Cindy Osborne, president of Feminists for Life of Ohio. I went through the usual Committee, and a Committee representative informed me that Ms. Osborne was welcome to speak and would receive a $75 to $100 honorarium. I checked back with the Speaker Committee representative throughout the month to make sure that the plans for the speaker were secure; the representative always gave the impression that everything was running smoothly.

This impression became doubtful, however, when I attended a Speaker Committee meeting just three days before Ms. Osborne's presentation. Apparently, there was some turmoil within the committee about a prolife speaker coming to Antioch, and Ms. Osborne would receive only $50, the lowest honorarium of all the speakers. Another local speaker, who had petitioned at the last minute, would receive a $100 honorarium. Why should Ms. Osborne receive this discriminatory treatment in a community that encourages diversity and the "search for truth"? The committee grants honoraria on merit, and had apparently decided that she has little merit.

One Speaker Committee member stated that he did not want his money going to the prolife cause. How does he think I feel when part of my tuition and community fees goes toward the prochoice cause? Act for Choice is provided with a place to meet and a small quarterly allowance. In Antioch's co-op job listings, four of the jobs deal with work in actual abortion clinics; none of the listings deal with prolife groups. How many times has the "politically correct" stance of prochoicism been alluded to in Community Meetings … and classes? Where is the diversity I hear so much about?

Another justification for my speaker's low honorarium was that no one would attend her presentation. Yet how can one justifiably claim herself/himself to be prolife or prochoice without listening to all sides of the issues? Feminists for Life is no ordinary prolife organization and I doubt seriously that most Antioch students have ever heard the feminists' prolife argument. I guess the search for "truth and justice" is deemed an unnecessary, foolish waste of time when the majority rules.

I am disillusioned by my experience at the Speaker Committee meeting. I was a dissenter, seeking true heterogeneity and equal treatment, pleading for this privilege that theoretically and financially is my right as a member of this community. I am angry at having to justify the principle of equal honoraria for Ms. Osborne and the other local speak of hype as well. "Politically correct" is an elitist, unprogressive term. It excludes all who disagree with the status quo.

Are we truly liberal, or have we become a mere inverse of the conservative mentality—trying to maintain the status quo of Antioch's brand of liberalism, stomping out any dissension from the "ignorant" or "misinformed" masses? "My goddess!" Are we just a bunch of conservatives in Birckenstocks? Or, as I read on a politically correct bathroom wall on campus, maybe we're so open-minded that our brains have fallen out!

Carol Nan Feldman Crossed

After teaching in Kentucky and Maryland, Carol Crossed extended her talents to peace and justice issues, including feminist prolife work, for which she has become an extraordinary activist and organizer. She got her start in social activism during the civil rights movement and the Vietnam War protests of the sixties, risking arrest on numerous occasions. Her protesting since then has focused on human rights issues in Central America and the rights of the unborn, for which efforts she has been arrested on at least 16 different occasions.

As an organizer, Crossed has coordinated, chaired, fundraised, and/or served as a delegate to conferences, commissions, workshops, and community hearings committed to spreading the messages of justice and nonviolence and effecting their reality. Her native American heritage has provided her insight concerning issues of diversity and inclusiveness; and she has applied her expertise to such efforts as Project Roothold, an Indian rights cooperative promoting relations between Native North Americans and indigenous peoples in Latin America, the Third World Visiting Journalist Program, the Women's Peace Encampment, the World Health Organization Conference on Women and Children, and the Soviet Realities Conference. In May of 1993, she testified before the U.S. Senate Judiciary Committee on nonviolent civil disobedience.

She has served the consistent life ethic movement as Vice President of JustLife and Executive Director of Common Ground of Upstate New York; and she currently serves as Executive Director of the Seamless Garment Network and is involved with the Faith and Resistance Community, a Rochester prayer and action ecumenical group. Her articles have appeared in various feminist and pacifist publications; she was editor of *Seeds of Change* from 1980–1986, a news magazine focusing on justice issues surrounding hunger; and she has been a guest speaker for conferences on world hunger, non-violence, and various other issues affecting women.

In spite of Carol's impressive credentials in the area of justice and nonviolence issues, she has experienced great injustice herself when it comes to her attempts to spread the feminist prolife message. In the following article, she recounts her local chapter's experiences when they sought to participate in a local "Take Back the Night" rally. The dignified protest of these women against those who would question their commitment to women victimized by violence sets an example of how nonviolent direct action against censorship and oppression can prove a powerful tool.

FFL Chapter Declines to be Silenced
by Carol Nan Feldman Crossed

Gandhi would have been proud of FFL of Western New York on the evening of October 1, 1991. Our chapter decided to participate in the local "Take Back the Night" march and rally, despite the fact that the NOW organization demanded that the Women Acting Against Violence committee take an abortion rights position or they would boycott the event. After all, they claimed, not giving women the right to choose (to be violent?) was a violence against women.

Previously, WAAV had agreed to avoid any pro-abortion expression as a courtesy to FFL of Western New York, and the chapter's participation was welcomed at the first "Take Back the Night" in February 1990. But pressure from NOW caused the position in favor of abortion to be resumed, and our chapter was told we could not be a sponsor in the month-long program, nor could we be promised that abortion would not be promoted at the rally.

The Rochester *Democrat and Chronicle* ran an article on this situation, quoting FFL and WAAV steering committee member Suzanne Schnittman as saying, "this does not feel like our interpretation of feminism. This feels like a gag rule." The paper also editorialized against the foolishness, saying that "the campaign to eliminate violence against women needs all the support it can get. It doesn't need ideological litmus tests that only weaken the effort."

Our chapter grappled with the question of what our response should be. We had participated in last year's march, and we were certainly against violence to women (isn't that why we are prolife?). These women were our friends and co-activists when it came to peace and justice issues. They knew us and we knew them. They were our sisters, weren't they?

Yes, we would march with them. Not protest on the sidelines, but be with them. And so we did, over 60 women walking in silence, composing a fourth of the total number present. We carried signs of the true violence of abortion: symbolic tombstones, each with the name of a different woman who died in a legal abortion. Carrying such a testimony of the horror of abortion affected us each deeply.

One participant, Mary Nicholson, later wrote: "I carried a memorial of a woman who bled to death after she was refused follow-up care at the abortion clinic. There is nothing "alleged" about a death certificate that states a cause of death: hemorrhage. These are the statistics no one dares to publicize. Abortion is the most anti-woman, anti-feminine violence against women in history. The act of suctioning or scraping the inside of her uterus to intentionally cause the death of her baby can hardly be described as non-violent or humane."

As we arrived at the place where the rally would be held, we once again asked each other, "Should we go in?" Do we sit here and listen to euphemisms like "choice" and "rights" which mean violence against women? Or could we trust them, in the spirit of unity, to focus on those varieties of violence we all oppose?

After some hesitation we decided to go in and found—you guessed it—that all the seats were taken except the ones in the front rows. We filled in those seats, and listened as the emcee, president of the local NOW chapter, gave the introduction. Within three sentences she had gotten to "the violence against women who are exercising their constitutional right to have an abortion."

As if on cue, we all stood. We had no other alternative. We walked out of the hall.

But wait. As we made our way out through the lobby, a woman ran after us, asking where we were going. We explained that we were women who saw abortion as violence, and so could not in conscience stay. The woman asked us please to stay and to listen.

What happened next was non-violence in action. The woman happened to be Ester Ostertag, founder of a safe house for prostitutes, and the main speaker for the evening! Ms. Ostertag walked up on stage and asked the group to invite us back in. "We need their vision of what violence is. We need to be united," she said. As we resumed our seats, Ms. Ostertag suggested that the group show us a warm welcome, and led a round of applause. At the conclusion of her speech, she left the stage to join us in the front row, greeting us with hugs. The feeling of exhilaration for our chapter was indescribable!

We had another high point just three weeks later, when our chapter sponsored leftist feminist historian Elizabeth Fox-Genovese in a talk at the University of Rochester entitled, "Feminism Without Illusions: Rethinking Abortion." Fox-Genovese is concerned that insisting on individual rights, without considering responsibility to the community, is leading to a fragmented society, "a multiplicity of unrelated cultures and selves." She feels that feminism has been taken over by white, upper middle class women who expect all women to share their expectations and values, and who deny many women's sense that they have rightful obligations to their children and society. Fox-Genovese is ambivalent on the abortion question, saying that it makes her "queasy" and that it is always a taking of life. However, she feels that this could be justified in the first trimester—but not as a woman's unilateral right. Such an action would have to represent the consensus of the community. While not agreeing with every facet of Fox-Genovese's stand, we were pleased to hear the views of one who is in the process of "rethinking abortion."

All kinds of social change have their origin, one way or another, in similar "rethinking." FFL of Western New York hopes that we've opened some minds to new ideas recently, and we look forward to more such opportunities in the future!

Kay Castonguay

Kay Castonguay is the President of Feminists for Life of Minnesota, one of FFL's largest and most active state chapters, and the Vice President for Chapter Development of the national office of Feminists for Life. A consummate social activist, Kay's efforts extend from taking the lead in helping to pass the nation's first state parental leave legislation to helping keep the death penalty out of Minnesota. She played a major role in launching the consistent life ethic movement in Minnesota and she continues to serve on the board of directors of Minnesota JustLife, a Christian consistent life ethic group concentrating on peace, social justice, and prolife issues. She was instrumental in the formation of the Gay-Lesbian Pro-Life Alliance, and she is also a member of Amnesty International, the Animal Rights Coalition, Minnesota Sanefreeze, World Population Balance (a prolife environmental group) and Hand-Gun Control. She lends her support to children through the Christian Children's Fund, the Minnesota Special Olympics, and the Committee to End Child Abuse, along with several other local organizations; and venturing where only brave prolifers dare to tread, she continues to be active in the Democratic party.

Ms. Castonguay's expertise on the death penalty places her in demand for public debates, and she is a frequent speaker and guest on radio and television talk shows. Her writings have appeared in magazines, newspapers and other local publications; we have included here two articles from the Minnesota FFL newsletter. In the first article, Castonguay discusses her consistent life ethic approach to abortion, and in the second, she records her own observations concerning two relatively recent issues of interest to feminists: the Clarence Thomas Supreme Court nomination hearings, during which Anita Hill came forward with her accusations of sexual harassment, and the William Kennedy Smith rape trial. Both articles illustrate the tendency of some prochoice feminists to create an either/or situation in which those who support abortion rights are the good guys and those who don't are the bad guys, in spite of where they may stand on other issues of critical importance to women. The revelations concerning sexual harassment by Senator Robert Packwood, Oregon, which surfaced after Castonguay wrote her article, may perhaps persuade some of these feminists to reexamine their uncritical view of prochoice legislators as feminist heroes.

In any event, Kay Castonguay will continue to labor on behalf of those born and unborn, old and young, female and male, able-bodied and handicapped, who suffer such oppression. You can find her agitating for justice from her home in Minnetonka, where she resides with her three children.

Enough Violence, Enough Hatred, Enough Injustice
by Kay Castonguay

Recently I took part in a two-day leadership training course. Continuing education is absolutely essential to good leadership. Apparently, the instructor's curiosity got the better of her, and, during a break, she walked over to my table and asked the inevitable question: "You're really in the heat of things, aren't you? Tell me about Feminists for Life." Everyone at the table turned to look at me expectantly, as I mentally braced myself, and responded.

Few words generate stronger feelings than the words "feminist" and "prolife." Sometimes I know how celebrities feel when they don their sunglasses and try to fade into the background. Every once in a while, it's nice to go incognito, to know that occasionally one can function socially without generating controversy. As I started to go into the history of the early feminists, and progressed into our present-day platform, I could sense a growing awareness and understanding among my listeners.

Just as the early feminists did, we take a consistent life ethic approach to issues. The end result is that we don't think like other people do—in spite of societal conditioning, we reject an "either/or" approach to life and justice concerns. The rest of the world tends to pit one group of human beings against another, then decides which group gets to survive and which group gets sacrificed (some people refer to that as "choice"). It's either women against their unborn children, blacks against whites, the innocent against the guilty, Americans against foreigners, straights against gays, etc.

The end result of this "lifeboat ethics" philosophy is discrimination, war, abortion, the death penalty, and other assorted forms of violence.

We view human life as a continuum, from conception to natural death, and act accordingly. Unlike most, we don't look at a major human problem and then attempt to decide who gets to live and who doesn't. We look at major problems and attempt to solve them as constructively and as peacefully as possible.

Violence, too, is interconnected. One of the training session participants shared with us her work in the prison system. She found in the course of her work that most violent offenders were themselves victims of violence earlier in their lives—they never learned any other way of dealing with their problems. I added that the death penalty is part of that pattern of perpetuating violence. Studies have shown that a high percentage of death row inmates were themselves victims of various forms of child abuse.

I went on to explain how violence perpetuates itself—no matter what its form, abortion, sexism, social neglect, abuse, military aggression, the death penalty. All of these things demean us as human beings and invite further abuses. What this society needs is not further abuses nor increases in violence. This society needs real solutions. That's what we're here for.

Instead of placing human beings in either/or situations, our job is to encourage people to see the interconnected nature of human life. The unborn child killed by abortion, the abused child, the battered woman, the homeless man who dies of society's neglect—all are victims of violence. If we write off any group of people because of convenience or our own prejudices, we effectively write off ourselves. It's not a case of either/or, it's a case of "and." We as a society will be judged by future generations on how we treat those among us who are unable to defend themselves. Instead of taking the Hatfield v. McCoy approach to life like most others have taken, FFL, along with other consistent life ethic groups, is willing to stand up and say, "enough violence, enough hatred, enough injustice. It stops here, with us. We will not continue along this path of continuing violence."

One of the key phrases in the leadership training course was the following: "Do not follow where the path may lead. Go instead where there is no path and leave a trail." I believe that we are doing just that. By our actions, our vision of the world, and our direction, we are travelling down a new path.

Hopefully, the rest of the world will follow.

Of Clarence and Anita and Willie and the Unknown Woman

by Kay Castonguay

Undoubtedly, one of the biggest winter headlines was the William Kennedy Smith rape trial. Following closely on the heels of the Clarence Thomas/Anita Hill controversy, it, too, held most of us captive to our TV sets for several days. Both cases bore a great deal of similarity—a woman claiming mistreatment and oppression at the hands of a powerful male figure—a familiar scenario that has been played out with minor variations throughout history. But there seemed to be a crucial difference between the two cases. I couldn't quite put my finger on it until I received a phone call from a very frustrated woman during the William Kennedy Smith trial. "Where are all the women's groups?" she asked. "I haven't heard of any demonstrations on this poor woman's behalf!"

Of course! That was it! Gone from our TV sets was the omnipresent face of Kate Michelman and other self-proclaimed "feminists" who had repeatedly spoken of their concern for women at the Clarence Thomas Senate hearings. The William Kennedy Smith trial seemed to produce no slogans, buttons, or organized protests. The editorials appearing in major newspapers relating to both cases also markedly differed. During the Thomas nomination hearings, columnists (many of them women) unreservedly threw their hats in Anita Hill's corner: "She's right, he's wrong, case closed."

During the William Kennedy Smith trial, however, many political writers and commentators were singing a far different tune. "Well, she could be telling the truth, but let's not be too hasty. Didn't she fail to prove her case?"

So, why the rush to judgment on Clarence Thomas but not William Kennedy Smith? Some have put forth the theory that since the stakes (meaning the Supreme Court) were higher in the Thomas hearings, more attention was necessarily focused on keeping him out. True, but by the same token, isn't rape a more serious crime than sexual harassment?

And it may have also been a bit harder for the American public to bond with a woman whose name and face were not revealed to them, unlike Anita Hill's.

But I really don't think that either of these theories is the answer. The one glaring difference in both these cases is ABORTION. Think about it. Let's put aside the issue of actual guilt or innocence (we'll leave that can of worms for another time). Just use your imagination for a minute and make a few basic changes: What if Clarence Thomas were suspected of being an abortion supporter instead of an abortion opponent? Would Anita Hill have received the same backing from groups such as NOW and much of the media? And what if William Kennedy Smith were the nephew of Orrin Hatch rather than Ted Kennedy? Get the picture?

This, of course, begs the next question: "Should a plaintiff's or defendant's feelings on abortion determine his or her perceived credibility, the amount of political or organizational support received, even guilt or innocence?"

Of course, it shouldn't. Verbal and physical abuse are serious offenses and both accused and accuser should be entitled to due process and even-handed treatment by groups who purport to speak for women and minorities.

This doesn't seem to have occurred here. Moira Lasch, the plaintiff's attorney in the William Kennedy Smith trial, was lambasted for supposedly being inept and for being either too emotional or too unemotional. No criticism was heard of the female juror who was interviewed on TV's "Inside Edition" after the trial. She was not only blatantly pro-Kennedy (she seemed about ready to confer sainthood on both Willie Smith and Uncle Teddy), she also made an incredibly inept, unprofessional, and anti-woman statement. It seemed that one of the biggest factors that led her to vote for his acquittal was her feeling that Willie Smith was just TOO handsome and TOO charming to have to force himself on any woman!

The case did have its notable exceptions. Anti-pornography crusader Catharine MacKinnon wrote an excellent editorial and didn't allow her feelings on abortion bias her judgment. She referred to the trial as the "second public hanging of a woman who accused a powerful man of sexual violation. ..."

We've said repeatedly that feminism and abortion advocacy are a contradiction. I think we've just proved it.

Part One Endnotes

Introduction

1.   Mary Wollstonecraft, *A Vindication of the Rights of Woman*, ed. Carol H. Poston, New York: W.W. Norton, 1975, 139.

2.   See Sally Roesch Wagner, *A Time of Protest*, Carmichael, CA: Sky Carrier Press, 1988.

3.   "What the Press Says of Us," *Revolution*, February 5, 1868; "The Revolution will discuss …," *Revolution*, January 15, 1868.

4.   See Marvin Olasky, *The Press and Abortion, 1838–1988*, Hillsdale, NJ: Lawrence Ehrlbaum, 1988.

5.   "Important Movement," *Revolution*, April 8, 1868.

6.   Tennessee Claflin, "My Word on Abortion, and Other Things," *Woodhull and Claflin's Weekly*, September 23, 1871.

7.   Kristen J. Leslie, letter, *Daughters of Sarah: the Magazine for Christian Feminists*, November/December 1990, 28.

8.   Jane A. Usher, letter, *Utne Reader*, September/October 1990, 12.

9.   Cynthia Bogard, letter, *Utne Reader*, November/December 1990, 15–16.

10.   Melanie Gross, personal communication with Mary Krane Derr, Spring 1991.

11.   Rosalind Pollack Petchesky, *Abortion and Woman's Choice*, Boston: Northeastern University Press, 1985, 44.

12.   James Mohr, *Abortion in America,* New York: Oxford University Press, 1978, 112.

13.   Terry Cosgrove, "Distorted History," (letter) *Chicago Sun-Times,* February 8, 1991; Annette Ravinsky, letter, *Daughters of Sarah,* November/December 1990, 28. Both of these letters were written in response to Feminists for Life's use of feminist foremother quotations.

14.   Isabella Beecher Hooker, *Womanhood: Its Sanctities and Fidelities,* Boston: Lee and Shepard, 1974, 33–37.

15.   See Adrienne Rich, *Of Woman Born: Motherhood as Experience and Institution,* New York: W.W. Norton, 1976.

16.   *Elizabeth Cady Stanton as Revealed in Her Letters, Diaries, and Reminiscences,* Volume 2, eds. Theodore Stanton and Harriet Stanton Blatch, New York: Harper and Brothers, 1922, 312–13.

17.   *The History of Woman Suffrage,* Volume 1, eds. Susan B. Anthony, Elizabeth Cady Stanton, and Matilda Joslyn Gage, New York: Fowler and Wells, 1881, 18.

18.   Wollstonecraft, *A Vindication of the Rights of Women,* 1792/1975.

19.   *The History of Woman Suffrage,* Volume 1, 71.

20.   Frederick Hollick, *The Marriage Guide,* New York: T.W. Strong, 1850, 356.

21.   Hollick, *The Marriage Guide,* Chapter Nine.

22.   *The History of Woman Suffrage,* Volume 2, 10.

23.   Quoted in Emanie Sachs, *The Terrible Siren,* New York: Harper and Brothers, 1928, 223–24.

24.   William Leach, *True Love and Perfect Union: the Feminist Reform of Sex and Society,* New York: Basic Books, 1980, 39.

25.   Carl Degler, *At Odds: Women and the Family in America from the Revolution to the Present,* New York: Oxford University Press, 1980, 243.

26.   Mohr, *Abortion in America,* Chapter Seven.

27.   Ann Braude, *Radical Spirits: Spiritualism and Women's Rights in Nineteenth Century America*, Boston: Beacon Press, 1989, 3.

28.   See, for example, Amelia Bloomer, "Have Women Souls?" in *The Radical Women's Press of the 1850's,* eds. Ann Russo and Cheris Kramarae, New York: Routledge, 1991, 198–199.

29.   Degler, *Women and the Family*, 247.

30.   Evidence of feminist involvement in the anti-slavery movement is ubiquitous. On feminist opposition to capital punishment, see, for example, "Capital Punishment," *Woodhull and Claflin's Weekly*, April 22, 1876; "Horrible," *Revolution,* March 11, 1869; Nelson Kent, "Capital Punishment—Murder By Law," *WCW*, March 8, 1873; and "Another Deliberate Murder," *WCW*, May 6, 1876. On support for the rights of born children, see, for example, Parker Pillsbury, "Foundling Hospitals Again," *Revolution*, April 30, 1868; "Bergh On Babies," *WCW*, May 16, 1874; "State Nurseries," *WCW*, November 22, 1873; and "Children in Massachusetts Factories," *Revolution,* April 9, 1868. Many of the activists represented in this collection experimented with a vegetarian diet. Some did this for health reasons, but others agreed with Frances Willard that meat-eating was "savagery" which progress would eliminate from society. (See Ruth Bordin, *Frances Willard: A Biography*, Chapel Hill: University of North Carolina Press, 1986.)

31.   "A Cry From the Condemned Cell," *Water Cure Journal and Herald of Reform,* September 1848, 85.

32.   Horatio Storer, *Why Not?—A Book For Every Woman*, Boston: Lee and Shepard, 1866, 27, 70, 85. But Storer, unlike others of his ilk, such as Augustus K. Gardner and Anthony Comstock, was not *utterly* incorrigible in his views. When feminists, especially the anonymous "Wife of a Christian Physician" (*Boston Medical and Surgical Journal*, November 1, 1866), challenged him to have compassion for aborting women, he took the criticism to heart and wrote *Is it I?—A Book for Every Man* (Boston: Lee and Shepard, 1867), which exhorted men to sexual responsibility.

33. Quoted in the *Wheeling (WV) Evening Standard,* November 17, 1875, reprinted in Victoria Woodhull, *The Human Body the Temple of God*, London: privately printed, 1890, 470.

34. bell hooks, *Ain't I A Woman*, Boston: South End Press, 1981; *Black Women in White America*, ed. Gerda Lerner, New York: Vintage Books, 1992.

35. *Narrative of Sojourner Truth*, ed. Margaret Washington, New York: Vintage Books, 1993.

36. Shawnee Sykes, "Multicultural Issues in Post-Abortion Healing," panel discussion at "Abortion Healing" Conference, Milwaukee, WI, November 3, 1993.

37. Toni Morrison, *Beloved*, New York: Knopf, 1987. See also Anne Ramirez, "There Could Have Been A Way, But There Wasn't," *Daughters of Sarah*, Fall 1992.

38. Sarah Grimké, "Marriage," in *The Female Experience*, ed. Gerda Lerner, New York: Oxford University Press, 1992, 87–97.

39. Linda Gordon, *Woman's Body, Woman's Right: A Social History of Birth Control in America*, New York: Penguin Books, 1977, Chapter Five.

40. Mary Krane Derr, "Margaret Sanger's Insufficiently Recognized Debt to Victorian Feminism," paper accepted by the 1990 National Women's Studies Association Conference.

41. John Cowan, *The Science of a New Life*, New York: Cowan and Company, 1878, 108–109.

42. Hollick, *The Marriage Guide*, 333.

43. *The Queen v. Charles Bradlaugh and Annie Besant*, London: Freethought Publishing Company, 1877, 172.

44. Edward Bond Foote, *The Radical Remedy in Social Science*, New York: Murray Hill, 1886, 52.

45.   Cowan, *The Science of a New Life,* 109.

46.   Sallie Tisdale, "We Do Abortions Here," *Harper's Magazine*, October 1987, 70.

47.   Rich, *Of Woman Born,* 269.

48.   Catharine MacKinnon, *Feminism Unmodified*, Cambridge, MA: Harvard University Press, 1987, 95–96.

49.   *History of Woman Suffrage,* Volume 1, 167.

Dr. Charlotte Denman Lozier

50.   In addition to the two pieces about her in the present volume, the major source of information about Lozier's short but amazing life is Abraham W. Lozier, *In Memoriam: Mrs. Charlotte Denman Lozier, M.D., Died January 3, 1870*, New York: Press of Wynkoop and Hollenbeck, 1870. See also Parker Pillsbury's obituary "Charlotte Denman Lozier, M.C.," *The Revolution,* January 13, 1870; William Leach, *True Love and Perfect Union: the Feminist Reform of Sex and Society*, New York: Basic Books, 1980, 55; "Death of Mrs. Charlotte D. Lozier," *Herald of Health,* February 1870; "Death of Dr. Charlotte Lozier," *New York Times,* January 4, 1870; and "Clemence Sophia Lozier," in *Lamb's Biographical Dictionary of the United States,* Volume 5, Boston: Federal Book Company, 1903, 156.

51.   See, for example, "Female Practitioners of Medicine," *Boston Medical and Surgical Journal 76*: May 2, 1867, 272–274.

52.   Quoted in Graham Barker-Benfield, *The Horrors of the Half-Known Life: Male Attitudes Toward Women and Sexuality in Nineteenth Century America*, New York: Harper and Row, 1976, 87.

53.   Clemence Lozier was born in 1813, the daughter of a female lay healer whom whites and Native Americans both respected. She taught herself physiology and then taught it in the school she ran to support

herself after she was orphaned. She was motivated to enter medicine by the memory of her mother and by a series of tragedies in the family she had with the man she married at sixteen: the deaths of five of their six sons in accidents or from illnesses, and then her husband's long terminal sickness. Lozier later married a man who turned out to be abusive. After hearing about Elizabeth Cady Stanton's call for woman-sensitive divorce laws, she gained the courage to extricate herself from this marriage and create a new life for herself. She entered medical school at age forty and graduated near the top of her class. She became involved with suffrage and served for many years as the president of the New York Suffrage Association. She also was active in the Moral Reform Society, which concerned itself with the plight of prostitutes and single pregnant women. She built up a flourishing practice in obstetrics and gynecology that emphasized self-help and preventive care. After giving weekly physiology lectures and organizing a medical library for her patients, she founded her medical school in 1863, despite the machinations of conservatives to prevent the state from granting it a charter. It flourished until the economic hard times of the 1870's. But Lozier persisted in her medical and feminist work until her death in 1888. At the huge celebration that Susan B. Anthony organized for Elizabeth Cady Stanton's eightieth birthday in 1895, Lozier was remembered in a tribute to great women of the past. See Elizabeth Cady Stanton, *Eighty Years and More*, New York: Schocken Books, reprinted 1970, 461, and Gena Corea, *The Hidden Malpractice*, New York: Harper, 1985, Chapter Two.

54.   Harriot K. Hunt, *Glances and Glimpses, of Fifty Years Social, Including Twenty Years Professional Life*, Boston, 1856; reprinted 1970, 152. See also Elizabeth Blackwell and Emily Blackwell, "Medicine as a Profession for Woman," in *The Feminist Papers*, ed. Alice Rossi, New York: Columbia University Press, 1973, 354–55; Mary Roth Walsh, *Doctors Wanted: No Women Need Apply*, New Haven: Yale University Press, 1977; and Virginia G. Drachman, "Women Doctors and the Women's Medical Movement: Feminism and Medicine 1850–1895," Ph.D. dissertation, State University of New York at Buffalo, 1976.

55.   *Thornburgh v. American College of Obstetricians and Gynecologists*, 476 U.S. 747 (1986). See also *Akron v. Akron Center for Reproductive Health*, 462 U.S. 416 (1983).

56.   Rosalind Pollack Petchesky, *Abortion and Woman's Choice*, Boston: Northeastern University Press, 1984, 314.

57.   James Mohr recounts this incident in his *Abortion in America*, New York: Oxford University Press, 1978, 113. He cites "Restellism Exposed," but incorrectly concludes that it discussed Clemence Lozier, not Charlotte. He obviously was unaware of other articles from *The Revolution* which clearly show that Charlotte was the object of the article's praise.

58.   Abraham W. Lozier, *In Memoriam*, 1870.

Paulina Wright Davis

59.   "Death of Mrs. Charlotte D. Lozier," *Herald of Health,* February 1870.

60.   Parker Pillsbury, "Charlotte Denman Lozier, MD," *The Revolution,* January 13, 1870.

61.   Elizabeth Cady Stanton, "Reminiscences of Paulina Wright Davis," *History of Woman Suffrage,* Volume 1, New York: Fowler and Wells, 1881, 283–89. See also Volume 1, 37, 46, 221, 246, 255–56, 273, 533, 827; Volume 2, Rochester: Susan B. Anthony, 1881, 367, 391, 428; and Volume 3, Rochester: Susan B. Anthony, 1886, 823. Information on *Una,* as well as reprints from it, can be found in *The Radical Women's Press of the 1850s,* ed. Ann Russo and Cheris Kramarae, New York: Routledge, 1991.

62.   Paulina Wright Davis, *History of the National Woman's Rights Movement*, New York: Journeymen Printer's Cooperative, 1871, 32.

Dr. Elizabeth Blackwell

63.   Olive Banks, *Faces of Feminism*, London: Basil Blackwell, 1986, 39.

64. Elizabeth Blackwell and Emily Blackwell, "Medicine as a Profession for Women," in *The Feminist Papers,* ed. Alice Rossi, New York: Columbia University Press, 1973.

65. See William Leach, *True Love and Perfect Union*, New York: Basic Books, 1980.

66. See Mary Roth Walsh, *Doctors Wanted: No Women Need Apply*, New Haven: Yale University Press, 1977; and Gena Corea, *The Hidden Malpractice*, New York: Harper and Row, 1985; and Ishbel Ross, *Child of Destiny: the Life Story of the First Woman Doctor*, New York: Harker and Brothers, 1949, 88. Ross is the source for this quotation from Blackwell's diary, revealing her motives to become a physician. Ross personally knew Alice Stone Blackwell, Elizabeth's niece and the daughter of Lucy Stone and Henry Blackwell, as well as other surviving family members. They granted her "full and free access" to family diaries, letters, and other papers, in addition to sharing their personal memories and anecdotes.

67. Ross, *Child of Destiny*, 88.

68. Ross, *Child of Destiny*, 88 and passim.

69. See Elizabeth Blackwell, *Rescue Work in Relation to Prostitution and Disease*, New York: Fowler and Wells, 1882.

70. Elizabeth Blackwell, *The Human Element in Sex,* London: J.A. Churchill, 1884.

Dr. Anna Densmore French

71. William Leach, *True Love and Perfect Union: The Feminist Reform of Sex and Society*, New York: Basic Books, 1980, 56–57, 59, 184; Virginia G. Drachman, *Women Doctors and the Women's Medical Movement: Feminism and Medicine 1850–1895,* Ph.D. dissertation, State University of New York at Buffalo, 1976, 207. The original "Minutes" of the New York City Sorosis are now in the Sophia Smith Library of Smith College.

Dr. Alice Bunker Stockham

72.   "Feminine Enterprise: Chicago Women Who Have a Business of Their Own," *Chicago Tribune,* September 14, 1890; "Alice Bunker Stockham," in *Woman of the Century,* eds. Frances E. Willard and Mary Livermore, Buffalo: Charles Wells Moulton, 1893, 690–691.

73.   Alice Bunker Stockham, *Tolstoi, A Man of Peace*, Chicago: Alice B. Stockham and Company, 1900.

74.   "Sanitary Science—Report read before the Illinois Social Science Association by Dr. Alice B. Stockham," in "Woman's Kingdom" column, *Chicago Daily Inter-Ocean,* October 26, 1878.

75.   Alice Bunker Stockham, *Karezza: Ethics of Marriage*, Chicago: Alice B. Stockham and Company, 1898.

76.   Alice Bunker Stockham, *Tokology: A Book For Every Woman,* 2d., Chicago: Sanitary Publishing Company, 1887. (Sanitary Publishing was the earliest name of her publishing house, before her daughter became her partner.)

77.   John C. Spurlock, *Free Love: Marriage and Middle-Class Radicalism in America, 1825–1860*, New York: New York University Press, 1988, 229.

Elizabeth Cady Stanton

78.   For other material on and by Stanton, see Elisabeth Griffith, *In Her Own Right,* New York: Oxford University Press, 1984; Alma Lutz, *Created Equal*, New York: John Day, 1940; Elizabeth Cady Stanton, *Eighty Years and More: Reminiscences, 1815–1897*, New York: Schocken Books reprint, 1971; *Elizabeth Cady Stanton as Revealed in Her Letters, Diaries, and Reminiscences,* eds. Theodore Stanton and Harriet Stanton Blatch, Volumes One and Two, New York: Harper and Brothers, 1922; and Elizabeth Cady Stanton, *The Woman's Bible*, Seattle: Coalition Task Force on Women and Religion, 1974.

79.   Elizabeth Cady Stanton, "Address at the Decade Meeting on Marriage and Divorce," in Paulina Wright Davis, *A History of the National Woman's Rights Movement*, New York: Journeymen Printers' Co-operative Association, 1871, 63.

80.   Lutz, *Created Equal*, 236.

81.   Stanton and Blatch, *Elizabeth Cady Stanton*, Volume 2, 44–45.

82.   "A Girl as Good as a Boy," *Woodhull and Claflin's Weekly*, September 30, 1871.

83.   "Infanticide" and "Child Murder" were not actually signed by Stanton. However, her authorship can be confidently inferred from their appearance in her paper, and from their similarities to each other and to texts known to be penned by her. See William Leach, *True Love and Perfect Union*, New York: Basic Books, 1980, 147, for a passage from a Stanton speech which is strikingly similar to the conclusion of "Infanticide." See also Mattie Brinkerhoff, "Woman and Motherhood," in this volume. Brinkerhoff specifically credits to Stanton *The Revolution's* insistence on "the true education and independence of woman" as the solution to "child-murder."

84.   As mentioned in the Introduction, Stanton's comments here reveal eugenicist, racist anxieties that were common among middle- and upper-class whites in reaction to increased immigration and a growing African-American population. Contemporary prolife feminists deplore such attitudes. However, Stanton's analysis of "Infanticide" can hardly be reduced to them.

85.   See Ida Husted Harper, *The Life and Work of Susan B. Anthony*, Volume 1, Indianapolis: The Hollenbeck Press, 1898, 309–310.

Matilda Joslyn Gage

86.   *History of Woman Suffrage*, Volume 1, 528–30.

87.   *HWS* Volume 2, 630.

88.   *HWS* Volume 1, 466.

89.   Matilda Joslyn Gage, *Woman, Church, and State*, Chicago: Charles Kerr, 1893; Watertown, MA: Persephone Press, reprinted 1980.

90.   Gage, *Woman, Church, and State*, 14, 43.

91.   Gage, *Woman, Church, and State*, 4.

92.   Gage, *Woman, Church, and State*, 543.

93.   Lynne Spender, "Matilda Joslyn Gage: Active Intellectual," in *Feminist Theorists: Three Centuries of Key Women Thinkers,* ed. Dale Spender, New York: Pantheon Books, 1983, 137–145.

Mattie H. Brinkerhoff

94.   Louise R. Noun, *Strong-Minded Women: The Emergence of the Woman-Suffrage Movement in Iowa*, Iowa State University Press, 1969, 70; "Mrs. Brinkerhoff," *The Revolution,* December 31, 1868.

95.   *The History of Woman Suffrage,* Volume 3, eds. Elizabeth Cady Stanton, Susan B. Anthony, and Matilda Joslyn Gage, Rochester, NY: Susan B. Anthony, 1886, 614; Mattie H. Brinkerhoff, "The Lecturing Field," *The Revolution,* November 12, 1868.

96.   "Mrs. Brinkerhoff."

97.   Noun, *Strong-Minded Women,* 97.

98.   Noun, *Strong-Minded Women,* 99.

Susan B. Anthony

99.   For further information on Anthony, see Kathleen Barry, *Susan B. Anthony: Biography of a Singular Feminist*, New York: New York University Press, 1988; Alma Lutz, *Susan B. Anthony: Rebel, Crusader, Humanitarian*, Boston: Beacon Press, 1959; *Elizabeth Cady Stanton-Susan B. Anthony—Correspondence, Writings, Speeches,* ed. Ellen Carol

Dubois, New York: Schocken Books, 1981; and Ida Husted Harper, *The Life and Work of Susan B. Anthony*, Indianapolis: the Hollenbeck Press, 1898.

100.   Frances E. Willard, *Glimpses of Fifty Years: the Autobiography of an American Woman*, Chicago: Woman's Temperance Publishing Association, 1889, 598.

101.   Barry, *Susan B. Anthony*, 123–24.

102.   This piece was signed "A." in the pages of the *Revolution*. The paper's staff often signed articles with their initials, if at all. Writers of that day and age did not fully share in our modern notions of intellectual property. However, additional signs point to Anthony's authorship. The piece clearly resonates with opinions she voiced elsewhere; some of these are recounted in the above biography of Anthony. See also the comments in the Introduction regarding the *Revolution*'s policy against patent medicine advertisements. Anthony, as proprietor of the paper, probably would not have allowed this policy, which caused a loss of revenues, unless she agreed with it. At the very least, Anthony surely condoned the antiabortion sentiments of this piece.

Henry Clarke Wright and Anonymous Correspondent

103.   The only published full-length biography of Wright is Lewis Perry, *Childhood, Marriage and Reform: Henry Clarke Wright*, Chicago: University of Chicago Press, 1980. A comprehensive listing of Wright's voluminous reform writings can be found on pages 345–50, although many of these are not readily available. Among his better known and more widely circulated works are *Defensive War Proved to Be a Denial of Christianity and of the Government of God,* London and Dublin: Charles Gilpin, 1846; *Anthropology; or, the Science of Man: In Its Bearings on War and Slavery*, Boston: Bela March, 1850; *A Kiss For a Blow; or, a Collection of Stories for Children Showing Them How to Prevent Quarrelling*, Boston: Bela Marsh, 1842; *Marriage and Parentage; or, the Reproductive Element in Man, as a Means to His Elevation and Happiness*, Boston: Bela March, 1854; and *The Unwelcome Child; or, the Crime of an Undesigned and Undesired Maternity,* Boston: Bela Marsh, 1858.

104. "Free Convention at Rutland, Vermont," *Banner of Light,* July 10, 1858.

Elizabeth Edson Evans

105. "Elizabeth E. Evans Dead," *New York Times*, September 15, 1911; "Edward Payson Evans," in *The National Encyclopaedia of American Biography,* Volume Nine, New York: James T. White, 1907, 433–434.

106. Edward Payson Evans, *Evolutionary Ethics and Animal Psychology*, New York: Appleton, 1898, 221.

107. Carl Degler, *At Odds*, New York: Oxford University Press, 1980, 234.

108. The pamphlet to which this woman refers is undoubtedly A. M. Mariceau's *The Married Woman's Private Medical Companion*, New York, 1847. Mariceau was actually a printer named Charles Lohman, the husband of the notorious abortionist Madame Restell. While others who wrote on the topic of sex and reproduction intended to help women as well as support themselves, Lohman's manual was no more than a device to drum up business for his wife. It exploited women's rightful resentment over the unjust conditions in which they were expected to mother and touted abortion as a painless, harmless panacea for their problems. On the advertising strategies employed by the Restell business, see Marvin Olasky, *The Press and Abortion, 1838–1988*, Hillsdale, NJ: Erlbaum, 1988.

Eliza Bisbee Duffey

109. See William Leach, *True Love and Perfect Union*, NY: Basic Books, 1980.

110. Dr. Edward H. Clarke, *Sex in Education*, Boston: Osgood, 1873.

111. Eliza Bisbee Duffey, *No Sex in Education*, Philadelphia: J.M. Stoddart, 1874. For an overview of the debate, see Mary Roth Walsh, *Doctors Wanted: No Women Need Apply*, New Haven: Yale, 1977, 119–32.

112.   Eliza Bisbee Duffey, *What Women Should Know*, Philadelphia: J.M. Stoddart, 1873.

Sarah F. Norton

113.   Sarah F. Norton, "Notes From the Lecturing Field," *The Revolution,* March 4, 1869.

114.   Quoted in William Leach, *True Love and Perfect Union*, New York: Basic Books, 1980, 190.

115.   *History of Woman Suffrage,* Volume 2, 390.

116.   Sarah F. Norton, "Notes From the Lecturing Field," *The Revolution,* March 4, 1869, and April 1, 1869, and "Dr. Bushnell Again," July 15, 1869.

Woodhull and Claflin

117.   *Woodhull and Claflin's Weekly: The Lives and Writings of Notorious Victoria Woodhull and Her Sister Tennessee Claflin,* ed., with biographical notes, by Arlene Kisner, Washington, N.J.: Times Change Press, 1972, 19. Other works about the sisters and their adventures include the following: Emanie Sachs, *The Terrible Siren*, New York: Harper, 1928; Johanna Johnston, *Mrs. Satan*, New York: Putnam, 1967; and M.M. Marberry, *Vicky*, New York: Funk and Wagnalls, 1967. See also Tennessee Claflin, *The Ethics of Sexual Equality*, New York: Woodhull and Claflin, 1873; Victoria Woodhull Martin, *A Fragmentary Record of Public Work Done in America, 1871–77*, London, 1877; and *The Human Body the Temple of God*, London, 1890.

118.   Could there be contemporary evidence to support this variation on the belief that "violence begets violence"? One psychiatrist has documented several cases of patients who mysteriously attempted suicide at the same time each year. The psychiatrist was unable to make sense of the particular dates "chosen" by these patients—until he discovered that the dates coincided with abortion attempts on the part of their mothers.

See "Almost Aborted," Chapter Eight in Ellen Curro, *Caring Enough to Help: Counseling at a Crisis Pregnancy Center*, Grand Rapids, MI: Baker Book House, 1990.

These nineteenth-century arguments are all the more intriguing in light of modern findings about the considerable damage that violence—whether in the media, within the home, in the community or the culture as a whole—causes postnatal children. Perhaps as we learn more about prenatal psychology, it will turn out that some of these findings apply to the period before birth as well. For a popularized resource on prenatal psychology, see Thomas Verny, *The Secret Life of the Unborn Child*, New York: Dell, 1981.

Isabella Beecher Hooker

119.   On Harriet, see Forrest Wilson, *Crusader in Crinoline*, New York: Greenwood Press, 1972. On Catharine, see Kathryn Kish Sklar, *Catharine Beecher: A Study in American Domesticity,* New Haven: Yale University Press, 1973. No one has yet written a full-length biography of Isabella; however, *The Limits of Sisterhood: The Beecher Sisters on Women's Rights and Woman's Sphere,* ed. Jeanne Boydston, Mary Kelley, and Anne Margolis, Chapel Hill: University of North Carolina Press, 1988, is a rich and helpful source of information about Isabella, along with the rest of the family. See also "Isabella Beecher Hooker," in Frances Willard and Mary Livermore, *Woman of the Century*, Buffalo: Charles Wells Moulton, 1893, 390–392, and *The History of Woman Suffrage* Volume 2, 425, 458, 486, 489, 496, 499, and 534, and Volume 3, 73, 99, 194, 103, 105, 320, and 327.

120.   Boydston, et al., *The Limits of Sisterhood*, Chapters Four, Seven and Ten.

121.   Willard and Livermore, *Woman of the Century,* 391. See also Isabella Beecher Hooker, *A Mother's Letters to a Daughter on Woman Suffrage*, Hartford: Press of Case, Lockwood, and Brainerd, 1870; and *The Constitutional Rights of the Women of the United States: An Address Before the International Council of Women*, Hartford: Case, Lockwood, and Brainerd, 1900. Portions of these two works are reprinted in Boydston, et al., *The Limits of Sisterhood*, Documents 59 and 63.

122. Willard and Livermore, *Woman of the Century,* 391.

123. On the estimable Rev. Dr. Todd, see Graham J. Barker-Benfield, *Horros of the Half-Known Life: Male Attitudes Toward Women and Sexuality in Nineteenth Century America*, New York: Harper and Row, 1976, Part Three. Todd's misogynist masterpieces include *Woman's Rights*, Boston: Lee and Shepard, 1867, and *Serpents in the Dove's Nest*, Boston: Lee and Shepard, 1867. "Fashionable Murder," the piece to which Hooker is responding, is a tract reprinted in the latter volume. For a feisty response to the former book, see Gail Hamilton (Mary Abigail Dodge), *Woman's Wrongs: A Counter-Irritant*, Boston: Lee and Shepard, 1868.

Laura Cuppy Smith

124. *History of Woman Suffrage,* Volume 2, eds. Elizabeth Cady Stanton, Susan B. Anthony, and Matilda Joslyn Gage, Rochester, NY: Susan B. Anthony, 1881, 390.

125. *HWS* Volume 2, 379.

126. Emanie Sachs, *The Terrible Siren,* New York: Harper, 1928, 207.

127. Sachs, *The Terrible Siren,* 207.

128. *History of Woman Suffrage,* Volume 3, eds. Matilda Joslyn Gage, Susan B. Anthony, and Elizabeth Cady Stanton, Rochester: Susan B. Anthony, 1886, 755.

129. Sachs, *The Terrible Siren,* 207.

Eleanor Kirk

130. *History of Woman Suffrage,* Volume 2, eds. Elizabeth Cady Stanton, Susan B. Anthony, and Matilda Joslyn Gage, Rochester, NY: Susan B. Anthony, 1881, 390.

131. *HWS* Volume 2, 379.

132. Eleanor Kirk (Nellie Ames), *Up Broadway*, New York: Carleton, 1870.

133. Eleanor Kirk, "Woman's Adversity," *The Revolution,* February 11, 1869.

134. Ida Husted Harper, *Life and Work of Susan B. Anthony,* Vol. 1, Indianapolis: The Hollenbeck Press, 1898, 309. For more information on Kirk, see "Mrs. Eleanor M. Ames," in *Woman of the Century,* eds. Frances E. Willard and Mary Livermore, Buffalo: Charles Wells Moulton, 1893, 22.

Frances E. Willard

135. See Ruth Bordin, *Frances Willard: A Biography*, Chapel Hill, University of North Carolina Press, 1986, and Frances E. Willard, *Glimpses of Fifty Years*, Chicago: Women's Christian Temperance Union Publishing Association, 1889.

136. Frances E. Willard, *Nineteen Beautiful Years*, New York: Harper, 1884; *A Great Mother,* Chicago: WCTPA, 1897; with Helen Winslow and Sallie White, *Occupations for Women*, New York: Success Company, 1897; with Mary Livermore, *A Woman of the Century*, Buffalo: Charles Wells Moulton, 1893; and *Woman in the Pulpit*, Chicago: WCTPA, 1888. Willard wrote several other works as well, including the engaging *How I Learned to Ride the Bicycle*, ed. Carol O'Hare, Sunnyvale, CA: Fair Oaks Publishing, 1991.

137. The term comes from Sara Ruddick, "Maternal Thinking," *Feminist Studies* 6(2), Summer 1980, 342–67.

138.   See Frances E. Willard, *Address Before the Second Biennial Convention of the World's WCTU ...*, Chicago: World's Columbian Exposition, 1893, 37; *Report of the National Women's Christian Temperance Union, Twenty-Second Annual Meeting*, Chicago: WCTPA, 1895, 298–99; and Charles N. Crittenton, *The Brother of Girls*, Chicago: World's Events Publishing Co., 1910. Numerous references are also made to the Crittenton Homes in the *Union Signal,* the National WCTU's newspaper.

139.   Frances E. Willard, "How the Chicago WCTU was Founded, What It Has Accomplished, and Who Have Assisted," *Union Signal,* December 5, 1895; *Alumnae of the Woman's Medical College of Chicago, 1870–1896*, Chicago: H.G. Cutler, 1896, 134, 136–37; and "Dr. Kate Bushnell," in Frances E. Willard and Mary Livermore, *Woman of the Century*, Buffalo: Charles Wells Moulton, 1893, 141.

140.   On the abortion-prostitution link, and on other early crisis pregnancy efforts, see Marvin Olasky, *Abortion Rites: A Social History of Abortion in America*, Wheaton, IL: Crossway, 1992.

141.   *Twenty-First Annual Report of the Erring Women's Refuge*, Chicago: Knight and Leonard, 1883, 6.

142.   This title has been taken from a short brochure about the Mission's work. The brochure is in the possession of the Chicago Historical Society.

143.   As adoption was then not so institutionalized as it is today, the alternative may have been sending the babies to orphanages.

144.   "Negro" or "colored" clients are conspicuously absent from the Mission's annual reports during this period. The national policy of the Florence Crittenton Homes was to serve all racial groups, including African-Americans; however, local affiliates took a great deal of latitude with the official policy. Many excluded African-American clients from the central maternity home, preferring to send them out to boarding homes or foster homes in the community: the old familiar trick of separate-but-supposedly-equal. See Rickie Solinger, *Wake Up, Little Susie: Single*

Pregnancy and Race Before Roe v. Wade, New York: Routledge, 1992. Ironically, the Mission's present-day descendant serves predominantly African-American clients.

145.   This may sound like a paltry, limited financial involvement on the part of the father, but it was actually quite progressive for the times. And it is certainly more than some fathers pay in child-support today, given the widespread lack of child support enforcement.

Dr. Mary Ries Melendy

146.   Melendy, *The Ideal Woman: A Book Giving Full Information on All the Mysterious and Complex Matters Pertaining to Women*, Chicago: J.R. Peper, 1911, 8.

147.   Mary Ries Melendy, *Cure of Disease Simplified: A Modern Vadi Mecum for the Household*, Chicago: Guiding Star Publishing Company, 1893, passim.

148.   Melendy, *The Ideal Woman*, 7.

149.   Melendy, *The Ideal Woman*, Chapters 11–13, 18.

150.   Melendy, *The Ideal Woman*, Chapter 22.

Estelle Sylvia Pankhurst

151.   On Sylvia's life, see Patricia Romero, *E. Sylvia Pankhurst: Portrait of a Radical*, New Haven: Yale University Press, 1987, and Richard Keir Pethick Pankhurst, *Sylvia Pankhurst: Artist and Crusader*, New York/ London: Paddington Press, 1979. (Richard Pankhurst is Sylvia's son.) Information on Sylvia's life and work can also be found in her own writings. In addition to editing such newspapers as *The Women's Dreadnought* and *The New Times and Ethiopia News,* she wrote a number of books. These included *The Suffragette Movement*, London: Virago reprint, 1977; *The Homefront,* London: 1932; and *Save the Mothers*, London: Knopf, 1930. For additional material on her famous family members, see Emmeline Pankhurst, *My Story*, London: 1914; Christabel Pankhurst, *Unshackled: The Story of How We Won the Vote*, London:

Hutchinson, 1959; David Mitchell, *The Fighting Pankhursts*, London: Jonathan Cape, 1967, and *Queen Christabel*, London: McDonald and Jane's, 1977; Sheila Rowbotham, *Hidden From History*, New York: Vintage, 1976; and Elizabeth Sarah, "Christabel Pankhurst: Reclaiming Her Power," in *Feminist Theorists,* ed. Dale Spender, New York: Pantheon, 1983, 256–284.

152.   Quoted in Romero, *E. Sylvia Pankhurst,* 115.

153.   Pankhurst, *Save the Mothers*, 122.

154.   Romero, *E. Sylvia Pankhurst,* 37, 185.

Further Evidence

155.   F.W. Stella Browne, "The Right to Abortion," in Sheila Rowbotham, *A New World for Women*, London: Pluto Press, 1977, 113, 114, 117.

156.   Browne, "The Right to Abortion," 119, 112, and 118.

157.   Browne, "The Right to Abortion," 121.

158.   See Beverly Wildung Harrison, *Our Right to Choose*, Boston: Beacon Press, 1983, and Ellen Willis, "Putting Women Back Into the Abortion Debate," *Village Voice,* July 16, 1985. For some very different views on the relationship between abortion and the liberation of female sexuality, see Karyn Milos, "Feminism and 'Choice': The Sexual Issues," *Feminists for Life of Minnesota Newsletter,* January 1991; Rivolta Femminile, "Female Sexuality and Abortion," Comitato Romano per l'Aborto e la Contraccezione, "Programme of the CRAC," and a group of women from the feminist collective of Via Cherubine, Milan, "We are working on a different political approach," in *Italian Feminist Thought: A Reader*, eds. Paola Bono and Sandra Kemp, Cambridge, MA: Basil Blackwell, 1991.

159.   Browne, "The Right to Abortion," 123.

160.   Rowbotham, *A New World for Women*, 34, 35.

161.   See Dorothy Kelly, "Abortion and the Law," *The Woman Rebel* 1(2):2 (April 1914), and Annette Charreau, "The Penal Code of Bale and Abortion," *Birth Control Review* 3(11):12 (November 1919).

162.   Margaret Sanger, *Family Limitation,* n.d., 5. The copy examined for this book was donated by Emma Goldman's lover Ben Reitman to the University of Chicago Library.

163.   Linda Gordon, *Woman's Body, Woman's Right*, New York: Penguin Books, 1977, 223.

164.   James Reed, *The Birth Control Movement and American Society*, Princeton: Princeton University Press, 1983, 119.

165.   Margaret Sanger to Dr. Hannah M. Stone (letter), January 30, 1933. Margaret Sanger Papers, Library of Congress. Thanks to Charlotte Paris for obtaining a copy of this memo.

166.   Minutes of the Staff Meeting of the Clinical Research Bureau, April 29, 1929. Margaret Sanger Papers, Library of Congress. Again, thanks to Charlotte Paris for obtaining a copy of this memo.

167.   Cited in Reed, *The Birth Control Movement*, 119.

168.   Laurence Lader, *Abortion II*, Boston: Beacon Press, 1973, 20.

169.   Margaret Sanger, *My Fight for Birth Control*, New York: Farrar and Rinehart, 1931, 133.

170.   Sanger, *My Fight,* 155.

171.   Margaret Sanger, *Woman and the New Race*, New York: Truth Publishing Co., 1920, 25.

172.   Sanger, *Woman and the New Race*, 79.

173.   Margaret Sanger, *An Autobiography*, New York: WW Norton, 1938, 449.

174.   Evelyn K.S. Judge to Mary Krane Derr (Letter), September 21, 1989.

175.   Evelyn K.S. Judge to Mary Krane Derr (Letter), September 12, 1989.

176.   *Ibid.* Thanks to Ms. Judge for sharing her recollections of Alice Paul. For an account of the hostility and indifference Ms. Judge faced when she courageously attempted to share them at a ceremony honoring Paul, see Bette Duganitz, "Alice Paul: Reality v. Propaganda," *Feminists for Life of Minnesota Newsletter,* April 1992.

177.   Cynthia Harrison, *On Account of Sex: The Politics of Women's Issues, 1945–1968,* Berkeley: University of California Press, 1988, 205. Thanks to Richard Stanley for bringing this information to the editor's attention.

178.   "Conversations With Alice Paul: Woman Suffrage and the Equal Rights Amendment." Transcript of an oral interview conducted by Amelia R. Fry, November 1972/May 1973, Berkeley: University of California Oral History Project, 1976, 535.

179.   Robert S. Gallagher, "'I Was Arrested, of Course': An Interview With Miss Alice Paul," *American Heritage: the Magazine of History* 25(2):16ff (February 1974).

180.   Gallagher, "'I Was Arrested of Course.'"

181.   Lader, *Abortion II*, 37.

182.   Letter from Clare Booth Luce to Ms. Carol Burris, President, Women's Lobby, Inc., February 21, 1978, recorded in the *Congressional Record*, "Clare Booth Luce Withdraws From Women's Lobby, Inc.," March 7, 1978, E-1061.

Part Two Endnotes

Introduction

1.   At a panel discussion in 1990 in which I spoke in favor of informed consent legislation which would include providing the abortion-seeker with an information packet prepared by a bipartisan group (comprised of both prochoicers and prolifers) concerning the abortion procedure and general information concerning reproduction and fetal development, a Planned Parenthood representative expressed her outrage at my "patronizing" position which suggested that young women do not know how their own bodies work. When the discussion later turned to sex education, she described some of her young clients who do not even know where their vagina is. When I pointed out the inconsistency of her position concerning the education of these young women, she responded in anger. To say that all young women know everything they need to know about their reproductive capacity is to suggest that they have all had equal access to education. Unfortunately, this is not the case.

[Linda Naranjo-Huebl, Ed.]

2.   Adrienne Rich, *Of Woman Born: Motherhood as Experience and Institution,* New York: Norton, 1971.

3.   Germaine Greer, *New Republic,* October 5, 1992.

4.   Catharine MacKinnon, "Abortion: On Public and Private," *Toward a Feminist Theory of the State,* Cambridge: Harvard University Press, 1989.

5.   MacKinnon, "Abortion," 186.

6.   Elizabeth Fox Genovese, "Feminist Theory to Feminist Politics," *Feminism Without Illusions,* Chapel Hill: University of North Carolina Press, 1991.

7.   Fox Genovese, "Feminist Theory to Feminist Politics," 84.

8.   MacKinnon, "Abortion," 186.

9.   We acknowledge the criticism that many of these centers have disguised themselves as abortion referral offices just to get women in the door and then bombard them with prolife information. We reject such dishonest tactics, but we also believe the actual instances of such practices are becoming rare. It takes sincere concern to continue to provide one's time and resources to young women in need; and few communities, whether they be predominantly prochoice or prolife, will tolerate such deceptive practices for any length of time. Some of the early criticism stemmed from the fact that many of these centers advertised themselves under "Birth Control Services" in the telephone directory with abortion referral services. This writer can attest to early work with other women in such a center who were told by the telephone company that we had to be categorized with abortion services agencies because there was simply no other category under which we fell (which bespeaks of the dearth of services, besides abortion, available at the time to women facing crisis pregnancies). Most local telephone directories have since corrected that problem, and these centers are now more appropriately classified. Many of these community-based agencies have become respected providers of services to women and even receive referrals from local prochoice organizations.

Fannie Lou Hamer

10. Fannie Lou Hamer, "It's In Your Hands," in *Black Women in White America: A Documentary History*, ed. Gerda Lerner, New York: Vintage Books/Random House, 1972, 607-614.

11. Kay Mills, *This Little Light of Mine: The Life of Fannie Lou Hamer*, New York: Dutton, 1993, 274.

12. Mills, *This Little Light of Mine*, 260-261.

13. *See* Mills, *This Little Light of Mine*, 274.

14.   Jo Etha Collier was an African-American teenager who showed great promise in both athletics and academics. She never had the chance to use her college scholarships, because she was fatally shot on the night of her high school graduation by a group of white men. Hamer gathered financial and emotional support for the girl's family.

Mary Krane Derr

15.   Margo Anand, *The Art of Sexual Ecstasy*, Los Angeles: J.P. Tarcher, 1992.

16.   Sue Nathanson, *Soul Crisis*, New York: Signet Books, 1990, 168.

17.   Sappho Durrell, "Journals and Letters," *Granta* 37:55-92, Autumn 1991.

18.   Vicki Thorne, speech at "Abortion Healing" conference, Milwaukee, WI, November 3, 1993.

19.   Feminist Collective of Via Cherubini, Milan, "We are working on a different political approach," in *Italian Feminist Thought: A Reader*, eds. Paola Bono and Sandra Kemp, Oxford, UK/Cambridge, MA: Basil Blackwell, 1991, 223-225.

To find out more about life-affirming feminism, contact any of the following organizations:

Feminists for Life of America
733 Fifteenth St, NW, Suite 1100
Washington, DC 20005
202–737–FFLA

Seamless Garment Network, Inc.
109 Pickwick Drive
Rochester, NY 14618
716–442–8497

Feminism and Nonviolence Studies Association
811 East 47th Street
Kansas City, MO 64110
816–753–2130

To obtain or provide help for pregnant women in need, call or write:

The Nurturing Network
910 Main Street, Suite 360
Boise, ID 83701
208–344–7200

Heartbeat International
1213½ St. James Road
Columbus, OH 43227
614–239–9433

USA Birthright
PO Box 98363
Atlanta, GA 30359
404–451–6336

Care Net
101 W. Broad Street, Suite 500
Falls Church, VA 22046
703–237–2100

2/07
Stack